THE OWL, THE RAVEN, & THE DOVE

Detail of the original sketch drawn by Wilhelm and Jacob's younger brother, the artist Ludwig Emil Grimm, for the frontispiece of The Fairy Tales of the Brothers Grimm. *The angel lovingly watches over the two children who are asleep and leaning on each other. Providence is depicted as a protective spirit standing by the little brother and sister during the forest night and shielding them in the darkness from the nearby danger of a steep cliff. The natural adds its help to the supernatural as the stars shine above and the glowing moon rises on the horizon to provide light for the children. Redrawn by Laurence Selim from the original.*

the
° OWL,
the RAVEN,
& *the* DOVE

The Religious Meaning
of the Grimms' Magic Fairy Tales

G. Ronald Murphy, S.J.

OXFORD
UNIVERSITY PRESS
2000

OXFORD
UNIVERSITY PRESS

Oxford   New York

Athens   Auckland   Bangkok   Bogotá   Buenos Aires   Calcutta
Cape Town   Chennai   Dar es Salaam   Delhi   Florence   Hong Kong   Istanbul
Karachi   Kuala Lumpur   Madrid   Melbourne   Mexico City   Mumbai
Nairobi   Paris   São Paulo   Singapore   Taipei   Tokyo   Toronto   Warsaw

and associated companies in
Berlin   Ibadan

Copyright © 2000 by G. Ronald Murphy, S.J.

Published by Oxford University Press, Inc.
198 Madison Avenue, New York, New York 10016

Oxford is a registered trademark of Oxford University Press, Inc.

Library of Congress Cataloging-in-Publication Data
Murphy, G. Ronald, 1938–
The owl, the raven, and the dove : the religious meaning of the
Grimms' magic fairy tales / by G. Ronald Murphy.
p.   cm.
Includes bibliographical references and index.
ISBN 0-19-513607-1
1. Kinder- und Hausmärchen.   2. Fairy tales—Germany—Religious
aspects.   3. Grimm, Wilhelm, 1786–1857—Religion.   4. Grimm, Jacob,
1785–1863—Religion.   I. Title.
GR166.M87   2000
398.2′0943—dc21   99-42770

5/03

1 3 5 7 9 8 6 4 2

Printed in the United States of America
on acid-free paper

for

Popsy Den

who first read to me

and told me stories

❍

et

Eugenio

benemerenti

❍

PREFACE

The *Fairy Tales of the Brothers Grimm* is a national treasure of the German people. Among its 210 stories there are a dozen or so which are such master-pieces that they have become a treasure that belongs to the childhood and the adulthood of the whole world.

Ever since Bruno Bettelheim presented his psychoanalytic interpretation of the tales more than twenty years ago, scholars have been fascinated by the mysterious nature and continuing influence of these stories on the human imagination. In the interval since the appearance of Bettelheim's *The Uses of Enchantment,* rewarding studies of these Grimm tales have been published from many points of view. With approaches that are Jungian, Marxist, so-ciopolitical, dialectical, historical, text-historical, feminist, gender-related, mythological, and economic, with both affirmative and critical assessments, scholars have demonstrated the richness of the stories and their openness to many levels of interpretation.

One of the most intriguing suggestions originally made by Bettelheim was that underneath the psychological meaning of the stories he found hints of another, deeper layer of religious meaning, which he thought deserved seri-ous attention. This suggestion has largely gone unexamined by contempo-rary scholarship. This book is an attempt to explore that fascinating chal-lenge and delve into the religious roots of the tales' enchantment by studying them as the poetic expression of what the brothers Grimm thought they were—fragments of ancient faith.

This exploration is supported by my discovery and interpretation of the notations and markings made by Wilhelm Grimm in his personal copies of the Bible and in his texts of the medieval epics which he taught. The patterns of Wilhelm's Christian religious thought as derived from his notations point unambiguously to a diachronic, ecumenical spirituality woven around love and faith. The (roughly eleven) biblical patterns discovered are very helpful for a religious interpretation of the tales because Wilhelm was the principal poet-editor of the stories over a period of decades and because it was he who gave them their final shape and form. He rewrote narratives extensively, or minimally, from his poetic religious perspective, which was based ultimately on his conviction that the tales were fragments of ancient faith whose purpose was to awaken the feelings of the human heart. Of course, not every one of the Grimms' stories is a masterpiece, but the five chosen here would be acknowledged by all the world as being among the most persistently enchanting ever written. With captivating affection and a magical sense of composition, they narrate the human confrontation of faithful love with death. This volume attempts to trace the religious roots of the abiding magic which, I believe, has made these five fairy tales among the most well-known and loved stories in the world.

Washington, D.C.   G.R.M

June 1999

ACKNOWLEDGMENTS

Let me begin in Germany, and in the Hessian town of Steinau where the brothers Grimm spent their childhood. I would like to thank the sexton and the pastor of the Reformed Church for guiding me and giving me the key to the medieval Church of St. Catherine where the Grimm family worshiped and where their grandfather had once been the pastor. I would like to acknowledge in a special way the kindness to a stranger of the people of Steinau who went out of their way to be helpful and make me feel at home. When I told some of them that I came from an American town once occupied by their fellow Hessians in the year 1776, Trenton, they surprised me by being familiar enough with such ancestral things as to ask me for the names of the regiments.

I am indebted to the staff of the Hessian State Archives in Marburg for giving me access to their Grimm holdings and especially to Wilhelm Grimm's textbooks. It was there that I found the leaf from the grave of the Hessian princess with Wilhelm's writing on it. In Berlin the staff of the *Staatsbibliothek* and the Humboldt University Library gave me generous assistance with their Grimm collections so that I was able to study the religious and theological books from the Grimms' personal library. Hundred-year-old flower petals fell from pages of some of these books, which seemed not to have been opened for extensive examination since the hand of Wilhelm Grimm last closed them. In Kassel I was assisted by the staff of the *Brüder Grimm Museum* and by Dr. Bernhard Lauer, the director of the *Brüder Grimm Archiv*, who encouraged me with his enthusiasm for my approach and gave me permission to copy from their holdings many of the drawings and prints for the fairy tales made by Ludwig Emil Grimm.

I would like to thank Sieglinde Bandoly, who not only welcomed me to the comfortable town museum in Haldensleben in Lower Saxony but also had warm coffee and cake ready for the weary traveler on a very stormy day. She proudly brought me Wilhelm Grimm's German Bible with his inscription on the flyleaf and told me I was the first to open it in her time there as director of the museum more than twenty-five years. I am grateful for her welcome and for her pride in the collection of the museum.

I am indebted to Karl-Heinz Draeger, conservator of Hessian antiquities, who showed me the holdings in the castle museum in Bad Homburg and arranged to have the Grimm family's Bibles on exhibition in the castle museum in Steinau unlocked so that I could study them.

In the United States, patient librarians have been my principal benefactors. Christa Sammons, curator of the German Literature Collection of the Beineke Library at Yale University supplied me with invaluable access to the Beineke's rare and treasured copy of the first edition of the *Kinder- und Hausmärchen*. The Firestone Library at Princeton University not only let me go through the copy of the second edition of the *Kinder- und Hausmärchen* in their rare book collection but also provided me with the atmosphere and space in which to finish the manuscript of this book. The Hamilton Public Library in my hometown was a comfortable working place with a much appreciated quiet room enjoying a peaceful view. For the grant of a sabbatical year in which to complete this work, I thank Georgetown University, and I thank Georgetown's interlibrary-loan librarians for their universally successful searches.

A very special word of thanks is due to the professional artist and my former student, Laurence Selim. She went out of her way to provide this book with illustrations that would do justice to the importance of the now faded sketches made in the early nineteenth century by Ludwig Emil Grimm, younger brother of Jacob and Wilhelm, for his brothers' book of fairy tales. Those sketches and prints from 1825 and earlier whose doorways and windows provide the reader with a visual path to the meaning of the story as seen by the Grimms, have suffered from deterioration and poor initial printing, and do not always hold up well when mechanically reproduced from previous copies. Laurence graciously attended to restoring them to effectiveness for this book. We gratefully acknowledge our indebtedness to the Brüder Grimm Gesellschaft in Kassel, and to Karl Dielmann, for the very helpful photographs of the sketches and drawings of Ludwig Emil reproduced in *Märchenillustrationen von Ludwig Emil Grimm*, which were a guide and inspiration. Further gratitude is due to Houghton Mifflin's Clarion books for permission to use sections from Neil Philip and Nicoletta Simborowski's charming version of Perrault's fairy tales, to Rowohlt Verlag for their compact and useful *Jubiläumsausgabe,* and to the Martin Bodmer Foundation for their publication of the earliest known collection of the Grimms' tales.

I thank my confreres in Georgetown's Jesuit Community, at Sankt Georgen in Frankfurt, and at the Canisius-Kolleg in Berlin, as well as my family and friends, who have lived through my enthusiastic discussions of the Grimms' tales over the years with great patience. I hope their gracious encouragement is now finally rewarded. A thank you to the editor of *America* for "Yggdrasil."

Finally, who can I thank more than Cynthia Read, the editor who has persisted in providing encouragement, perceptive reading, and a profound understanding of academic work in the humanities. The Grimms would have found her a gracious and gifted reader. For her efforts in shepherding this volume through to completion, I am now thrice grateful.

CONTENTS

one • The Roots of Spiritual Stories   3

two • Scholars and the Religious Spirit of the Tales   17

three • The Spirituality of Wilhelm Grimm   31

four • *Hansel and Gretel*   45

five • *Little Red Riding Hood*   67

six • *Cinderella*   85

seven • *Snow White*   113

eight • *Sleeping Beauty*   133

nine • Afterword   153

Appendix A The Verses Marked by Wilhelm Grimm in

His Greek New Testament   155

Appendix B *Little Red Riding Hood,* 1st edition, 1812   165

Appendic C Yggdrasil, the Cross, and

the Christmas Tree   171

Select Bibliography   179

Index   185

THE OWL, THE RAVEN, & THE DOVE

One

THE ROOTS OF SPIRITUAL STORIES

The brothers Grimm thought of fairy tales as remnants of ancient faith expressed in poetry. Through all the revisions of their collections of tales, their preface always begins with a description of gleaning, a biblical image recalling the command that the poor are not to be prevented from gathering the remnants that survive the harvest or the storm, nor the grain that has grown unnoticed by the hedgerow or the roadside.[1] The brothers, and especially Wilhelm, who continually revised the tales over a period of forty years, found those untouched grains of wheat still surviving on the margins of religious and poetic consciousness in traditional figures of speech, common superstitions, and, above all, in old stories. Wilhelm was a gleaner, he believed, of remnants of ancestral Germanic religious faith surviving on the margins of culture in popular poetic tales. The gleaner, however, was also a kneader and blender of other ancient stories embodying religious faith. He collected and reexpressed the religious faith found in the poetic tales primarily of three ancient traditions: Classical Greco-Roman, Norse-Germanic, and Biblical. In all three he was at home as a fluent reader, student, and storyteller, and in one of them, Christianity, he was a devout believer. His personal style of Johannine spirituality with its emphasis on love as the divine and life-giving form of faith, enabled him to have a serene reverence for pre-Christian, pagan religious awareness in Germanic and Greek forms, especially insofar as they too spoke of the primacy of love and the tragic and violent nature of its violation. To do justice to Wilhelm Grimm's retelling of the tales it is not enough to treat them as narratives that ignore the spiritual feelings of the past and integrate only the middle-class morals of the nineteenth century as some scholars seem to maintain.[2]

Through many editions over the years the preface to the brother's collec-

---

1. Brüder Grimm, *Kinder- und Hausmärchen, Ausgabe letzter Hand mit den Originalanmerkungen der Brüder Grimm, (Jubiläumsausgabe)*, hrsg. Heinz Rölleke (Stuttgart: Reclam, 1993), I, p. 15.

2. See, for example, Marina Warner, *From the Beast to the Blonde, On Fairy Tales and Their Tellers* (New York: Farrar, Straus and Giroux, 1994), p. 211.

tion of fairy tales always ends with a religious thought parallel to that at the beginning: the tales enable a blessing. The brothers stated that their book consists of stories which are precious crumbs of ancient faith, gleaned wheat, made into bread, and that they wished to place it only into benevolent hands which have the power to bless, hoping that these "breadcrumbs of poetry" will never come to the attention of those who would withhold them from the poor.[3]

My first acquaintance with the work of the brothers Grimm made an unforgettable impression. It was a long time ago when I first saw *Snow White* in Walt Disney's film version of the Grimms' story. To tell stories as affecting as that, I thought as a child, is a great human achievement. I am aware that since then Disney has been criticized for his alterations to the story, especially for his naming of the seven dwarfs, and so when I was almost finished with this book, after the lapse of many years I saw the movie again. Disney did well. His rendition of the ending with the sleeping Snow White surrounded by the kneeling dwarfs, a candle placed on either side of her glass casket, music changed to solemnly religious, and the slowly paced entry of the prince into what is unmistakably a church atmosphere, captures well Wilhelm Grimm's religious spirit. It occurs to no one viewing the film to think that Germanic elves are out of place amidst the candles and organ music of Christian piety, and that is the style and achievement of the brothers Grimm, well depicted by Disney. When the princess is awakened from death with the kiss of the king's son, the prince and Snow White leave, going hand in hand up the hillside toward his father's castle. Disney then has the father's castle appear in the distance, not on the horizon as one might expect in a Disney film, but high above and ahead of the prince and his bride, radiant in the sky, shinning like a golden city made of sunlight. My mother, eighty years old at the time, turned to me and asked quietly, "Is she dead?" That question in its astonishing clarity shows how effectively Disney perceived and presented the Grimms' style in his *Snow White*.

The curious and inclusive religious richness of German Romanticism came to its most classical and effective expression in the fairy tales of the brothers Grimm. Not in all 210 of them, to be sure, but most tellingly, even in their own day, in certain stories that were recognized as their *Zaubermärchen*, "magic fairy tales." Five of those have become so beloved throughout the English-speaking world that they constitute our most well known and familiar works of German literature, so familiar to us and to our newspapers as often to be thought of as our own. Our own they have become. The Grimms and their tales have also become controversial. Some maintain that the Grimms' stories are really French tales retold in German (and now English) translation; this claim we will examine in each case. Some feel that they are

3. Rölleke, *Jubiläumsausgabe*, I, p. 24.

neither religiously inspired nor inspiring and much too violent to be of spiritual value—notwithstanding the bible's own faithful accounts of cannibalism in besieged cities, royal adultery, and murder, not to mention mockery and crucifixion. There is also the criticism that the Grimms thoroughly reworked the tales while at the same time publicly maintaining that they were faithfully retelling ancient stories transmitted to them orally by folk storytellers. This criticism is very important. There is truth on both sides of the fence in this argument, and the religious nature of the tales, especially as perceived by Wilhelm, is pivotal in resolving the issue.

The Grimms were professors and librarians whose great area of interest was the literature of the Middle Ages, philology, the history of stories, words, and languages. They enjoyed uncovering the hidden verbal connections of the past to the present. Jacob's concentration was on law and linguistics, Wilhelm's was on stories and literature, and both followed the historical method first introduced to them by Karl von Savigny, co-founder of the historical school of the interpretation of law, which they did as much by their personal inclination as by his instruction. Together the brothers initiated publication in 1854 of what has become the great historical dictionary of the German language, the *Deutsches Wörterbuch*. In this they most likely inspired the English Philological Society to begin their great project three years later, in 1857, of a dictionary "to begin at the beginning," with dictionary entries to use quotations from "all the great English writers of all ages, and from all writers whatever before the sixteenth century," in order to give an account of the "meaning, origin, and history of English words now in general use."[4] This is an exact description of the procedure of the Grimms' *Deutsches Wörterbuch*, then well under way. The Philological Society's dictionary has now come to be called the *Oxford English Dictionary*, but its original title when it first appeared in 1888, *A New English Dictionary on Historical Principles*, pointed to its source of inspiration.

On his trip to Paris to work for and with Savigny, Jacob continually attempted to collect and save all the fragments of medieval German literature and law that he could. I say this only to emphasize the curious fact that the oldest known piece of secular German literature, the *Hildebrandslied*, was published by the brothers Grimm without alteration or addition, much less any attempt to supply an ending to make this single-page fragment an effective piece of literature. When it came to the remnants of ancient religious stories however, which the Grimms believed the fairy tales to be, they often reworked the material extensively and for effect. Why?

---

4. *A New English Dictionary on Historical Principles*, ed. James A. H. Murray, M.A. Oxon., Ph.D. Freiburg im Breisgau (Oxford: Clarendon, 1888), I, pp. iii–iv. It is significant that Murray's doctorate was taken in Germany where the historical method of the Grimms and Kluge would have been a strong influence on him.

The answer may lie partially in their observation and criticism of the uneven quality of many of the variants created in oral and written transmission, but it lies also in Wilhelm Grimm's concept of the fairy tales as being remnants of belief, in his affective approach to belief, and, in the concrete, in his intense liking of German medieval models of effective transcultural religious storytelling. This is true of the many epics which he taught and read, but especially of *Parzival* and the *Heliand,* in which Christianity reexpressed itself in Northern, Germanic forms, reimagining the Christian story and accepting "pagan" religious values. At the time when the Grimms' fairy tales were first published, their curious pagan-Christian nature was noted immediately by an English reviewer and was republished with obvious approval in the second edition of the *Kinder- und Hausmärchen (Grimms' Fairy Tales)*: "Among the most venerable remains of ancient Teutonic literature we should rank the abundant stores of popular legends and traditions, which often preserve most curious illustrations of heathen mythology and still more frequently exhibit it in a most incongruous combination with the Christian faith."5

Christian faith was so important a subject for the Grimms that, even though they were evidently not theologians, the entry in the seventh volume of their German dictionary covering *Glaube* (faith, belief) extends from page 7777 to page 7847! Significantly, the entry begins with the Greek word *pistis* and the Latin *fides,* and it goes on to note the relationship of the word to its medieval Low German equivalent, *gelof,* a form not entirely distant from the English "love." The word is directly related to medieval English *leaf* meaning "dear" or "esteemed." The Grimms briefly note Aquinas's definition—"faith is an act of the intellect moved by the will" (fides est actus intellectus secundum quod a voluntate movetur)—and then extensively and affirmatively cite Luther's counter to that definition:

> Against this there is Luther's rejection of any definition of belief as essentially something of the intellect: "this sort of faith is more a kind of science. . . . They (the papists) define faith as accepting all the things which they have heard and keep from Christ as true, but the devils believe the same things and that doesn't make them any more holy. . . . [True faith] is not just a type of acknowledgment in which I hold everything which God has revealed to us in his word to be true, but it is also a trust that comes from the heart which the Holy Spirit works up in me through the gospel. . . . Faith is a firm, unwavering, unshaking position taken by the heart. . . . Faith is always belief in a person."
>
> (dagegen Luthers ablehnung einer wesentlichen intellectuellen bewertung: "diszer glaub ist mehr eyn wissenschafft. . . . sie (die papisten) heiszen das

5. *The New Monthly Magazine,* no. VIII (August), London, 1821, p. 148. Cited in Rölleke, *Jubiläumsausgabe,* III, p. 293.

glauben, das sie von Christo gehört haben und halten, es sey alles war, wie denn auch die teuffel auch glauben und werden dennoch nicht frum da durch. . . . [warer glaub] ist nicht allein eine gewisse erkandtnusz, dardurch ich alles für war halte was uns gott in seinem wort hat offenbaret: sondern auch ein hertzliches vertrauen, solches der heilige geist durchs evangelium in mir würket. . . . der glaub ist und sol auch sein ein standfest des hertzens, der nicht wancket, wackelt. . . . Der glaub geht allezeit auf eine person.")

To further bolster this definition, the Grimms give five individual citations from German antiquity's unique version of the gospel story, the *Heliand,* including "hluttro habas thu an thinan herron gilobon" (You should have transparent trust in your Lord). The Grimms therefore saw faith as effective only if it moves the heart of the reader of the gospel to trust. "The devils hear and know all the same things and it does them no good, because they are not moved." This Luther-inspired insight on the nature of faith is important if the Grimms regarded the fragments of religious poetry, the fairy tales, as documents of faith. Such documents would then do the reader no good if the reader were not moved by them in his heart. Wilhelm said as much when he wrote that the reason for telling fairy tales was to awaken the thoughts and feelings of the heart. The theology of the Reformed church in which the brothers were raised would have said much the same thing on the importance of faith as a felt movement of the heart. Calvin in his *Institutes of the Christian Faith* would perhaps go even further than the gospel story and say that the purpose of the sacraments themselves, of Baptism and Communion, is to strengthen the faith of the recipient and the congregation, since it is through their feeling of the emotion of belief that they know that they are saved. Arousing such feelings of the heart is the very purpose of the Reformed preacher whose office Wilhelm so admired as a vocation when he mused in the little church in Steinau where his grandfather had been the preacher and pastor. The purpose of the preacher and the purpose of telling fairy tales coincided for Wilhelm Grimm, and if the tales were only fragments, and as such had become incapable of arousing the religious feelings of the heart, then Wilhelm would and did restore them to religious life, giving them back their ancient ability to move the spirit. In sum, to leave a secular fragment as it is and publish it meticulously as it is, a possibly ineffective remnant of a story, is to do no injury to it. To publish a fragment of a poem of belief in the same manner would be to publish it not for what it is, but rather for its value as information, effective perhaps as a secular document, ineffective as a story of faith, a fragment without its heart. A religious poem requires resuscitation in order to be published as what it is. The challenge which Wilhelm faced was how to revive the religious feelings in fragmented ancient pagan stories in such a way that they would elicit a religious reaction of the heart of Christian contemporaries.

Early Models of Religious Storytelling

Over the years from 1808 to 1857 the brothers, and especially Wilhelm Grimm, had many medieval models for effective transcultural religious storytelling at their fingertips. The *Heliand* was first written c. 830 and first published, with the help and encouragement of Grimm scholarship, in 1830 by a printing press. In Northern Europe and England in the early Middle Ages the *Heliand* had been a well-known religious epic poem. When I went to Berlin to see the copy that had been in Jacob's library, I was quite astonished by the stark brevity of the two-word dedication of the work printed by Schmeller, the publisher, in inch-high letters: *Iacobo Grimmio,* "to Jacob Grimm." Nothing could have been more appropriate. The *Heliand* would have amazed the English reviewer mentioned above, who was taken aback by the juxtaposition of the pagan and Christian in the *Grimms' Fairy Tales.* The entire story of Jesus is recast in pagan Germanic terms. There are no trolls or dwarfs, but the Holy Spirit does land and perch on the shoulder of Jesus, following the iconography of Woden. The prophets Simeon and Anna are "soothsayers," Jesus is the "chieftain" of mankind, and his most dangerous enemy is not Satan but "the workings of fate." Jacob did note in his realism, however, on the rear flyleaf of his copy of the *Heliand,* that the jackass which carried Jesus into Jerusalem on Palm Sunday had been omitted from the story. That absence was probably a deliberate adaptation, to avoid inappropriate Germanic laughter.

Wilhelm also had his own copy of the *Heliand,* now in the Hessian state archives in Marburg. In it I found his notation of the fact that the preface is parallel to the Caedmon story in Bede. There is an *arbor vitae* sprig marking Song 32 in which Christ is not thrown over the cliff at Nazareth because it is not yet his fated time, and a second marker at the story of the birth of John the Baptist. The latter story is one whose beginning has a very familiar parallel in the fairy tales: it begins with a childless couple who are promised an infant. The author of the *Heliand* is also quite concerned at this point to find a proper role for pagan fate within the Christian gospel:

> [The angel is speaking in the temple to priest Zachary.] My name is Gabriel, I always stand before God, I am always in the presence of the All-Ruler, except when He wishes to send me off on His affairs. Now He has sent me on this journey and told me to let you know that a child will be born to you—from your elderly wife a child will be granted to you in this world—and he will be wise in words. Never in his lifetime will he drink hard cider or wine in this world: this is the way the workings of fate made him, time formed him, and the power of God as well. . . .
>
>   Soon thereafter the power of God, His mighty strength, was felt: the wife [Elizabeth], a woman in her old age, became pregnant—soon the husband, that godly man, would have an heir, an infant boy born in the hill-fort.

The woman awaited the workings of fate. The winter skidded by and the year measured its way past. John came to the light of mankind. His body was beautiful and his skin was fair, as were his hair and fingernails, and his cheeks shone![6]

The *Heliand* provides a unique example for the attempt to weave pagan piety into the gospel story itself. The unknown author's method is to allow God the ultimate power to bring things and people into existence, but fate and time play their ancient roles as well. Fate and time determine the physical characteristics of the baby, the length of pregnancy, and assign the time and hour of death. Even winter is woven into the tale of John the Baptist's birth. The religious tone and pagan-Christian compositional style of Wilhelm's revision of the tales are here, including the beauty of the child, the passing of winter, the combined decrees of fate and the power of God, worked into a Christian narrative. And, if the *Heliand* depicts Jesus as a chieftain, might not the Grimms have felt it appropriate to see him as a prince?

Wilhelm Grimm's other model may well have been the knight Wolfram von Eschenbach's early thirteenth-century *Parzival*. In that sweeping, medieval crusader's epic, faith is reimagined as a knightly quest for the grail. Belief as acceptance of Jesus is changed, reimagined as arriving at feelings, arriving at loving interest in the suffering of Anfortas who is in pain caused by a mysterious bleeding lance (Crucifixion story) and by the zenith of the planet Saturn (Roman god of time). The surprising thing about Wolfram's story of salvation is that it is ecumenical. At the end of the epic, when Parzival the Christian knight is engaged in a last desperate fight with a pagan knight, Feirefiz, who is disconcertingly his equal in swordsmanship, Parzival's sword shatters. Though Parzival is helpless, his pagan enemy, a character created by the author in order to make his point, refuses to kill Parzival because there would be no glory in killing an unarmed man. The two equally chivalrous and exhausted knights sit down on the ground among the flowers and gradually recognize each other as sons of the same father, Gahmuret of Anjou. They are brothers biologically and also religiously, since, as they talk on, they agree that Christian and Moslem, and all human beings, have only one Father who created them. The crusader then realizes that this makes killing a Moslem an act of fratricide—which means the central activity of the Crusades must be divinely forbidden. This religious epic of the thirteenth century, which so acknowledges the spirituality of the chivalry of knights of other religions because it is rooted in feelings of belief and love, even has a passage at the end in which the Moslem decides to be baptized because of love—he has fallen in love with Parzival's aunt, a Christian woman. Before anything can happen, Parzival notices that tears of love are streaming down

---

6. *The Heliand, The Saxon Gospel,* trans. G. Ronald Murphy, S. J. (New York: Oxford University Press, 1992), pp. 7–10.

the face of his pagan brother and realizes further that those flowing waters of human love are a kind of baptism.

This surpassing masterpiece of pagan-Christian harmony within the love of the one Father is one of the works which Wilhelm Grimm taught at the University of Marburg. His copy of the text is still there in the Hessian state archives in Marburg, and it still has his underlining and marginal notes on difficult expression requiring explanation during class. When I went through it, looking at his notes in his precise and minute handwriting, I realized how close its world of human and religious feelings was to the world of the Grimms' fairy tales.

The most important lines of *Parzival* noted by Wilhelm in this regard may be the following realization, which the hero of the tale arrives at after finally feeling enough interest in his uncle's suffering to break the rules of decorum to ask Anfortas what is troubling him. (It is marked with a vertical line alongside the text and one verse is underlined.) As he rides along, Parzival is filled with happiness over Anfortas's healing from the spear wound in his genitals and from his years of lying poisoned in his bed made of the skin of a snake. The scene thus alludes sexually to the results of the Fall in the Garden of Eden, with the effect of the "poisoned apple" and the original sin being human weakness, a possible meaning of "An-fortas." Parzival has cured Anfortas by bringing compassionate interest to the snake-skin bed of "human weakness" simply by asking his uncle what the problem is. Parzival has become a spontaneously goodhearted person, he now feels great happiness for Anfortas's sake. He is thinking out loud: God has enormous greatness. Who ever sat in council to give him advice? Or who knows any limit of his strength? All the companies of angels could never get to the bottom of it." (797,23ff). The next three lines are the ones noted by Wilhelm:

> Got ist mensch unt sins vater wort
> got ist vater unde suon,
> sin geist mac groze helfe tuon. (797, 28–30)

> (God is human, and also the father's word,
> *God is father and son:*
> this spirit of God can be of great help.)

The Divinity itself gives an example of how two religiously separate persons are one: God is the Father and the Son, Christ is both human and the divine Word. The crusader is being prepared to see himself and the Moslem as brothers, united by the baptism of love. The Holy Spirit is in the passage because it is by the waters of baptism that the effects of the Fall are taken away, and this very passage is repeated by the priest at the moment of the baptism of Feirefiz. The second occurrence of this passage was underlined as above and also marked by Wilhelm with a double line in the margin, and is therefore of importance to him. The "Spirit" who as the dove is everywhere in the fairy tales is seen here in its transcendent identity as the divine spirit of love and unifying harmony. In his revised fairy tales, Wilhelm has the dove play this role in *Hansel and Gretel* and in *Cinderella*—in the one case leading the children home when the bread crumbs cannot, and in the other creating a transcendent unity between the belief-filled daughter and her dead mother. The dove in *Parzival* is ubiquitous because it is the insignia of the knights of the Holy Grail, but also because it unites heaven and earth by bringing down the communion wafer to rest on the stone of the Grail. As in the fairy tales, therefore, the dove is the manifestation of the harmonizing and communicating function of the Holy Spirit.

Wilhelm also underlined the simple question asked about Christ by the gray knight. He is speaking to Parzival, who is oblivious that it is Good Friday, "Do you mean God to whom the virgin gave birth?" ("meint ir got den diu magt gebar?" 449, 29). Wilhelm underscored the passage about the shield brought to Parzival painted inside and out with the pierced man (42, 28) and the reference to weeping and providence in the blessing said to Gawain: "May He whose hand salted the sea give you support in your trouble" ("des hant dez mer gesalzen hat, der geb iu für kumber rat" 514, 15).

Passages of feelings of love are marked everywhere. After describing the lips of two daughters of the gray knight in the Good Friday passage as red, hot, and thick, Wilhelm put a double line in the margin next to the comment that follows in the text, "however, the lips were not held sensuously, in accordance with nature of the day" (449. 29–30), and wrote in the margin "Vor scham bewegt wie am Karfreitag" (moved by shame as on Good Friday). For Wilhelm it seems that shame, in good medieval style, is a very good thing because it shows that the hero has a sense of religious honor; he is capable of feeling ashamed of himself, especially in comparing his own demeanor to the modesty exhibited by the two young women in honor of Good Friday. Love as the force that leads the good knight on to chivalry by putting the capability of feeling shame in his heart is also able to "conduct" high feelings into his heart. This passage is marked with an "X" in the margin:

> die minne condwierte
> in sin manlich herze hohon muot,
> als sie noch heute dem minne gernden tuot. (736, 6–8)
>
> Love led
> exalted feelings into his manly heart,
> as she still does to lovers today.)

"Love leads the way" is also the name of the woman whom Parzival loves, "Condwiramurs," lightly disguised by using a French form. The same disguised form is used for the place of the Grail to which Parzival is destined and being led by her (but where he initially fails the test for lack of loving interest). It is called "Munsalvaesche," probably from *mons salvationis*, "Mount

Salvation." Wilhelm's "little house deep in the forest" serves as the parallel destined place of testing and eventual rescue or salvation, to which the dove leads Hansel and Gretel and Little Red Riding Hood and Snow White.

On the front flyleaf of his *Parzival*, Wilhelm wrote in very minute script, "Gawain findet auf dem weg eine haarflechte . . . drei blutstropfen im schnee, die ihn an seine geliebte erinnern" (Gawain finds a braid of hair on the road . . . three drops of blood in the snow which remind him of the woman he loves). Granted the many variants on this image in the fairy tale tradition of *Snow White*, it is obvious that the *three* drops in *Parzival* made the brothers change the manuscript version, "*a couple of* drops" to "*three*" drops, trusting to the authenticity of the medieval text to show the oldest Germanic tradition. The same is true for the snow. In alternate versions of *Snow White* the blood falls on cheese, or even on milk. The Grimms would consider only "snow" appropriate, because of the light snow on the ground in the parallel scenes with Parzival and Gawain in the thirteenth-century epic.

Wilhelm placed a double vertical line alongside another passage referring to love: "Parzival's radiance [beauty] would be good as a set of tongs, it holds his faithfulness fast." He also marked Wolfram's complaint that love makes his head spin and takes his sense away (287, 11–18), which follows on the passage in which Parzival is supposed to be defending himself in combat, but is utterly entranced by the image of three drops of blood in the snow and the memory they bring of his beloved. The blood comes from a bird just downed by a hawk, the common medieval symbol of the amorous, searching heart. Wilhelm underlined the word "jewel" in the passage marked with a vertical line (371, 27–30) in which love promises to grant the power which she possesses to make her servitor unsurpassable and invincible. "I will take pains to prepare my *jewel* for you. Whenever you wear it, in fame no one will ever be able to surpass you" (371, 27–30). The tone of *amor vincit omnia* is heard in all these passages and finds its echo in the Grimms' version of the ending of *Sleeping Beauty.*

There are two mentions of fairy tales in the margins of the *Parzival* text, the one noted above with regard to the drops of blood in the snow, and another next to the curious passage with the analogy of the short cow's tail and infidelity, "his faithfulness has such a short tail that even the third bite doesn't make it swat, he just runs off with the horseflies into the woods" (2, 21). Wilhelm's comment is interesting: "refers to an unknown fable, cf. *Grimms' Fairy Tales* 2, 101—" (Wilhelm's reference is to the persevering fidelity of a promised bride to her wildman-like husband). The interesting thing is that Wilhelm was clearly attempting to establish connections to the Grimms' fairy tales, and making reference to them even on obscure or unclear matters, while reading *Parzival*. In another passage he seems again to have been fascinated by an apparent allusion to a story that he is unfamiliar with. He wrote "unknown reference" next to "then he made a thrust with the knife through the hand." (310, 10) Several vertical lines appear next to remarks about the importance of stories' never lying and always telling the truth "It would be better if a lying story ("maere") were left outside in the snow for its mouth to freeze" (338, 17–21); for Wilhelm, apparently it was equally important for a fairy tale (*maerchen*) to tell the truth, the ultimate truth. His conviction that fairy tales could and should do this was, I think, the principle that guided (*condwirte*) his retelling of them as stories of the spirit.

Finally, Wilhelm noted three texts on the passage of time which may bear on the fairy tales. At the very end of *Parzival* he underlined the two lines which mention casually that there are many people in Brabant who may still know about the happy couple (826, 10). Wilhelm trusted that stories were handed down over time, even if with distortions imposed by the imperfection of human memory. The second passage is one of a more haunting memory. "*It is still for him as it was then,* when the people after the tournament were all in the windows" (*im ist noch wirs dan, end die gent/nach porte alda die venster stent*) (171, 5–6). The knight is aging, and this is at the beginning of the story, and already he sees his present reality through the eyes of the way it once was. He is conscious of an audience that once was there. This moving half-line almost betrays the whole way in which Wilhelm Grimm and many of the German Romantics felt about human consciousness of the world and the concomitant passage of time. One has only to look at the touching passage in his autobiography about his visit to his hometown of Steinau, many years after his parents had died, and his experience there of the past coming back to him in the church, and his experience outside his childhood house in which he almost thought he could see his mother moving across the field toward him as she once did, clothes blowing in the wind. "It is still for him as it was then." There is no wonder that he found it moving to discover this short and compassionate line written 700 years before him, and perhaps no wonder that he had such reverence for the Germanic religion which felt that memory was a divine attribute, a spiritual raven on the shoulder of Woden.

The last text which we will consider in the *Parzival* epic is one that Wilhelm noted as special by putting double lines alongside it both on the left and on the right side. It reads "hiest der aventiur wurf gespilt, / und ir begin ist gezilt" ("here the dice of the story has been rolled, and its beginning has been set") (112, 9–10). Parzival is fatherless at birth; Gahmuret is fourteen days in the grave as he is born. The ending of the story has been set, aimed at, too, since the death prevents father and brothers from knowing each other from the beginning, and all paths will lead to the two brothers, sons of a father they will never find, into recognizing each other in the midst of a religious fight. They will realize late that they are spiritual brothers as well, because of having another Father, and it all happened this way because the story began with such a curious cast of the dice. The thread of the narrative is determined from the first, just as the Greeks felt in the myth of the three spinners, the parcae, that the narrative of each life was set and predetermined. Greek myth is also a root of Indo-European heritage, and it too finds its way into Wilhelm's artistic efforts at bringing the old fragments of tales back to life.

Among the most important spiritual roots of the Grimms' tales are Wilhelm Grimm's own Christian spirituality. Instead of relying on his membership in the Reformed church to be the guide as to what his religious feelings must have been, I searched in the little town of Haldensleben and in Berlin at the Prussian State Library and in the adjacent Humboldt University Library for more concrete evidence. Wilhelm Grimm's New Testament, in the original Greek, was in Berlin, and his German Bible was in Haldensleben. The results of examining the numerous critical passages which he underlined and annotated are in their own chapter in this book. The results are gratifying. Wilhelm has been made out to be a moralizing type, he was, rather, more of a private, mystic soul. His biblical Christian devotion seems to have centered on three mysteries: the Holy Spirit as the divine awareness of human events, the Resurrection of Christ, and the two great commandments, love for God and for neighbor. The influence of this spirituality will be examined in each of the five fairy tales that follow.

In the following chapters I will first review some of the work of scholars who have dealt with the question of religion in the Grimms' tales. I will then detail the results of studying Wilhelm Grimm's markings in his choice of Scripture and consider five of the better-known stories from point of view of his spirituality as found therein, looking at the stories in their earliest manuscript form, contrasting them with Perrault and Basile's version to show the difference in tone and intent, and this will lead to the interpretation of the Grimms' final version of the five tales. I have appended the rarely seen first version of *Red Riding Hood* and an essay on that most revered of Germanic, pagan-Christian symbols, the Christmas tree.

It should surprise no one that the Grimms thought of religious belief in diachronic, or historical, terms. As they thought of words in terms of their historical roots, they thought in the same manner of the persistence of little spiritual stories as stemming from ancient roots in human faith, hope, and love. They thought of faith as a diachronic phenomenon. Thus, if asked to explain the theological importance of "fairy tale," they might begin in verbal chronological order as they did in what they called "witnesses" to fairy tales: the Greeks called them myths, the Romans called them fables, the Germans call them little stories, the English and French have come to call them fairy tales. The stories express changing forms of religious awareness over the course of time. The fables and myths express a feeling that nature is aware of us. We in turn are afraid of the passing of time and aging, the fates. Religious wisdom is to be conscious that nature is aware of us, and to be in awe of the parcae: the owl of Athena. Another form of religious awareness is to feel reverence for human thought and memory as divine phenomena, like twin birds perched on the shoulders: the ravens of Woden. Another form of religious consciousness is to be touched by the phenomenon of love when it occurs between us, or hovers between us and the world of nature: the dove from heaven.

The form of the bird has changed over time. For Wilhelm Grimm's story-telling that would be merely the effect of time passing. What always remains is the patient alertness of the bird's eye, the human feeling of faithful love, and the curious ability which both of these give the heart to awaken and fly.

Two

SCHOLARS AND THE RELIGIOUS SPIRIT OF THE TALES

My interest in religious meaning in the *Grimms' Fairy Tales* began with the appearance of Bruno Bettelheim's *The Uses of Enchantment, the Meaning and Importance of Fairy Tales*.[1] Bettelheim's application of psychological models to explain the tales struck me then, and now, as a brilliant work of interpretation, even though there are places, such as his reading of the seven dwarfs, where it seems he got carried away. Bettelheim consistently maintains a Freudian-Oedipal approach throughout the book and forcefully defends the therapeutic usefulness of the stories in raising children, but he also repeatedly makes reference to his feeling that the tales have unexplored religious significance. In referring to the return journey of Hansel and Gretel after they have defeated the witch, he comments: "Their way home is blocked by a 'big water' which they can only cross with the help of a white duck. The children do not encounter any expanse of water on their way in. Having to cross one on their return symbolizes a transition, and a new beginning of a higher level of existence (as in baptism)."[2] When he comments briefly on *The Seven Ravens*, Bettelheim speaks more fully on what he sees as baptismal symbolism in the tale:

In the Brother Grimm's story "The Seven Ravens" seven brothers disappear and become ravens as their sister enters life. Water has to be fetched from the well in a jug for the girl's baptism, and the loss of the jug is the fateful event which sets the stage for the story. The ceremony of baptism also heralds the beginning of a Christian existence. It is possible to view the seven brothers as representing that which had to disappear for Christianity to come into being. If so they represent the pre-christian, pagan world in which the seven planets stood for the sky gods of antiquity. The newborn girl is then the new religion, which can succeed only if the old creed does not interfere with its development. With Christianity, the brothers who represent paganism become relegated to darkness. But as ravens,

---

1. Bruno Bettelheim, *The Uses of Enchantment, the Meaning and Importance of Fairy Tales* (New York: Random House, 1976). I am here using the Vintage Books paperback edition.
2. Bettelheim, p. 164.

they dwell in a mountain at the end of the world, and this suggests their continued existence in a subterranean, subconscious world.[3]

When he discusses the possible survival of Greek mythology in Basile's tale of Talia, mother of the sun and the moon, who does not know that she had intercourse nor that she has "conceived without pleasure or sin," Bettelheim first comments that Basile is probably being influenced by the story of Leto, lover of Zeus, who bore him Apollo and Artemis, and then, thinking of the Virgin Mary, Bettelheim adds: "Most fairy tales of the Western World have at some time included Christian elements, so much so that an account of those underlying Christian meanings would make another book."[4] Thinking of the white birds which are present in so many of the Grimms' classical fairy tales, he comments on the dove in *Hansel and Gretel*, "The behavior of the birds symbolizes that the entire adventure was arranged for the children's benefit. Since early Christian times the white dove has symbolized superior benevolent powers. . . . Another white bird is needed to guide the children back to safety."[5]

In *The Three Languages* a young man learns to speak the languages of the frogs, the dogs, and the birds, which Bettelheim reads as mastering the urges of sex, violence, and the superego. Having achieved this mastery of self and created internal harmony, the young man is made pope, since he now deserves the "highest office on earth." At the end of the tale the young man celebrates his first Mass, and has no trouble with the Latin, nor perhaps even with the sermon, because two white doves alight on his shoulders and whisper into his ears everything that he has to say and do. Bettelheim adds an integrating comment:

> Learning the language of the birds follows naturally from having learned that of the dogs. The birds symbolize the higher aspirations of the superego and ego ideal. . . . White doves—which in religious symbolism stand for the Holy Ghost—inspire and enable the hero to achieve the most exalted position on earth; he gains it because he has learned to listen to the doves and do as they bid him. The hero has gained personality integration.[6]

What Bettelheim does not notice is the similarity of the image of the whispering doves perched on the shoulders of the young pope to the standard iconography of Woden and his two ravens, Hugin and Munin "mind and

---

3. Bettelheim, pp. 12–13, 14.

4. Bettelheim, p. 228. See also his discussion of "safe" stories, p. 8: "'Safe' stories mention neither death nor aging, the limits on our existence, nor the wish for eternal life. The fairy tale, by contrast, confronts the child squarely with the basic human predicaments."

5. Bettelheim, p. 164.

6. Bettelheim, p. 102.

memory," standing on his shoulders and whispering into his ears all that happens on the earthly middle world below.

Though Bettelheim can be criticized for using an amalgam of each tale for his interpretation of it, it is also interesting to note that he is biased in favor of the French version of tales for psychological interpretation, and yet his observations on the religious symbolism of water and baptism in the fairy tales are almost without exception references to the versions of the brothers Grimm.

The most distinguished scholar of the textual history of the Grimm versions is Heinz Rölleke, who has published not only the final versions of the tales with the notes on the fairy tales made by the brothers Grimm themselves, but more important, the earliest Grimm versions in the manuscripts and earliest printed editions, enabling scholars to examine the scope of the rewriting of several of the tales from the earliest versions of 1810 to the final edition of 1857. It is interesting, therefore, to contrast Rölleke's ideas on the religious element in the tales with the ideas of Bettelheim. In an essay published in 1985 he addressed the question of the role of God in the *Grimms' Fairy Tales*.[7] He gives four categories of ways in which God is present in the Grimms' versions of the tales. First, God is present in colloquial expressions (*redensartlich*), and as is appropriate to this form of presence, no one is really concerned with Him, and He is just as unconcerned about anything at all. He gives examples such as "Oh God," "dear Lord," and so on. Second, God is present in certain middle-class, Victorian exclamations that have made their way into the fairy tales via the middle-class Christian Zeitgeist incarnate in Wilhelm's quill, not in order to move the plot forward, but simply to be an adjunct contributor to general atmosphere.[8]

He gives examples from *Hansel and Gretel*. Hansel reassures Gretel, "God will not abandon us," and "Don't cry Gretel, go to sleep, God will help us." Rölleke assures us that it is not God in the story but the dumbness of the witch and the cleverness of the children which make the happy end possible. It is not God, he says—in contrast to Bettelheim's suggestion about the significance of the way the children come home over the water—who brings the children home to their father, but a magic duck. Christianity in the tales is just a layer of varnish.

In his third category, Rölleke maintains much the same concerning the rare personal appearances of God in the two hundred tales. He plays a totally insignificant role and never one that is critical of society. God is like the exclamations addressed to Him: a cliché, an insignificant add-on. In his fourth

---

7. In "Wo das Wünschen noch geholfen hat," *Gesammelte Aufsätze zu den "Kinder- und Hausmärchen" der Brüder Grimm* (Bonn: Bouvier Verlag, 1985).

8. "Wo das Wünschen," p. 212. "Also darf man auch diese intensiven und inständigen Nennungen und Anrufungen Gottes nicht als handlungsfördernd, sondern lediglich als atmosphärisches Beiwerk betrachten."

category, however, Rölleke acknowledges the intrusion of Christianity deep into several of the tales. This is for Rölleke a melancholy matter. In the story of *The Goose Girl*, he sees a story line deeply structured by the intrusion of a Christian philosophy of life: an interconnected plot of guilt, healing, and reconciliation. At the end of the tale the thirsty princess bends over the flowing water of a brook and drinks. As she drinks, the little cloth with the three magic drops of blood falls out of her bosom, and, without her noticing it, disappears forever downstream. The magic is gone as she drinks from the waters. For a moment even Rölleke is allowing himself to see in the flowing water something of Bettelheim's baptismal vision, albeit in a negative version. With the waters, he believes, the old pagan magic is gone.[9] Rölleke regrets that the tales have not remained in a pure animistic form. He sees the Christianity in them as an "add-on," usually harmless, and does not see the animistic-pagan and Christian elements in the stories in transhistorical, mutually supportive synthesis.

Rölleke also brings up a theological/aesthetic question that justifies the non-inclusion of Christianity in the Grimms' tales as he sees them. He refers to the realization of the brothers Grimm concerning the nature of fairy tales: "Fairy tales are survivals of an ancient faith that goes back to the earliest times, a faith which is expressed in the pictorial representation of things that go beyond the senses (*Märchen sind Überreste eines in die älteste Zeit hinaufreichenden Glaubens, der sich in bildlicher Auffassung übersinnlicher Dinge ausspricht*).[10] In other words, the oldest levels of the fairy tale faith go back to animism, Christianity is intrusive if one wishes to read the tales for their oldest level. "Oldest," however, is a term that needs a great deal of clarification. The oldest written European tales go back to Basile, older yet are those in the Norse tradition, still older are the Greek myths. The "oldest level" of a Grimm tale could mean anything from the above available myths, such as the Norse *Snaefrið* as the oldest form of *Snow White*, or a manuscript version of 1808, or a projected "oldest level of the tale *an sich*" which would be a Platonic abstraction created by the scholar. This latter would be of dubious helpfulness and objectivity, not to mention antiquity, and it would not get at the poetic religious nature of the stories as published by the brothers Grimm, where many ages or levels are skillfully woven together.

Theologically, Rölleke maintains, Christianity in fairy tales would have the problem of the Incarnation. In Christian belief, in the life of Jesus of Nazareth the eternal God entered into the world of time and was restricted by his humanity to a specific time and place, whereas the fairy tale hero is beyond time ("Gott ist in diese Zeit gekommen, der Märchenheld aber steht außerhalb jeder Zeit").[11] Granted that this is so, were Christianity to be pre-

---

9. "Wo das Wünschen," p. 217.
10. "Wo das Wünschen," p. 215.
11. "Wo das Wünschen," p. 216.

sent theologically in the tales, following the Grimms' insight above, it would be present in perceptible images of faith, *in bildlicher Auffassung* and in the depiction of the supernatural in natural things or symbolic persons intruding into the plot. In other words, Christ incarnate could not be depicted in the tales except in the form of faith-caused outcomes of the plot, or as the symbolic rescuer, or even in the form of "things" such as water, trees, and birds, when used to indicate the presence of spiritual awareness and providence. I maintain that this is indeed the case and that Wilhelm realized the aesthetic-theological problem which Rölleke has broached. Wilhelm solved the problem in good medieval Christian style: Christ is depicted not in biblical glory but rather in plotlines and endings that reflect Christian faith, in a rescuing prince coming from "beyond" the forest, and in things, magic things (the water of the river, doves)— in which the invisible is depicted happening— things that depict the spiritual and supernatural in a sacramental view of the natural world. This we will take up again when we examine Wilhelm Grimm's spirituality.

Rölleke's view is markedly different from Bettelheim's, and rests on the acceptance of the tales' rootedness in reconstructed unknown oral "Germanic" versions of the tales that are not merely pre-Wilhelm Grimm, but also pre-medieval. Such core versions would have to be scholarly reconstructions. Non-reconstructed tales which are that old do exist: the written tales of the classical Greeks and Romans. Most important, however, Rölleke is persuaded that, even if the word "the Lord" is a meaningless nineteenth-century addition in the fairy tales, the religion and faith, especially the ancient animistic form of faith, found in them is constituitive of their power of enchantment. Christianity, he maintains, as a later addition, often of Wilhelm, is not constitutive of the magic of the *Grimms' Fairy Tales*. In this he offers reassurance against the fear of historical-analytic scholars that in their attempts to find the earliest recoverable written versions of the Grimms' tales, they will lose the very magic that drove them to study the tales in the first place.[12] The earliest manuscript versions presumably, from 1808, before Wilhelm rewrote them, one must conclude from Rölleke's exhortation, are the ones that contain in pure form the familiar Grimm fairy-tale "magic." In this I disagree with him entirely.[13] For me it is the stories as rewritten by Wilhelm (and Jacob) in their final versions which are the works of art that charm us all with diachronic religious magic. In the words of Donald Ward, "Had Wilhelm Grimm not revised and restored the tales, no one other than a handful of

---

12. See "New Results of Research on Grimms' Fairy Tales," in *The Brothers Grimm and Folktale,* ed. James M. McGlathery (Urbana: University of Illinois Press), p. 109.

13. An effective example of how spare the first Grimm versions can be is given by Ellis in his *One Fairy Story Too Many, The Brothers Grimm and Their Tales* (Chicago: University of Chicago Press, 1983), pp. 54ff.

philologists and narrative researchers would have heard of them today."[14] In general for researchers on the literary side of the fence this sentiment is agreeable, regardless of point of view. The "handful of philologists" and folklore researchers, however, are not of the same sentiment and have found rather explosive expression in the writing of John M. Ellis. Their disappointment is acute that the Grimms' tales are not literally preserved remnants of ancient lore passed on in oral form by the "folk" from generation to generation, but rather that many of them are also in part what the title of most translations imply: "the Fairy Tales of the Brothers Grimm." This knowledge of the Grimms' rewriting of the tales leads Ellis to call the Grimms liars about their collected folklore and to call their stories "fakelore." His shock that these famous paragons of the simple *Märchen*, unadorned folk tales, are actually *Kunstmärchen*, tales that are deliberate works of art, is quite apparent. Ellis writes:

> The Grimms, it will be remembered, said in their preface that Dorothea Viehmann was the ideal story teller, a German peasant who told from her memory ancient tales from the old tradition of the Hessen region—"from the heart of the German-speaking area," as Gerstner later put it. But the facts were shockingly different: Dorothea Viehmann's first language was French, not German, and she was a member of a large community of Huguenots who had settled in the area, in which the language of church and school was still French. She was not a peasant but a thoroughly middle-class woman; she was not an untutored transmitter of folk tradition but, on the contrary, a literate woman who knew her Perrault; she was not a German but of French stock. The discrepancy between the Grimms' account of her and the real facts is astonishing, but what is just as astonishing is the way in which scholars have alluded to some of those facts seeming not to notice the way in which they made nonsense of what the Grimms had said. Already in 1959, Schoof reported: "She was the daughter of the innkeeper Johann Isaak Pierson and came from an old Huguenot family . . . Frau Viehmann whose source was Perrault, just like the Hassenpflugs."[15]

It is immediately clear why this gradual realization would disconcert two groups of scholars. For one thing, if the fairy tales were really works of Wilhelm Grimm's creative art, *Kunstmärchen*, then the proper literary study of them would necessarily treat each one of them as an individual aesthetic entity, would insist on the priority of the final version of 1857 as the proper object of study, and would subject them, as poetry, to literary analysis and inter-

---

14. In "New Misconceptions about Old Folktales" in *The Brothers Grimm and Folktale*, ed. James M. McGlathery (Urbana: University of Illinois Press), p. 95. See also in the same volume the essay of Lutz Röhrich on the need to interpret the tales, "The Quest of Meaning in Folk Narrative Research," pp. 1–15.

15. John M. Ellis, *One Fairy Story Too Many*, p. 32.

pretation involving their place, and Wilhelm Grimm's place, in the history of German literature. Folklorists would have to abandon any idea that the final versions of 1857, nor even the earliest versions of 1810 and 1812, would provide them with a royal road to ancient Germanic mythology via the generational continuity of the simple voice of the people. The reticence of the first group and the angry disappointment of the second (the Grimms are considered the founders of the scientific study of folklore) is what Ellis expresses. The anger of the second group may have abated somewhat as other scholars reasonably pointed out that it is foolish to expect that the Grimms would have had tape recorders and video cameras to do the literal collecting of storytelling as one might imagine it in our world. The Grimms did indeed acknowledge in their second preface, 1819, that they were responsible for the way in which the tales were expressed. Even in the example that Ellis gives,[16] it is clear that the brothers carefully copied down the plot of the story which they were told, accepting in good Aristotelian fashion that the plot contained the essence of the story, so that they could later re-create the full tale. What they copied down from the teller is little more than a sketch, somewhat useful perhaps to the folklorist, but completely unappealing as a work of art. Even Jacob wrote critically in the margin of one tale "the ending isn't right" (*"Endung stimmt nicht"*), a judgmental statement unambiguously calling for restorative or creative work (or both) to get the ending right. If then there are strong Germanic and Christian plot elements in the completed final versions of the tales, and not just some reworking in the realm of morals and language, and if these elements did not come down through history by way of Perrault via the Huguenot German families of the Viehmanns and the Hassenpflugs, then they must be the additions of Wilhelm (and Jacob) Grimm. If the final versions of the tales are the creative reworkings of traditional story material, as Goethe reworked the Faust tradition to the point of giving it a "happy end," then it is important to study Wilhelm Grimm as someone engaged in a task no more reprehensible than Goethe's.

Ruth Bottigheimer approaches the task of interpreting the corpus of 210 tales in the Grimm collection with a realistic view of their authorship. Quoting from a legal brief in which Wilhelm's sons, after Wilhelm's death, attempted to claim right of ownership of the collection she then gives her opinion of the importance of the Grimms' reworking of the tales:

> "Their collection came to be the mother of all subsequent collections. . . . In it lies the distinct individuality which authors manifest, [and] if any claim of authorship may be asserted it lies with them. Not in the sense that they composed and invented an uncomposable, uninventable material, but far more in the higher [sense] that they understood how to save this material from degeneration and how to breathe new life into it."

16. Ellis, p. 54.

This letter is meant to define the tales legally not literally, but it nonetheless clearly sets forth the terms in which Jacob Grimm understood their, and particularly Wilhelm's effort. The letter states that this collection legally belongs to them because of the formative effort they had upon it, an evaluation that provides the basic premise of my study, namely, that any consideration of the content of the *Kinder- und Hausmärchen* [the Grimms' Fairy Tales] must include an appreciation of the extent and nature of Wilhelm Grimm's reformulation of the text.[17]

I could not possibly agree more.

When it comes to the actual religious nature of the tales and of the extent to which they have been Christianized by Wilhelm, Bottigheimer comes to a conclusion that I find wide of the mark. First, in her chapter entitled "Christian Values and Christian Narratives," she accepts Rölleke's views that God in the tales is merely a very occasional and completely irrelevant intruder, and even then only in the form of a pious exclamation. She does state that "German and Christian are two concepts that have been inextricably linked in Germany for centuries,"[18] but instead of going back to the instances in medieval or later German literature, which might have led to consideration of Wilhelm's love of Wolfram's *Parzival*, and the *Heliand's* first edition being dedicated to Jacob, Bottigheimer gives a number of household examples, accurate enough, but from the realm of mottos and other clichés taken from parlor samplers or lintels rather than from literature. Her point, however, is clearly made: the concept of German and Christian have been linked in German culture, whether in harmony or in discord, for a millennium. While I agree with her observation that *Hansel and Gretel* does not become a Christian tale by the addition of a few pious exclamations, it becomes quite necessary to examine the symbolism and the plot alterations, as well as Wilhelm's own spirituality, to come to a more rounded poetic judgment on the religious spirit of the tale. If Wilhelm Grimm is the principal agent in this process, it might be appropriate to examine what he did of substance to the tales in reworking them, especially to the one he reworked the most, *Snow White*, rather than accepting that *The Sparrow and His Children* is the most Christian tale in the collection on the basis of the presence of the virtue of humility in a sparrow.

On the other hand, however, Bottigheimer speaks favorably or at least neutrally of a suggestion concerning Christian narrative material in the *Handwörterbuch des deutschen Märchens* which contradicts the view that a thoroughly non-Christian mentality underlies folk narrative:

---

17. Ruth B. Bottigheimer, *Grimms' Bad Girls and Bold Boys, The Moral and Social Vision of the Tales* (New Haven: Yale University Press, 1987), p. 7.

18. Bottigheimer, p. 144.

Dietz-Rüdiger Moser represents the antipodal position in "Christliche Erzählstoffe," which claims that the extent of Christian material in oral narrative has been underestimated in the past, citing the Catholic church's active role in disseminating Christian tales that then entered the oral tradition, especially during the Counter Reformation. The final word on this subject is not yet in.[19]

If one is open to the suggestion that both a symbolic approach and an examination of Wilhelm Grimm's spirituality are appropriate tools for ascertaining the role of religion in the tales, then it might be possible to determine which tales have been religiously modified, and to what degree and in what particular direction Christianized. Bottigheimer's view might then be open to the suggestion of rejecting Rölleke's sweeping negative judgment and of reexamining the basis for the use of the term "Christian" as applying par excellence to the sparrow tale. It might then be appropriate to modify her conclusion that "Christianized tales in the Grimms' collection separate the characters not so much into good and evil as into male and female, their fates determined and defined not according to the ethical and moral quality of their lives, but according to their sex."[20] The surprise in all of this might well be that it is precisely the most Christianized tales (without excluding the two earlier faith forms) which have become the most popular throughout the world.

In a brief but perceptive aside, moreover, Bottigheimer noted what I think is the very heart of Wilhelm's religious style of poetic composition:

In "The Juniper Tree" (no. 47), an elaborately intricate and beautiful symbol links classical allusions to immortality with Germanic and Biblical ones and narrates the first stage of the murdered boy's return to life:

"Then the juniper tree began to stir itself, and the branches parted asunder, and moved together again, just as if someone were rejoicing and clapping his hands [Germanic, the tree Yggdrasil]. At the same time a mist seemed to arise from the tree, and in the center of this mist it burned like a fire, and a beautiful bird flew out of the fire singing magnificently [Classical, the phoenix], and he flew high up in the air, and when he was gone, the juniper tree was just as it had been before, and the handkerchief with the bones was no longer there [biblical, Resurrection]."[21]

In other words, Wilhelm does indeed speak of immortality, but through a beautifully complex interweaving of the mytho-poetic imagery of three ancient faiths, which he both finds present and also weaves in, and in no way

19. Bottigheimer, p. 143.
20. Bottigheimer, p. 155.
21. Bottigheimer, p. 27.

can his transcendent religious poetry be restricted to the pious exclamations found in a few very circumscribed and relatively unknown "Christian tales." When writing his comments on the meaning of the phoenix in *The Golden Bird* (*Vom goldenen Vogel*), a tale in which brothers toss their youngest brother into a well from which he is later rescued by a compassionate fox, Wilhelm's poetic faith sees "the falling into the well" in this Germanic fairy tale as related to the biblical story of Joseph who was thrown by his brothers into a well. He then adds "and Joseph himself is none other than the phoenix, the golden bird."[22] The religious spirit in the tales, or religious faith as the Grimms maintained, is an ancient one and speaks in diachronic pictures of the unseen. The pictures, moreover, in strikingly close parallel to the Grimms' method of defining a word in their German dictionary, are arranged in a harmonized historical order, and this harmony we will examine in five of the most well-known stories.

Max Lüthi, looking at the Grimms' tales in the context of German literature, wrote: "The fairy tale is the poetic expression of the confidence that we are secure in a world not destitute of sense, that we can adapt ourselves to it and act and live even if we cannot view or comprehend the world as a whole."[23] He furthermore considers the authors of fairy tales to be great religious poets dealing with the great question, "What is man?" "Fairy tales certainly do not originate among simple folk but with great poets; and, in a sense, they provide an answer. . . . The fairy tale . . . presents its hero as one who, though not comprehending ultimate relationships, is led safely through the dangerous world."[24] In considering Mircea Eliade's view that listening to fairy tales was a sort of initiation rite, a baptism of the imagination, he cites with approval,

> "The folk tale transposes the initiation process into the sphere of imagination. . . . Without rendering account to ourselves but rather in the full belief that we are merely relaxing and being entertained, modern man too enjoys the imaginative initiation that the fairy tale affords us." How correct this scholar's assertion is can be shown in any folk fairy tale. It is not surprising that it becomes especially clear in the best known, most popular tales.[25]

It is precisely in these tales that the hero-heroine is led by supernatural forces acting through natural ones and that Wilhelm Grimm has most advanced the notion of divine providence acting through nature.

---

22. "Das Stürzen in den Brunnen . . . ist mit der Sage von Joseph, der ja auch sonst selbst der Phönix, (d.h. der Goldvogel) ist. . . ." Rölleke, *Synopse*, p. 331. I am indebted to Colin Bezener, a graduate student of mine, for noting this comment made by Wilhelm.

23. Max Lüthi, *Once Upon a Time, On the Nature of Fairy Tales* (New York: Ungar, 1970), p. 145.

24. Lüthi, p. 142.

25. Lüthi, p. 60.

Other critics, however, see either relatively little of the religious in the tales or a very great deal. An example of the first is Jack Zipes, who feels that the tales have a socially liberating function that he characterizes as the "progressive pursuit of home." This is a very appealing and insightful notion, one that could readily find authorial confirmation in the dogged pursuit of home which was a regular occurrence, and one of the sadder ones, in the lives of the brothers Grimm.[26] It certainly is a driving force in many of the most popular tales. Zipes, however, does not list religious spirituality in the form of a sublimated pursuit of home as one of the contributions of Wilhelm to the tales. In his introduction to his remarkable translation of the Grimms' tales he lists Wilhelm's authorial/editorial contributions as: stylistic smoothness, concern for sequential structure, liveliness and imagery, reinforcement of motives for action, infusion of psychological motifs, and the elimination of non-rustic elements from the tone.[27] When he ends his introductory essay, however, Zipes adds, "Though the Grimms imbued the tales with a heavy dose of Christian morality, the Protestant work ethic, and patriarchalism, they also wanted the tales to depict social injustices and possibilities for self-determination."[28] Is it really Christian morality and Protestant work ethic that give Wilhelm's revised versions of the tales their universal power of enchantment—or is it their multiple strands of spiritual faith?

On the other side, Norbert Glas seems to feel that the tales are entirely Christian. He gives a reading of them in which he remarks, "The fairy stories collected by the brothers Grimm are an infinite source of . . . pictures of events taking place within the human soul."[29] He is described with some annoyance by Dundes as interpreting *Little Red Riding Hood* in such a way that the grandmother is an old woman weak and in need of help. Red Riding Hood comes to her aid bringing bread and wine, just as in the Church Christ comes to the weak in the Bread and Wine to bring healing. The huntsman signifies wisdom. In the end the grandmother eats the cake, the bread, and the wine, thus receiving Holy Communion. The fairy tale *Little Red Riding Hood* describes thus in a most wonderful way the victory of the human soul

26. See Jack Zipes, "Dreams of a Better Bourgeois Life: The Psychosocial Origins of the Grimms' Tales," in McGlathery, *The Brothers Grimm and Folktale*, pp. 205–19.

27. *The Complete Fairy Tales of the Brothers Grimm*, trans. Jack Zipes (New York: Bantam, 1987), p. xxv.

28. *Complete Fairy Tales*, p. xxxi. Zipes too agrees that the Grimms substantially revised the tales, but for purposes of "sanitizing" them for the "bourgeois socialization" of children. "The Grimms gathered their tales primarily from petit bourgeois or educated middle-class people, who had already introduced bourgeois notions into their versions. In all cases the Grimms did more than simply change and improve the style of the tales: they expanded them and made substantial changes in characters and meaning." Jack Zipes, *Fairy Tales of the Brothers Grimm, The Classical Genre for Children and the Process of Civilization* (New York: Wildman Press, 1983), "Who's Afraid of the Brothers Grimm," pp. 45–70; citation, 47.

29. Cited by Alan Dundes in his "Interpreting Little Red Riding Hood Psychoanalytically," in McGlathery, ed., *The Brothers Grimm and Folktale*, p. 29.

over the wild and tempting forces of the wolf which want to prevent it from treading the true path into the future.[30] In my opinion Glas' reading may do justice to the Christian element in the tales, but at the fatal price of blindness to the importance of the religious charm that comes from the lively presence of the pagan figures and poetry in the narrative.

Maria Tatar, who has studied so extensively the surprising level of violence and grisly behavior in many of the tales, comes to a very interesting conclusion that final success does not go to those in the fairy tales who are brave and strong, neither the wolf nor the hunter, so to speak, but to the humble and the compassionate.[31] In this regard she emphasizes that the help that comes from the natural-supernatural world often comes after the humiliation of the heroine, such as Cinderella, has taken place. She also mentions from the history of German literature that the initial failure of Parzival at Munsalvaesche on the feast of St. Michael is his lack of compassion.[32] Wilhelm Grimm would have heartily agreed.

Two recent scholars have commented on the influence of Herder, the theologian of Romanticism. Judith Ryan comments on form: "The German Romantic poets followed in Herder's footsteps by combining an interest in oral traditions with scholarly research into written traditions.[33] Their familiarity with a wide variety of literary works from earlier periods provided models for the mixed-form texts they developed."[34] Christa Kamenetsky's admirable *The Brothers Grimm and Their Critics, Folktales and the Quest for Meaning*,[35] gives an additional basis for accepting the role of compassionate human feelings in the Grimms' tales, the influence of the humanistic thought of the theologian Herder. In her very encompassing and useful study, she highlights Herder's belief in the symphonic harmony of the ancient and natural poetry of all nations. "He believed that each ancient nation's voice was lovely in its own way, yet in harmony with the songs of other nations, they created a symphony that was symbolic of God's creation of the world."[36] The Grimms certainly

---

30. Dundes. Cf. Glas' *Red Riding Hood* (East Gannicox: Education and Science Publications, 1947), p. 3; and *Once Upon a Fairy Tale: Seven Favorite Folk and Fairy Tales by the Brothers Grimm*, translated and interpreted by Norbert Glas (Spring Valley, N.Y.: St. George Publications, 1976).

31. Maria Tatar, "Born Yesterday," in *The Hard Facts of the Grimms' Fairy Tales* (Princeton: Princeton University Press, 1987), pp. 85–105.

32. Tatar, "Born Yesterday," pp. 103–104.

33. Herder's collection of folksongs, "natural poetry" in his description, as opposed to "work-of-art poetry," was published in 1778–1779.

34. In "Hybrid Forms in German Romanticism," *Prosimetrum, Crosscultural Perspectives on Narrative in Prose and Verse*, ed. Joseph Harris and Karl Reichl (Cambridge: D. S. Brewer, 1997), p. 165. Ryan emphasizes the "wildness" of variety encouraged here, using the example of the English garden rather than the French. This is useful when thinking of the hidden variety involved in Wilhelm's weaving of diverse religious traditions in his retelling of the fairy tales.

35. Christa Kamenetsky, *The Brothers Grimm and Their Critics, Folktales and the Quest for Meaning* (Athens: Ohio University Press, 1992).

36. Kamenetsky, pp. 56–57.

must have been inspired with regard to the presentation of diverse images in the tales in harmonized, diachronic form, and by Herder's insistence in the story on rewarding the good and punishing the bad, but they differed from Herder as well. Herder thought little of violence in the tales and made a great deal more out of biblical stories and their usefulness than did the Grimms. They were completely with him, however, throughout their lives and their scholarly work, in balancing a love for their own nation's tradition with a belief that other nations should equally treasure their own poetry's role in the human "symphony." Kamenetsky quite rightly takes to task those scholars who accuse the Grimms of ethnocentricity and nationalism, citing the Grimms' prominent work on Irish and Slavic tales in particular, and deplores the presence of a certain scepticism that has crept in among the folklore-oriented critics with regard to the Grimms' work. Her final conclusion is that literary and psychological studies offer the most enlightened perspectives on the Grimms' tales.

Marina Warner sees both the Christian and the classical in the tales: "The Grimm Brothers worked on the *Kinder- und Hausmärchen* in draft after draft after the first edition of 1812, Wilhelm in particular infusing the new editions with his Christian fervor. . . . Just as [*King Lear's*] Cordelia is a fairytale heroine, a wronged youngest child, a forerunner of Cinderella, so Goneril and Regan are the wicked witches, ugly sisters; the unnatural women whom fairy tales indict."[37]

From all of this it seems very important to determine as clearly as possible just what the religious outlook of the brothers was and to apply it to the reading of the final version of the Grimms' tales. This is especially true, of course, for Wilhelm. There are two sources that we can turn to for this information and evidence. The first are the two autobiographies written by the brothers, and the second and truly invaluable source is the copy of the Greek New Testament that Wilhelm read early in the morning to begin his day, and in which he carefully underlined more than seventy-one passages.

37. Marina Warner, *From the Beast to the Blonde*, pp. 211, 228.

Three

THE SPIRITUALITY OF WILHELM GRIMM

Jacob Grimm begins his autobiography with a description of one of his earliest memories.

I was my parents' second son, born in I Ianau on the 4th of Jan. 1785. When I was about six years old my father was named judicial magistrate (Amtmann) of Steinau an der Straße, the town of his birth. It is of this area with its plentiful meadows and its beautiful encircling mountains that I have the most vivid memories of my childhood. All too soon, however, on the 10th of Jan. 1796, my father died. In my mind I can still see the black casket as I look sideways through the window, the pallbearers carrying yellow lemons and rosemary in their hands, as it moved by. I can still picture my father clearly. He was a very hardworking, orderly, loving man. I can still see his study, his desk, and, most of all, his bookcases with their books, always kept clean, even the red and green titles of many individual books are still clearly before my eyes.

We children were all raised strictly Reformed, not that there was much talk about it, mainly by deed and example. The few Lutherans who lived among us in our little country town I usually regarded as strangers, people with whom one could not associate in confidence. About Catholics who used to ride through our town from Salmünster, about an hour away, but who were generally identifiable by their more colorful clothing, I formed strange, slightly fearful ideas. To this day it seems as if I can only be completely devout and recollected if I am in a church furnished in Reformed style—all faith depends so much on the first impressions of childhood—and, in any case, the imagination knows how to decorate and put life into bare and empty places. Never was greater devotion inflamed in me as on my confirmation day, after I had just received Holy Communion, as I watched my mother walking toward the altar of the church in which my grandfather had once stood in the pulpit.[1]

There is a very great deal of Jacob in this simple paragraph, but above all the historical lens through which he viewed everything. He remembers his fa-

1. *Jacob Grimm Selbstbiographie*, hrsg. Ulrich Wyss (Munich: DTV, 1984), p. 23.

ther's death in the same breath in which he says of Steinau that was the place of his father's birth. He remembers his father's bookcases and no doubt is seeing in them the origin of his own love of books. When he thinks of the style of church in which he feels most at home, he thinks of the plain gothic Reformed church in which he was raised, and when he recalls the moment of his greatest childhood religious devotion, his confirmation day, he recalls that it was not so much the moment of his confirmation, of which he says nothing, nor even directly his participation in the Lord's Supper itself that moved him as much as it was the sight before his eyes of three generations in a moment of historical continuity in the Reformed church: his grandfather, now deceased, but whose pulpit still stands there, his mother as she approaches it, and himself as the latest link in this chain of holy continuity. It was this awareness that brought him to tears. Jacob has often been accused of having a much more narrowly sectarian spirituality than his brother Wilhelm, and this is indeed true, but one can see here the basis for it. As in linguistics, Jacob sees things in a moving line that runs from origin to the present, and feels that it is wrong or unnatural to break that line, and beautiful to see its course, and one's place as the latest instance along it. Obviously that includes religion.

Jacob's appreciation of his own Reformed lineage occasionally led him to make disparaging remarks, in one case about the "brighter clothed" Catholics. As Peppard writes:

> Jacob believed very sincerely that the modern German language was a product of Protestant thinking and in the preface to the second edition of his German Grammar asserted: "One may well designate New High German as the Protestant dialect whose liberating nature has long since overwhelmed poets and writers of the Catholic faith, quite without their realizing it." In his defense, however, in his personal and social contacts and in his many friendships, he never allowed his bias to interfere or become an obstacle.[2]

Peppard also notes, "In the normal routine of life they [the Grimm brothers] were not ostentatious about religion, churchgoing, or the formal expressions of faith, but in times of stress they were able to find simple, sincere, and moving words for their belief in God's guidance of the universe. . . . When Aunt Zimmer died, he [Jacob] had found his faith reconfirmed and wrote Wilhelm to comfort him with the assurance that *God would continue to help*."[3] This curious phrase, which several critics would characterize as a mere cliché, seems by context and, one might say, faith-context, to be much more than that: it is a part both of the autobiographies and of the fairy tales. It occurs in Jacob's description of his acceptance of the position of librarian

---

2. Murray B. Peppard, *Paths Through the Forest, A Biography of the Brothers Grimm* (NewYork: Holt, Rinehart and Winston, 1971), p. 6.

3. Peppard, p. 23.

at Göttingen. He reports on the friendliness of his reception by colleagues at Göttingen, and more than hints at his sad feelings at having to leave his homeland,[4] but adds with an optimism also put into the mouth of Hansel,

> I know that the area around Göttingen cannot be compared to that of Cassel, but the same stars are in the skies, and *God will continue to help us.*

> (Zwar ist die Göttinger Gegend nicht zu vergleichen mit der Kasseler, aber die nämlichen Sterne stehen am Himmel, und Gott wird uns weiter helfen.)[5]

In the case of Wilhelm, there is a parallel description of religious experience in the Reformed church of Steinau, but it does not come from early childhood, but from 1826, when he was forty years old, and well on into continuing revisions of the fairy tales. The recollections below come from his autobiography, which he wrote in 1830–31.

> In the autumn of 1826 business affairs brought me to Steinau, where I had not been in 20 years. The castle's familiar rectangular keep from which on Sundays trumpets played a chorale as we walked after church in solemn silence in the castle gardens with our mother, the churches and other high buildings still stood out against the clear sky as they always had. Much in the vicinity, however, had changed. New houses had been built on fertile garden fields. Several towers on the city gates had been torn down. Part of the castle where once the mother of the deceased Elector had lived (she was a princess of England, daughter of George II) had been changed into a prison during the time of the French [seven-year occupation] and the windows barred up. We have a constant feeling of how relentlessly everything is sinking, but I can not prevent myself from being moved when a memory brings me back, for a moment, into the midst of a lifetime long past which had other sorrows and other joys. . . .
>
> I had them bring me the keys to the church in which my grandfather had given his inaugural sermon a hundred years ago, and I walked into it all alone. Through the high windows the sun was shining down onto the floor of the church which was completely covered with grave stones, many of which went back to the 16th century. On one of them, directly in front of the altar, I found the names of my family: two brothers of my father lay there (he was the only one who survived), one of them who was called Friedrich had died in his youth and an inscription in Latin recalled the exceptional gifts of this child and the deep grief of his parents at his loss. The other one had just become a preacher in Hanau. Above both of them, between the altar and the pulpit, lay

---

4. "Die geliebte und gewohnte Heimath aufzugeben schien uns hart und schmerzhaft wie vorher, aus dem Geleise genau bekannter Beschäftigungen und einer uns Frucht bringenden Muße herauszutreten, fast unerträglich." *Jacob Grimm Selbstbiographie*, p. 36

5. *Jacob Grimm Selbstbiographie.*

my grandmother, and thus, every Sunday for twenty years, my grandfather strode across her grave to the pulpit. Nowadays people shy away from memories like that, but to me it seems more worthy to honor the memory of the dead in this way. . . . [My grandfather] had been the preacher for 47 years in the same town. How enviable his lot seemed to me: a richly blessed position, the love and respect of the community, leisure for contemplation and reflection together with a vital and joyful feeling of being alive.

I also looked for the garden [outside the walls] which my parents once owned. The tree was still standing on which my mother's white cloak used to hang, we could see it in the distance when we were coming home after school, and [as I stood there] it seemed to me as if I could see her walking slowly over the meadow.[6]

Dantur lacrimae rerum one is often tempted to think when reading Wilhelm's personal reflections. He almost automatically sees again the events of long ago happening in the fields and buildings which have lasted to the present, and then he feels sadness that the people who lived in those buildings are irretrievably gone, and that even the buildings they once knew are fading and sinking away. When it comes to persons once loved, the existence of persons of the past in the present, there is something of a sadly mystical and romantic turn in "it seemed to me as if I saw her." It is indeed common to the spirituality of both brothers that a time dimension, whether in their stories or in their research, is never absent from their feelings. Wilhelm, like Jacob, possessed the ability to look at an old building—one in which a real princess did indeed live in a tower—and feel the joys and sorrows, though long past, which once were felt there. It is hard to miss the atmosphere and similarity to fairy tale in Wilhelm's description of his experience in the old church. It is not only the bright sunlight that impresses him, but the persons and feelings that lie under the flat gravestones on the floor. When he thinks of his relatives whose bodies lie there, he sees the position of his grandmother's stone and comes to the realization that whenever his grandfather wished to move from the altar to the pulpit he would have to walk across his wife's grave. The living, walking as they do on the basis of the dead, the preacher having to preach about death and resurrection, must truly realize what he is talking about, he passes over the grave of his wife on the way to the pulpit. It is almost as though there is a communion of saints suggested here just as there was in Jacob's experience of communion on his confirmation day. Wilhelm's praise of his grandfather's position of minister in the small community may reveal something of what he feels his position to be as he works not on sermons but on tales that one day the whole world will read.

Wilhelm's description of the tree and his mother's white cloak bears an uncanny affinity to Cinderella's visit to the tree-grave of her mother, and the

---

6. Wilhelm Grimm, "Selbstbiographie," in *Jacob Grimm und Wilhelm Grimm Werke*, hrsg. Ludwig Erich Schmitt (Hildesheim, Zürich, New York: Olms-Weidmann, 1992), XXXI, pp. 6–8.

beautiful clothes that the tree wafts down to her. Wilhelm, even more imagi-
natively than Jacob, sees a living connection between the people of the past
and those of the present in a communion of love, a love which is the only
thing that can possibly overcome the "irresistible" changes and deaths
wrought to Steinau and parents by the passage of time.

He was not immune to the effects of those forces on himself. Always rather
sickly compared to Jacob, he was regularly frightened by his possible death
during the early years of his work on the fairy tales. He suffered from asthma
and from a dangerous and frighteningly painful form of heart disease, recently
diagnosed as paroxysmal auricular tachycardia,[7] that would be treated at Jena
with the latest remedy, magnetism, without much help. The prolonged and
extremely painful attacks gave him a profound and frightening awareness of
human mortality.

> My sickliness had significantly increased after the death of my mother (1808).
> In addition to the restricted breath which made even climbing a few stairs an
> enormous burden as well as constant piercing pain in the chest, there now
> came cardiac sickness. I cannot compare the pain to anything except to the
> feeling that from time to time a red hot arrow was going through my heart,
> the pain was constantly accompanied by attacks of fear. Sometimes my heart
> would suddenly, without any external cause, begin a tremendous pounding
> which would then just as suddenly come to a stop. Once it lasted twenty hours
> without interruption and left me in a state of complete exhaustion. A feeling
> that I was then pretty close to death was certainly not without foundation.
>
> Many nights I spent sleepless, sitting upright [the doctors' advice was that it
> was safer to sleep in a chair] without moving, waiting for the gray light of day
> which always seemed to bring me some consolation. A quail [*Wachtel*, possibly
> the "waking" or "sentry" bird] hanging in a cage in front of a neighbor's win-
> dow was often the first one to announce the dawn, and to this day I cannot
> hear the peculiar sound of that bird with indifference.[8]

This passage says something about the person who felt his mortality so
soon in life and who had also experienced the loss of his father and mother at
an early age. His gratitude for the new day and his remembrance of the bird
that proclaimed at dawn that he was alive for the new day carries over into
the present. The enormous role of the helpful bird that occurs continually in
the Grimms' tales is therefore a matter of life experience for Wilhelm and
not just a result of reading or hearing stories.

---

7. I am indebted to Dr. John Collins Harvey and Dr. Josef Kadlec, S.J., of the Georgetown
Medical School for the diagnosis. It is based on Wilhelm's description of the symptoms as given
below. To this day there is apparently no known cure for the disease. While the patient's extreme fright is caused by the uncontrolled pounding of the rapidly beating heart, the "red-hot
arrow" pain is caused by the resulting acute lack of oxygen in the coronary arteries.

8. Wilhelm Grimm, "Selbstbiographie," pp. 15–16.

A last passage from his autobiography sounds almost like something from *Hansel and Gretel*. The two children, abandoned in the forest in the tale, fell asleep under a tree. Early in the morning, as with Wilhelm in his sick room, out of nowhere there was a white bird singing in a tree nearby to lead them on. In one of his earliest memories, from the time when the family was still in Hanau and he was about five years old, Wilhelm's description betrays the closeness of his feelings when he reflectively writes his own history to the imagery and feelings which he enhances in the fairy tales: "I can still remember no less vividly how the two of us, Jacob and I, walked hand in hand across the Newtown market area to the house of a French teacher who lived next to the church, and in childish glee stood still in order to watch the golden rooster on top of the spire as it turned back and forth in the wind."[9]

Wilhelm fell in love with and married the source of many of his fairy tales, Henriette Dorothee Wild, nicknamed Dortchen, a neighbor of French Huguenot ancestry whom his mother had also been quite fond of. Of his marriage with Dortchen, he said, "I never cease to be thankful to God for its happiness and wealth of blessings."[10] At the time of his writing, 1830, their third child, Rudolf, had just been born, and the second, Hermann, was thriving; but the couple's first child, who had been named Jacob after Wilhelm's brother, had died in 1826 only eight months after his birth. He was buried next to Wilhelm and Jacob's mother.

In order to find out more about the inner spirituality of this imaginative and loving teller of our most well-known and beloved fairy tales, I consulted with colleagues about the possible existence in Germany of copies of Scripture that might contain notes or underlined passages by Wilhelm. I was encouraged to proceed with the search, and Professor Bottigheimer assured me that Grimm-related Bibles existed in Hesse and that she had once seen a family Bible of the Grimms' great-grandfather there, but had not had time to examine it. I found two Bibles in Steinau, one a preacher's Bible with alternate pages empty for making sermon notes, and another in which Jacob, thinking diachronically as one might expect, had written a very extensive family tree on the flyleaf. There are however no notes or underlined passages in either. I was a bit disappointed.

As I later sat in Berlin at the Humboldt University Library, I watched the librarian approaching me with a full cart load of books from the Grimms' private library, I knew immediately the modest volume I had been looking for. I deliberately looked at a couple of other books first. And then I picked it up. A strange feeling came over me about looking into another person's private

---

9. Wilhelm Grimm, "Selbstbiographie," p. 1.

10. Wilhelm Grimm, "Selbstbiographie," p. 23. "Ich bin seit dem 15ten Mai 1825 verheiratet mit Henriette Dorothee wild und habe niemals aufgehört, Gott für das Glück und Segensreiche der Ehe dankbar zu sein."

The altar and pulpit from the position in the church in which Wilhelm stood on the day on which he visited Steinau as described in his autobiography. He commented on the light streaming in the windows and meditated on the family grave stones set in the floor (since placed outside in a "fit of renovation"). The sight of the altar and the pulpit moved him to think of his grandfather. In a thought reminiscent of the grave scene in Cinderella, *Wilhelm wrote of his admiration for the spiritual faith of his grandfather who, every time he went from the altar to the pulpit to preach, had to walk across the grave of his deceased wife. It is also on this spot that Jacob, as related in his autobiography, watched his mother approach the altar for Communion and was moved by the sight of his family's long religious continuity. Drawing by Laurence Selim, from a photo by the author.*

religious thoughts, feelings which had occurred a hundred and fifty years ago. Then I opened it, and a small shower of dark dried flower petals, color long gone, fell into my lap, along with bits and pieces of small leaves, and whole sprigs of rue, still green. It was Wilhelm's own copy of the Greek New Testament[11]—of course Wilhelm Grimm would read the New Testament in the original, he believed in continuity with origins. Then came an even happier surprise, the one in hope of which I had come to Germany. Wilhelm, who "was an early riser and often began his day with readings in the Greek New Testament"[12] had used his fine quill to write on the front flyleaf, "den 14ⁿ Julius 1820. W.C. Grimm" (the 14th of July 1820. W. C. Grimm) and over time had underlined seventy-one passages in the text. The importance of the discovery of these passages for an insight into the Christian spirituality of the poet of the final version of the Grimms' fairy tales is simply unparalleled.

Among the surprises: first, there is almost no trace of interest in the fatalism or predestination that might be presumed from Wilhelm's Calvinist Reformed forbears. Second, there are no markings reflecting a moralism, neither Pauline strictures that might support the Protestant work ethic nor any on sin and judgment, which might have been presumed from the same source or from the occasional reproaches of recent criticism. Third, there are no markings to be found in any of the Pauline letters nor in the Book of Revelation. Of the seventy-one passages carefully and precisely underlined by Wilhelm, twenty-one are from John's Gospel, nineteen are from Luke, sixteen are from Acts, twelve are from Matthew's Gospel, and three are from Mark's. Wilhelm's obvious predilection is for the teachings of Jesus in the gospel story and, within that context, for those teachings in the mystical form given in John's Gospel and in the humane-social form of Luke-Acts. Perhaps surprisingly indeed he shows very little interest in the miracles and wondrous cures that fill the pages of Mark. Love, in its many biblical manifestations, the Spirit of God, divine providence, love of God and of neighbor, faithful confidence, ecumenical acceptance of other faiths, the Resurrection to eternal life, is the common thread among the themes that moved him most in the pages of his New Testament. Love seems to have guaranteed him the hope for contact over time that he so longed for. I have grouped Wilhelm's underlined passages under eleven somewhat overlapping categories, the categories listed approximately in the order of the number of underlin-

11. *Novum Testamentum Graece,* Schott (Leipzig: 1811). The edition has a Latin translation on facing pages. The text corresponds almost in every detail with a modern critical edition, but there are variations, including verse numbering. For this reason in the listing of the verses in the Appendix, I have included the beginning and ending of each underlined verse as it is in Wilhelm's version. This is for the convenience of anyone who would like to locate it or compare it with Nestle-Aland. The English is my translation of the words that Wilhelm underlined.

12. Murray B. Peppard, *Paths Through the Forest, A Biography of the Brothers Grimm* (New York: Holt, Rinehart, Winston, 1971), p. 115.

ings in each one. This list of the passages together with the Greek text and suggestions for their relevance to the fairy tales is given in its entirety in Appendix A. The following is a summary of the main spiritual areas of interest indicated by the passages.

The Holy Spirit

"God is spirit, and those who worship him must worship in spirit and truth." The Spirit of God is understood in the citations marked by Wilhelm as the source of human awareness and life. "In him was life and the life was the light of men." "You have made known to me the ways of life . . . receive my spirit." "In him we live and move and have our being; as even some of your poets have said, 'For we are indeed his offspring.'" "John baptized with water, but you shall be baptized with Holy Spirit." "If you then who are evil know how to give good gifts to your children, how much more will the heavenly Father give the Holy Spirit to those who ask him!"

Passages connected with the Holy Spirit are the ones most frequently underlined by Wilhelm. The significance of the preoccupation with the indwelling of the divine Spirit in created beings makes it possible to suggest that Wilhelm felt an affinity between Christianity and animism, the ancient belief that all creatures have an anima, a soul or life principle, that makes them living, conscious beings and part of the universal Spirit.

Rölleke's theological observation, on the other hand, is that Christianity could not be in the fairy tales to any serious extent because Christianity is not based on a universal anima but rather on the Incarnation which is the historical reality of Jesus Christ as living in one very specific non-universal space and time. Wilhelm Grimm's spirituality however is quite Trinitarian, and is not solely concerned with the Incarnation of the second person of the Trinity and his life in first-century Palestine. Wilhelm Grimm's biblical notations reveal him to be equally preoccupied with the "Incarnation" of the third person of the Trinity, the Holy Spirit, as the breath of Adam and "the lord and giver of life" of all living creatures, "in Whom we live and breathe and have our being." It is the commonality of religious belief in the presence and consciousness of the provident Spirit of God throughout creation that enables Wilhelm's Christianity to be close to the tales' original animism. Furthermore, Wilhelm's emphasis on his belief in the divine Spirit may well explain the very prominent guiding presence in so many of those tales, as he rewrote them, of the animal which symbolically "incarnates" the Holy Spirit—the dove. Looked at over the long course of mythic time and religious faith, belief in the divine Spirit's diachronic awareness of human beings is expressed analogously as the raven of consciousness whispering into the ears of Woden, and the wide-eyed owl of wisdom at the feet of Athena.

Christ and Resurrection

The second most predominant focus suggested by the underlined passages is Christ and the Resurrection, the continuity of life. "I am the good[13] shepherd." "The Father is in me and I am in the Father." "I am the resurrection and life." "Peace I leave with you; my peace I give to you; not as the world gives do I give to you. Do not let your hearts be troubled and do not let them be afraid." One wonders if this last passage might have been underlined in memory of a night of tachycardia. "Remember me when you come into your kingdom." "For they [the dead] cannot die anymore, because they are equal to angels and are the sons of God being sons of the resurrection. Now he [God] is not the God of the dead, but of the living; for to him all of them are alive."

This selection of the second-largest group of citations suggests a clear bearing on Wilhelm's revision of the tales. Faith in resurrection is important to the introduction of the survival of Red Riding Hood in the Grimm version of the story, in contrast to her terminal death in the French version of Perrault. Belief in the survival of the dead and in their help is the heart of the enchantment of the Grimms' version of *Cinderella*, with its magic grave tree, something which is absent in Perrault, who uses a fairy godmother for the role, and this belief contributes to the endings of *Snow White* and *Sleeping Beauty*.

Love One Another

"This is my commandment: that you should love one another even as I loved you so you should love one another." "This I command you, to love one another." "The good person out of the treasure of his heart produces good." This latter passage echoes the ecumenical sentiment found in the *Heliand* that the source of revelation is the goodness of the human heart. "You shall love the Lord your God with your whole heart, and with all your soul, and with all your mind; and your neighbor as yourself." "Whatever you wish that people should do to you, do so to them." "Love one another."

In the revisions of the tales Wilhelm removes the satire of Basile and the cleverness of Perrault and replaces them with love, a love that reaches from

---

13. In the original Greek "good" is actually "beautiful"("καλος"). In other words the passage reads in Greek: "I am the *beautiful* shepherd." Christ is the beautiful shepherd in Scripture because he comes to rescue the lost sheep and to defend against the wolf. The passage suggests the identity of Christ with the hunter who saves Red Riding Hood and beautiful prince / rescuer of the classical tales who comes to save Snow White and Sleeping Beauty from the sleep of death. In the Grimms' fairy tales beauty is often a metaphor for internal goodness as it is here in the original language of this biblical passage. Wilhelm underlined this passage twice.

beyond the grave from a mother to her child in trouble, and to a soul made so lovable that even in death it attracts the prince to come from afar.

Humble Faith

"But he was beating his breast saying, "God, be merciful to me a sinner." "Why are you afraid, have you no faith?" "Not a hair of your head will perish." "Be it done for you as you have believed." Wilhelm copied out in his own hand the entire passage in which Paul notes to the Athenians that they have an altar dedicated "To the Unknown God." Not only is humility the characteristic which makes every hero or heroine in the magic tales savable, as Wilhelm writes them, but the acknowledgment by St. Paul of the validity of pagan worship "to the unknown god" gives a Christian theological standing to older forms of pagan faith. This verse was of great importance to Wilhelm, I believe, in justifying his manner of diachronically synthesizing the humility and faith, the piety, found in both pagan and Christian poetry.

In addition, Wilhelm underscored passages on the subject of poverty and wealth such as "seek first the kingdom of God and his righteousness, and all these things will be given to you as well"; on rejection, such as "I say to you that no prophet is accepted in his own country" and "Love your enemies and pray for those who persecute you;" on the Word, "The heavens and the earth will pass away, but my words will not pass away." He noted the need for family bread, for Christ as "the living bread that anyone may eat of and not die." Not unexpectedly and touchingly he underlined the New Testament's regard for a significant portion of his audience—children: "Let the little children come unto me and do not prevent them for to such belongs the kingdom of heaven."

Wilhelm's second copy of Scripture is at Haldensleben in Lower Saxony, brought there by his granddaughter who spent much of her life in that small town as a schoolteacher. Albertine was the daughter of Rudolf, the third son of Wilhelm and Dortchen. Rudolf's marriage to his intended was prevented by the disapproval of his older brother Hermann and his wife, who felt that she was not an appropriate match for a member of the Grimm family. Rudolf therefore simply lived with his "amie" and the daughter of their relationship was Albertine. When Albertine settled in Haldensleben she brought many interesting mementos, furniture, letters, Jacob's formal uniform from the Congress of Vienna, and her grandfather Wilhelm's German Bible. The small museum in the town is as warm and welcoming a place to a scholar or interested visitor nowadays as the Grimm household must have been, once upon a time.

On opening this Bible, once again a shower of flower petals and leaves, long ago placed there, fell into my lap. The volume contained two paper markers, three oleander leaves, two pink and one yellow ribbon markers, and three red markings next to texts relating to poverty and wealth, and a five-lobed flower that I could not identify, though I recognized one of its petals from the Greek New Testament at the Humboldt University Library in Berlin. The book was obviously subjected to much use—including that of drying flowers!

The Bible[14] is a corrected (*berichtigte*) version of Luther's translation which had been published only two years before Wilhelm acquired it. Inside, on the front cover, Wilhelm wrote the following: "Erhalten am 3n Febr. 1821. Morgens 11 Uhr bei Sonnenschein. W.C. Grimm," which indicates that the volume was "received on the 3rd of Feb., 1821, in the morning at 11 o'clock, the sun was shining."

The oleander leaves and ribbons may have marked places where Wilhelm was reading, but it is very uncertain what to make of their meaning, since they may be random placements, and nothing in the text itself is marked or underlined to assist in their interpretation. The two paper markers however are a different story. The first is at a familiar spot, the beginning of John's Gospel: "In the beginning was the word, and the word was with God." (This is the inscription later placed by the Grimms on the title page of their German Dictionary.) The second is also placed in John's Gospel, between Chapters 16 and 18, at Jesus' farewell speech at the Last Supper. In his final talk to his followers Jesus here makes the promise to send the divine Spirit to them from heaven, warns them that the world will hate them and begs them to remain lovingly as one. He prays to the Father that "the love with which you loved me may be in them and I in them." The paper marker has one word carefully written on it: "Göttingen." Much of the above in Jesus' words certainly was pertinent to the experience of the two brothers in that fateful period of their lives. Perhaps the marker was inserted in the year 1829 when the brothers had just received the good news that they had been appointed librarians in Göttingen, or, if one is more pessimistic, when they were coping with the news eight years later that they would have to leave. I favor the former, but only for the slim reason that the word "Göttingen" is written so clearly, almost proudly; on the other hand, the marker is at Jesus' farewell thoughts. The subtitle which the printer gave for this section of the Bible, in any case, is "Christ's prayer for himself, his disciples and community" (*Christi Gebet für sich, seine Jünger und Gemeine*).

The three oleander leaves indicate Wilhelm may have been reading 1 Maccabees 13–14 which includes the death of Jonathan, a period of peace, and the siege of Jerusalem. The second leaf is at 1 Maccabees 1:59–2:41, which deals with the refusal of the Jews to engage pragmatically in pagan worship—"It is better to serve God than men,"—a theme we have seen above—and their subsequent persecution and death. The third leaf was at Sirach 30:12–32:36,

---

14. *Die Heilige Schrift in berichtigter Uebersetzung mit kurzen Anmerkungen*, Johann Friedrich von Meyer (Frankfurt am Main: Verlag der Hermannschen Buchhandlung, 1819).

which advises moderation in eating and drinking, friendliness as a host, and a moderate attitude toward money. It is in this latter section that there are four unusual meandering colored lines in the margin next to four texts. These colored lines are not in Wilhelm's style and are almost surely by a later hand. They do not exhibit the fine precision characteristic everywhere else of Wilhelm's quill when noting a passage of interest. They are included in the appendix, however, for the sake of completeness.

Finally there is a last and very important notation by Wilhelm to consider. In the introduction to his corrected version of Luther's translation, Meyer as editor wrote very ecumenically. In speaking of the Bible and its long history of interpretation in the church, he wrote that Scripture is subject to no prejudgment except that of the Spirit who inspired it and inspires belief in it. Then he added a section which Wilhelm emphatically noted with carefully drawn double vertical lines in the margin. "Furthermore, it [the whole historical system of revelation and tradition] recognizes no essential difference between the members of different churches insofar as they have true faith in the world's Savior and his love. It recognizes only *one*, ecumenical, at the present time visible-invisible, community, which can be found wherever the Father is being worshiped through Christ in the holy Spirit"[15] (emphasis Meyer's).

This graciously ecumenical and Trinitarian passage, with its outgoing reverence for people of faith, might well be the best theological expression of the Christian spirit of Wilhelm Grimm, the spirit that he expressed poetically in his versions of the fairy tales.

15. "Es kennt ferner keinen wesentlichen Unterschied zwischen den Mitgliedern verschiedener Kirchen, sofern ihnen wahrer Glaube an den Weltheiland und seine Liebe eigen ist. Es erkennt nur *Eine* allgemeine, zur Zeit sichtbar-unsichtbare Gemeine, die da wohnt, wo der Vater durch Christum angebetet wird in dem heiligen Geist" (emphasis Meyer's) Meyer, *Vorrede*, p. vii.

Four

HANSEL AND GRETEL

"Children's fairy tales are told so that in the pure and gentle light of these stories the first thoughts and powers of the heart may awaken and grow."[1] *Hansel
and Gretel* is a story of such an awakening and growth occurring in deeply
threatened children, sharply contrasted with adults in whom the warm
thoughts of the heart have long shriveled and been replaced almost completely by pragmatic calculation. Thus the beginning of the story of the "Little Brother and Little Sister," of Hansel and Gretel. Where did the story come
from? Was it always as we now know it? Was the story possibly narrated to the
brothers by the same Dortchen (Dorothee) Wild whom Wilhelm later married? Rölleke is convinced that the narrator was indeed a member of the Wild
family in Cassel, mainly by the fact that Wilhelm wrote it down.[2] Ellis feels
strongly that if the story had been told to Wilhelm by Dortchen Wild he
would certainly have so indicated, as he did in other cases.[3] This omission of
Dortchen's name, of course, would not exclude the other members of the
family. The story itself in any case does not conceal its literary ancestry—it is
descended from the French tradition. Jacob even noted the fact on the very
earliest manuscript of the tale that scholars have uncovered, found at the Trap-
pist monastery of Ölenberg, the handwritten collection of stories sent to
Clemens Brentano in Berlin on Oct. 25, 1810. Brentano read it and judged it to
be boring and thin. The *Hansel and Gretel* tale was sent on paper with a faint
monogram "WK"—presumably Wilhelm Karl [Grimm]. It was then called
"Little Brother and Little Sister" (with *"alias Hänsel und Gretchen"* added by Jacob)

1. Wilhelm's first sentence in his "Über das Wesen der Märchen," *Jacob und Wilhelm Grimm
Werke, Abteilung II, Die Werke Wilhelm Grimms,* Bd. 31, hrsg. Otfrid Ehrismann (Hildesheim,
Zürich, New York: Olms-Weidmann, 1992), S. 333. "Kindermärchen werden erzählt, damit in
ihrem reinen und milden Lichte die ersten Gedanken und Kräfte des Herzens aufwachen und
wachsen."

2. *Die Älteste Märchensammlung der Brüder Grimm. Synopse der handschriftlichen Urfassung von
1810 und der Erstdruck von 1812,* hrsg. Heinz Rölleke (Cologny. Genève: Martin Bodmer, 1975),
p. 355.

3. John M. Ellis, *One Fairy Story Too Many,* p. 201, note 25.

Gretel holds a lantern as the witch tries to see if Hansel's finger shows that he has been fattened enough for eating. On the roof, in an interpretive parallel action, a black cat stalks the dove which is above Hansel's cage. Wilhelm directed his younger brother's efforts at illustrating the heart of each story, his only criticism seems to have been that he would have preferred a less naturalistic and more fanciful style of representation. Drawing by Laurence Selim after sketches by Ludwig Emil Grimm for the 1825 edition.

and is in Wilhelm's handwriting but with a second significant remark made by Jacob: "cf. Perrault, petit Poucet."[4] The Grimms themselves seem to have been a little reticent about giving the exact source and simply noted that the story was taken from "various Hessian stories" ("*nach verschiedenen Erzählungen aus Hessen*").[5] Perhaps they were somewhat embarrassed at this early stage to see the obvious French connection of this story which they wished very much to be purely Hessian. In order to see how Wilhelm retold the story it seems good first to follow Jacob's suggestion and "confer with *petit Poucet*."

Petit Poucet or "Little Thumb" or "Hop o' My Thumb," was written by Charles Perrault, member of the Académie Française and legal counsel to the court of the Sun King, Louis XIV. The good courtier published his stories using the salon-amusing conceit of having the name of his twelve-year-old son appear as author in 1697, a good 115 years before the appearance of the Grimms' Tales. Its title, *Histoires ou Contes du temps passé, avec des Moralités* (Stories or Tales of Bygone Days, Each with a Moral) is better known to us by its alternative title, *Contes de ma mère l'Oye* (Stories of Mother Goose). One pretended that the stories were by a child for children, but they were actually intended, as all who read them knew, both to enthrall children and to amuse the sophisticated and worldly wise adults at the height of the French Enlightenment. The praise of reason is everywhere in the story, cleverness and pragmatic deception are rewarded (financially), the prodigious ability of the lower classes to produce offspring is smiled at, and the reader is warned at the end: when it comes to judging your children, don't look down on the runt of the litter if he is the brainiest.

There once was a woodcutter and his wife who had seven children, all sons. The oldest was ten years old and the youngest only seven. People were astonished the woodcutter had managed to have so many children in so little time, but the reason was that his wife became pregnant quickly and never had fewer than two sons at once.[6]

The woodcutter and his wife were very poor and their seven children caused them a lot of hardship because none of them was old enough to earn a living. What troubled the couple further was that the youngest was extremely delicate and never uttered a word. They took this as a sign of stupidity, whereas in fact it was because he was so gentle. He was very small indeed. When he came into the world he was scarcely larger than your thumb, and so he was called Hop o' My Thumb. . . .

There came a year of such terrible famine that these poor people could no longer feed their children. One evening, when the children were in bed and the

4. *Die Älteste Märchensammlung der Brüder Grimm*, p. 70.

5. *Die Älteste Märchensammlung der Brüder Grimm*, p. 355.

6. *The Complete Fairy Tales of Charles Perrault*, trans. Neil Philip and Nicoletta Simborowski (New York: Clarion Books, 1993), pp. 82–95.

woodcutter was by the fire with his wife, he said to her, his heart pinched with sorrow, "We cannot feed our children anymore. I couldn't bear to watch them die of hunger before my eyes, so I've decided to take them to the woods tomorrow and lose them. It should be very easy. While they are enjoying themselves gathering wood, all we have to do is run away without them seeing us."

"Ah!" cried his wife. "Could you abandon your own children?" Her husband tried to convince her of their extreme poverty but she would not consent to losing the children: she was poor, but she was their mother. However, when she realized what agony it would be to watch them die of hunger, she gave in and went to bed in tears.

Hop o' My Thumb heard all that they said, for their voices woke him up, and hearing that they were talking about household affairs, he had got up quickly and slipped beneath his father's stool in order to listen without being seen. He went back to bed and didn't sleep for the rest of the night, thinking what to do. He got up early and went to a stream where he filled his pocket with tiny white pebbles and then came back to the house.

Everyone set off. Hop o' My Thumb did not tell his brothers of what he knew. They went into a part of the forest so thick that you couldn't see someone else only ten paces away. The woodcutter started to cut logs, and his children scattered to collect sticks for kindling. When the father and mother could see that the boys were busy at their task, they crept away unnoticed and then fled down a little path.

The similarities to the Grimm version are clear in the beginning of the story (excluding the aside on the astonishing fertility of the couple): the terrible famine is present, there is the secret parental decision to get rid of the children in the forest, the objection of one of the parents who eventually gives in with regret, the child overhearing the parents' plan, and the child's collecting of pebbles to mark the way home. Dissimilarities are also clear: it is the mother and not the father who objects to the plan, and Hop o' My Thumb tells no one what he has found out, whereas Hansel and Gretel tell each other what they know and share their sorrow and fear.

As the tale continues, Hop o' My Thumb lets his six brothers cry for a while (with no real compassion) since he knows how to get home by dropping the pebbles on the path, and then coolly has them follow him home. When they get there all is well. A local squire who owed the woodcutter ten sovereigns has finally paid up. The parents immediately buy meat, so much that they were able to eat only a third of it, and the wife begins "when they are full" as Perrault archly notes, to berate her husband for the loss of the children. At this point the children, who wisely have been listening at the door, know their cue and rush in. With his usual ironic treatment of the virtuousness of the poor, Perrault continues:

These poor folk were thrilled to have their children with them again, and this joy lasted as long as the ten sovereigns lasted. But when the money had been spent, they started to worry again. They decided once more to abandon the children and, to make sure this time, they led them much farther into the forest than they had the first time.

As before, the little hero overhears, but finds the door double-locked. So he uses his bread this time instead of pebbles to mark the path. The birds come and eat the bread crumbs, as in the Grimms' version, and as in the Grimms' tale the lost children come to a house in the forest where, in Perrault's version, a married ogre and his wife live. The wife is kindly and lets the children in to protect them from the wild animals, and tries as well to hide them in the house to protect them from her husband, who unfortunately detects the children by smell and finds them under the bed. Even Hansel's fattening is presaged here:

> He had already grabbed one of the children when his wife said to him, "Just look at the time! Wouldn't it be better to slaughter them tomorrow morning?" "Shut up!" said the ogre, "they'll only be more bruised." "But you've got so much meat left," his wife went on, "look, there's plenty for dinner: a calf, two sheep and half a pig." "You're right," said the ogre. "Give them a good supper so that they don't lose weight, and then put them straight to bed."

Hop o' My Thumb next saves his brothers during the night by taking the seven crowns off the heads of the ogre's seven daughters and placing them on the heads of himself and the brothers, and placed his and his brothers' seven nightcaps on the daughters. Perrault can't resist describing the seven little ogresses, whose throats their father is unwittingly about to slash. "These little ogresses had lovely rosy complexions, because they ate fresh flesh like their father, but they had mean little eyes, sharp noses, and huge mouths full of long, pointy teeth with gaps between them. They were not entirely evil, but they showed promise"—a bit of humor not to be found in *Hansel and Gretel*. After slaughtering his seven daughters by mistake in the dark, and his wife fainting dead away, the ogre puts on seven-league boots to chase the now escaped seven boys. Hop o' My Thumb spots a hollow boulder and hides his brothers inside (were the Grimms writing the tale, it would be a hollow tree, for the sake of Germanic mythology) and then also steals the seven-league boots when the exhausted ogre ("seven-league boots are very tiring to wear") takes a nap nearby. Hop o' My Thumb puts the boots on, races back to the good wife, and coolly tricks her into believing that her husband has been captured by robbers and is in mortal danger. The ogre sent him back in the boots to show he's no imposter, the boy tells her, and he is to collect all the couple's gold and silver as a ransom to pay the robbers. Needless to say, the good wife does as told, "for the ogre was her husband, even though he did eat little children. And so Hop o' My thumb, laden with all the ogre's riches, returned to his father's house, where he was welcomed with great joy." Deception wins the day, as in Gretel's treatment of the witch, and none of the principals in the story, if we omit the little ogresses, need pay with their lives.

Perrault said many people did not agree with this ending to the story and claimed that Hop o' My Thumb actually made a lot of money off the ogre's seven-league boots.

> The king paid him very well for taking orders to the army. Also an endless number of women gave him all he wanted in return for news from their lovers, and that is where he earned most. He found a few women who gave him letters for their husbands, but they paid so badly, and there was so little of such work, that he didn't even bother to account for what he earned in that area. . . . He made his entire family wealthy and accepted new titles for his father and brothers, and in this way established them all, and at the same time continued to serve at court.

The moral that follows the tale gives an equally pragmatic reason for why one should love the least of one's brethren, nicely rhymed by the translator:

> Boys who are bright, and look all right,
> Are always welcome to most folk,
> While one who's weak or doesn't speak
> Will be the butt of every joke.
> But for all that, the little brat
> May turn out useful, when you're broke.

The earliest version, which the brothers Grimm wrote down from oral versions of the tale told to them in Hesse, is both similar and different, analogous, to the version of Charles Perrault. As the young Grimms heard it told, the German tale retains the victims' attempts in the plot by cleverness and deception to outwit the creatures who wish to devour them and efforts of the children to save themselves by using their heads. The trail laid by pebbles and the trail laid by bread are kept. There is a happy ending with the treasure brought home by heroic children, there is even the same air of moral anomie, pre-right-and-wrong, in both tales. Other elements are different: it is the father in the Hessian version who has feelings for the children, not the mother; the ogre is male in the French version, female in the German one; there is no husband-wife household in the gingerbread house in the forest; the story is more domestic with a farmerly emphasis on fattening before cooking and the use of an outside oven. In general, the storytellers who retold the story of "Little Brother and Little Sister" had already done a great deal to adapt the tale to their German audience. If they used the Perrault version as one of the bases for their tale, as I think they did, the storytellers can be said to have changed the story from a courtly version to a country one.

The remark below referring to the textual removal of "the boy overheard" and the change to "they" overheard, shows that the Grimms were working on the text even when they were writing down the manuscript. The following is this version as composed from oral sources in Hesse by Wilhelm Grimm and found in the Ölenberg manuscript:

Once upon a time there was a poor woodcutter who lived close to a great forest. Things were miserable for him, he could scarcely feed his wife and his two children. One time he didn't even have any more bread and was very afraid. That evening his wife spoke to him in bed: take both of the children tomorrow morning and lead them into the great forest. Give them the rest of the bread, make a big fire for them, and after that go away and leave them by themselves. For a long time the husband didn't want to, but his wife let him have no peace until he finally agreed.

But the children had heard everything that their mother had said [alternative reading: the boy had overheard everything]. The little sister began to cry very hard, little brother told her to be quiet and comforted her. Then he got up quietly and went outside and stood in front of the door. There the moonlight was shining and the white pebbles in front of the house glistened. The boy picked them up carefully and filled his little coat pocket with as many as he could fit inside. Then he went back to his little sister in bed and fell asleep.

Early in the morning, before the sun had risen, the father and the mother woke the children up to go with them into the great forest. They gave each one a little piece of bread; little sister put them in her little apron because little brother's pocket was full of the pebbles. Then they set off on their way into the great forest. As they were walking along, little brother often stood still and looked back toward their little house. The father said: why do you keep stopping and looking back? Oh, answered little brother, I am looking at my little white cat which is sitting on the roof and wants to say goodbye to me; secretly however he was dropping one of the white pebbles. The mother said: just keep walking, it is not your little cat, it is the red morning light shining on the chimney. But the boy continued to look back and every time he would again drop a little stone.

So they walked for a long time and finally came to the middle of the great forest. There the father made a big fire and the mother says: sleep for a while, children, we want to go into the forest and look for wood, wait till we come back. The children sat down next to the fire, and each one ate its little piece of bread. They wait for a long time until night falls, but the parents didn't come back. Then the little sister began to cry very hard, but the little brother comforted her and held her hand. Then the moon came out and the little white pebbles glistened and showed them the way. And the little brother led the little sister all through the night, and in the morning they arrived in front of the house. The father was very happy because he hadn't been glad about doing it; but the mother was angry.

Soon afterward they once more had no bread, and little brother in the evening in bed heard again as the mother told the father that he should take the children out into the great forest. Once again little sister began to cry very hard, and little brother got up and tried to look for the little stones, but when he got to the door it had been locked by the mother. And then little brother began to be sad and was not able to comfort his little sister.

They got up again before daybreak, each one received again their little piece of bread. As they were on their way, the little brother often looks back; the father said: my child, why do you keep stopping and looking back at the little house? Oh, answered the little brother, I'm looking at my little dove which is sitting on the roof and wants to say goodbye to me. Secretly, however, he was crumbling his little piece of bread and kept letting a little crumb fall. The mother said: just keep walking, that's not your little dove, it is the red morning light shining on the chimney. But little brother still kept looking back, still kept dropping crumbs.

When they came to the middle of the forest, the father again started a big fire, the mother again said the same words, and both went away. [No dead tree is present.] The little sister gave her brother half of her little piece of bread since the little brother had dropped his on the path, and they waited until evening, then the little brother wanted to lead his little sister back by the moonlight. But the little birds had eaten up the bread crumbs and they couldn't find the way. They kept on walking and became lost in the great forest. [There is no tree under which they slept, no dove guiding the children from the tree to the house.] On the third day they came to a little house that was made of bread, the roof was a cover of cake, the windows of sugar. The children were very happy when they saw that, and the little brother ate some of the roof and the little sister some of the window. As they were standing there doing that and enjoying the taste, suddenly a thin voice called out:

> Nibble, nibble, gnaw like a mouse,
> Who's that nibbling on my house?

The children were completely terrified; soon a little old lady came out, she took the children by the hand in a friendly way, led them into the house and gave them a good meal, and put them into a beautiful bed. [No mention of the children thinking they were in paradise or heaven.] But the next morning she put little brother into a little animal shed, he was supposed to be a little pig and the little sister had to bring him water and good food. Every day she came to the shed and then the little brother had to stick his finger out and she felt to see if he would soon be fat. He always stuck out a little bone instead and then she thought he wasn't fattened yet, and so it went on longer. She gave nothing to the little sister to eat except crab shells because she wasn't supposed to be fattened. After four weeks, she said to the little sister in the evening, go out and get water, and tomorrow morning heat it, we are going to slaughter your brother and boil him; meanwhile I'll prepare the dough so that we can bake at the same time. The next morning when the water was hot, she called little sister over to the oven and said to her, sit on the board, I will push you into the oven, see if the bread will soon be done; what she wanted, however, was to leave little sister in there and roast her. Little sister noticed that and said to her: I don't understand, you sit on it first and I'll push you in. The old lady sat down on it, and the little sister shoved her in, closed the door and the witch burned up. After that she went to the little brother and opened up his shed. They found the whole house full of jewels and they filled every pocket with them and brought them to their father; he became a rich man; but the mother was dead. [There is no large body of water between them and their way home.][7]

Between 1810 and 1857 Wilhelm worked and meditated on this story until he made it a classical parable of the journey of the human soul from infancy to spiritual awareness of right and wrong, the journey of human salvation. He did this structurally by adding to the above story an ending that requires the crossing of a great water, and by inserting spiritual guidance in the form of the white dove which leads the children on. In vocabulary and tone he altered the function of the forest, the path, the unselfish love of the children for one another, so that there is hardly any person of religious faith who cannot but feel moved by this seemingly so simple tale.

Wilhelm regarded the tales as being remnants of ancient faith; in his essay on the nature of fairy tales, he described these remnants in detail for some tales but not for *Hansel and Gretel*. He describes *Hansel and Gretel* in that essay as one of the stories which move the heart to the basic human feelings that are the basis of religious faith, and associates this tale with others in the category "Remnants of Pagan Faith." Can one, with Wilhelm, detect such remnants in this tale? First, there is the unmistakable role of the forest as the dwelling place of the spiritual, the liminal natural world where the natural and supernatural meet. Long ago Tacitus wrote that the German tribes did not build temples because they considered trees and forests to be the dwelling places of the gods. This would have confirmed Wilhelm's view that the "witches forest" (*Hexenwald*), as he had Gretel call it in the final version, was a remnant of the long-ago Germanic religion. The cannibalistic witch of the forest is a figure about whom we have strictures from as long ago as the Frankish prohibitions in the Saxon capitularies dating from the reign of Charlemagne.[8] The moral dilemma of the impoverished parents, and its solution by exposure and abandonment of the children to nature, goes back to the world of classical antiquity and is familiar as the basis for the plot of Sophocles' *Oedipus the King*. The trail of pebbles may be a distant echo of Ariadne's thread. And the children's love for one another and their mutual

7. Rölleke, *Die Älteste Märchensammlung*, pp. 70–76 (my trans.).

8. Cf. G. Ronald Murphy, S. J., *The Saxon Savior, The Germanic Transformation of the Gospel in the Ninth-century Heliand* (New York: Oxford University Press, 1989), pp. 22–23, and the *Leges Saxonum und Lex Thuringorum*, hrsg. von Claudius Freiherrn von Schwerin (Hannover: Hahnsche Buchhandlung, 1918).

fidelity as enabling an escape from their situation echoes medieval Christian tradition. Thus remnants of all three traditions might have been seen by Wilhelm as present in the basic story, waiting only for resuscitation under his hand.

In reconceiving and filling out the tale in its religious spirit, Wilhelm intensifies the parents' moral dilemma by associating its solution, losing the children in the forest, with cold, logical reason, and by painting the father's love and fidelity to his children as appealing but, disastrously, too weak to resist his wife's arithmetical mind. He then adds the dove and the tree to the scene leading to the witch's house and, significantly, adds the broad waters that have to be crossed in order for the children to get home.

As Wilhelm's final version of the story begins the husband is tossing and turning in bed out of sheer worry that there is no food. He groans and says to his wife, "How can we feed our poor children when we don't have enough for ourselves?" The wife makes her suggestion about losing the children in the forest and then adds: "they won't find their way home again and we'll be rid of them." This coldness is countered by the husband's reply that he hasn't got the heart to do it to his own children. In the original manuscript this objection is merely an abstraction: "For a long time the husband didn't want to do it, but his wife let him have no peace until he finally agreed." The final version is very concrete:

> "O you fool," she said, "then all four of us will have to die of starvation, you can just go and plane the boards for the caskets."
> "But I feel sorry for the poor children," the husband said.[9]

The wife is a pragmatist and pointedly tells the woodcutter what his next carpentry task will be if he does not do as she wants. He is revealed as a weak but feeling person, one who will abandon his children, with tears. It occurs to neither parent to sacrifice; they have enough for themselves, and that's where it stays. Hansel overhears and gathers the white pebbles. When he comes back he comforts the crying Gretel. He had told her, "I will help us," and once back in bed with the pebbles in his pocket he does not say, "Now I can help us," but rather, "God will not abandon us" (though the parents have every intention of doing so), and he treats the pebbles as though they were divine creations. Wilhelm puts divine help and Hansel's efforts together.

9. Possibly influenced by Basile's Neapolitan version, *Ninnillo and Nennella*, the earliest (1634) written version in Europe, and surely the earthiest: "He took as second wife a hideous witch who was a malicious bitch. As soon as she set foot in the house she began to behave as if she were the cock of the roost, and said: "Have I come here to clean the lice from another woman's children? This is the last straw, that I should take on such a job, and have two plaguey brats about me." *The Pentamerone of Giambattista Basile*, trans. N. M. Penzer (London: John Lane the Bodley Head, 1932), II, p. 144.

Gretel releases Hansel from his stall. In the background is the oven from which the witch's black spirit is seen emerging with the chimney smoke. The oven drawn for the story is identical to the town bakery's oven still to be seen in Steinau. The date of 1800 is inscribed on the lintel of the now sealed oven door. The oven is fed from outside the building, where a trestle supports the baker's wooden board for shoving items to be baked into the oven. Drawing by Laurence Selim after sketches by Ludwig Emil for the 1825 "Little Edition" of the tales.

As the family sets out into the forest, Wilhelm has corrected the color discrepancy between Hansel's "little white cat," which he claims to be continually turning around to say goodbye to, and the mother's flawed response, "It's only the red light of dawn on the chimney." The mother's words are revised to the more plausible "It is the morning sun on the chimney." Neither parent catches the slight slip that Hansel has made. In saying that the white cat, and later the dove as well, is saying goodbye, he has let out that he knows why they are going into the woods. When they are deep in the forest and the father and mother have left them by the fire, Wilhelm made another addition to the text to show how cleverly reason can be used against a child's trusting love: "And since they could hear the strokes of the wood axe, they believed their father was nearby. But it was not the wood axe, it was a branch that he had tied to a dead tree which the wind was banging back and forth." The father may be goodhearted, but that does not prevent him from using his skill to devise a comforting ruse so that his children will not get nervous and come after him and his wife, but rather will be deceived into thinking that their father is not far away. For the children the noise is dangerously false comfort, the tree is a dead tree (in German, *dürr*: "dry," "lifeless"), and the father's feelings are shown to be as dead and vacillating as the swinging in the wind of a near-dead branch, artificially attached to a hollow dead tree.

Nature is not so unfeeling. When the full moon comes up, "Hansel took his little sister by the hand and followed the pebbles. They shone like newly minted coins and showed them the way." The love that the parents should have for them, but do not, the children possess for one another, and in its light the moon is able to do its magic for them, and even stones are able to reveal the way. Nature helps those who act naturally. Wilhelm's comparison is not accidental: the stones shone like "a new wealth" in the moonlight. There must be another kind of riches in the world that come to light when two people walk together in natural love. By morning they are home.

The father's dilemma and the mother's logic are made sharper the second time around. When the bread is almost gone again, the wife tells the husband that the children will have to be taken deeper into the forest. The husband's heart becomes heavy, and he thinks, "It would be better if you would share the last mouthfuls with your children." And so the thought of unselfishness and sacrifice does occur, but the wife will hear nothing of it. She throws reproaches at him and says, "He who says A has to say B" ("Wer A sagt, muß auch B sagen"), accusing him of being unable to draw a logical conclusion and to carry it out, to be *konsequent*, because of sentimentality. If you have four people, and you have food for two, then four minus two equals two. The mathematical logic of the cruelly enlightened mother considers her husband's love as sentimental, and regards murder by abandonment as a necessary, personally uninvolving, neutral act. To Wilhelm Grimm, logic undirected and controlled by love and faith, infanticide performed with not even a sense of tragedy, by a (step) mother in the name of cold logic, renders the soul ugly and kills the beauty of the person. The mother's clear thinking advocacy of the murder of her children is mortal sin—mortal not in the sense that it means mortality for its victims, mortal sin is the effect on the perpetrator. Such an act kills the beauty of the soul, rendering a person's humanity not just ugly but taking away its life-spirit, making it become a deceiver of the innocent, a desiccated tree waving an attached dead branch. No matter how apparently acceptable in the conventional world of society, the advocate of killing the children, the mother, is revealed in the forest world, the religious environment of the story, to be an ugly witch. Because her action, no matter how logical, is mortally sinful, the woman is found truly "to have died" at the end of the story, when the children return home.

The father, it could be argued, is no better. Indeed the children are his own. His lack of courage and strength make him an accomplice, even a clever accomplice, as when he adds the branch to the dead tree. Unlike the mother, however, he does not perform the sin with chilling indifference and fails to find comfort in its arithmetical necessity. He regrets what he does as he does it, whereas she does not.

When the children are being led into the forest for the second time, it is his "little white dove" that Hansel keeps turning around to see, as he drops his bread crumbs, hoping they will bring him back home. When his mother questions him for looking back (as he secretly drops the breadcrumbs) he answers that he is looking at his little dove on the roof. "'Fool!' the woman said. 'That's not your little dove. It's the morning sun shining on the chimney.'" The child-adult dialogue recalls the father-son conversation in Goethe's *Erlkönig*, with the same tragic adult incomprehension. The parents may be excused for not seeing the non-existent animals on the roof, but they cannot be excused for not hearing the son's hidden reproof and touching appeal, "They are saying goodbye to me." They do not even hear the contradictoriness and reproof in their own words, "The morning sun is shining on the chimney of our home," for the parents are determinedly leading their children to death. Witches, as Wilhelm will note sagely later in the story, have poor eyesight. The mother is walking down the path deeper into the forest of the spiritual world, ready to become a murderer, a killer of her own, a witch.

Abandoned in the forest, alone, and very frightened and hungry, as were their parents at home when the food ran low, the children do not share the premoral attitude of the mother. "When noon came, Gretel shared her bread with Hansel, who had scattered his along the way." The brother and sister deem it very natural, as does the reader unconsciously, for the one to sacrifice his bread to find a way back, and for the other to sacrifice half her bread for him.

Bettelheim has noted that to go back home would be to regress psychologically; thus nature, representing the natural growth one should undergo, eats up the crumbs so that the children are forced to go on. The same is true when reading the story spiritually. It would be most unfortunate for the children, who have advanced through genuine love and care for each other to a state of natural sacrificing for one another, to regress to the premoral, selfish state of their parents. It is for this reason that the representatives of the spiritual world come and eat up the breadcrumbs that would only lead them backward into becoming like their mother and father. Wilhelm Grimm thought of the doves in this tale as the messengers of divine providence, as guiding the children away from the wrong way and into the right one. He writes about the depiction of the human condition in the fairy tale:

> The parents have no more bread and in their desperation have to abandon the children in the forest . . . But God sends his help, he sends the doves. . . . As in a golden age, everything is still alive: the sun, moon and stars are approachable and give gifts; in the mountains there are dwarves mining ore, mermaids sleep in the water, the animals, the birds (doves are the most beloved and most helpful), plants, stones speak and know how to express their sympathy. . . . The ravens speak in prophesy, they know, like Odin's ravens Hugin and Munin (i.e., possessing Understanding and Memory), what is happening in the world. In general moreover, the birds are seen as spirits. Doves come and pick the lentils out of the ashes for the poor child, and poke out the eyes of the evil sisters.[10]

Hansel and Gretel, however, are as human as their parents, are just as dependent on bread, make use of the same rules of logic, and are as vincible as their father was before them. Can they avoid going back to the same material condition of their parents, or can they follow the spirit to another level of awareness? Can love lead them to what the heart of their father only feebly senses and the heart of their mother does not experience at all: the knowledge of rational actions as good and evil?

The quest begins under a tree. The tree protected the children as they slept during the night—as did a hollow stone in Perrault's version of the tale. The tree is Germanic pagan religion's highest symbol of constant salvation and eternal rescue. Yggdrasil is the tree which is the dynamic invisible structure of the universe; it upholds and preserves the universe, and it protects and is the savior of the human race. In the mythology of a thousand years ago, there will come a time when the world will end: *Ragnarök*, the Twilight of the Gods. At that time the whole of the middle world will be shaken by earthquakes and enveloped in raging flames that will reach up to the sun and moon. Fireballs will surge from the earth and will fall from the skies as the forces of heat engage in a terrible struggle with cold coming down from the North. All human beings will be destroyed—except for two. Before the final, terrifying cataclysm takes place, Yggdrasil will open up its great tree trunk to admit the last boy and girl and will then close around them to protect them

10. *Über das Wesen der Märchen*, pp. 333–34, 340.

and keep them safe throughout the time of the end of the world. When the end is over, the tree will have survived. And as a new sky appears with a new sun and a new moon and stars, and when the meadows first turn green again with new grass, the tree will open up and let the boy and girl emerge to start again in the new world. Yggdrasil is the tree of human salvation. In parallel to the book of Genesis, Yggdrasil is the Germanic name for the Tree of Life.[11] The Christmas tree is one of the "remnants" of this ancient faith, one the Grimms treasured in their home, and the "gingerbread house" would have been nearby in the living room of the very children to whom this story was read. This tree will play a role in almost every tale that we will consider. As in Germanic mythology, the world of the two children has just come to an end, an end totally cataclysmic in the dissolution of the family that surrounded them. But the tree is a symbol which guarantees that the children will continue on after the end of their world, protected by the Upholder. The Grimms have stated Hansel and Gretel's, and their own, childhood spiritual and psychological crisis in Germanic language by having the two children, at the end of their rope, fall asleep in front of the trunk of the tree. They will arise from the tree and be led on by the spirit of life.

Leaving behind a Germanic symbol for human life rescued, the story continues with a Christian one. At noon on "the third day [the Resurrection was on the third day] they saw a beautiful snow-white bird sitting on a branch. It sang so beautifully that they stood still and listened to it." It is curious indeed how close this is to Wilhelm's memory in his autobiography of the two little brothers standing in the town square of Hanau, holding hands and looking up in fascination as the weathercock on the church tower turned back and forth in the wind.

The story of *Hansel and Gretel* continues: "And when it was finished, it spread its wings and flew on before them, and they followed it until they came to a little house and it alighted on the roof."[12] The children did not stumble onto the little house, they were led to it, and by the snow-white bird. The journey is now one led by the Holy Spirit. Wilhelm has also paraphrased a well-known passage of spiritual quest in describing the flight of the bird: "And behold, the star which they had seen in the East went before them until it stood still over the place [the house] where the Child was."[13] They are indeed being led to a place of spiritual rebirth, as were the Magi, but a place of testing and new life, a place where gold, frankincense, and myrrh are gifts to the newborn spiritual Child.

The test is old: the food is forbidden. The children begin eating the house,

---

11. The above paraphrase of the story is taken from my "Yggdrasil, the Cross, and the Christmas Tree" in *America*, Vol. 175, No. 19 (Dec. 14, 1996), p. 17. It can be found in Appendix C.

12. *"auf dessen Dach es sich setzte."* This important final phrase in this line is, unfortunately, absent from the Zipes translation of the story.

13. Matthew 2:9.

enjoying what Hansel calls a "blessed meal" even though a voice tells them that the house belongs to someone, and is not theirs to consume. They pay no attention, they wish to eat, and they eat. They follow the example of their parents. Like their mother and father before them, they treat as their disposable personal property that which is surely not theirs to dispose of; they eat forbidden fruit. When they are warned off in a rhyming spell

> Nibble, nibble, gnaw like a mouse,
> Who's that nibbling at my house?

they continue eating and compound the problem by answering with a lie:

> The wind, the wind,
> the child of the heavens: the wind.[14]

The Fall has occurred again. The original sin of selfishness has been passed on, and it is not long before a familiar figure comes gliding out of the house: "Suddenly the door opened, and an ancient woman, leaning on a crutch, came shuffling out ("kam herausgeschlichen")." The snake had promised Adam and Eve that all they had to do was eat to become like God, knowing good and evil. The ancient woman promises as well that they will come to no harm, and she feeds them well. They thought they were in paradise ("sie meinten, sie wären im Himmel"). Actually they are, but in the garden of paradise, Eden. The punishments (except labor pains, which immediately followed the Fall in the Bible), mortality and hard work, are immediately visited upon the two children by the serpent/witch: Hansel will be fattened for killing, Gretel will be forced to do hard labor, and then she too will be killed. The witch's hand with which she leads the children to their fate is now described in the same terms as the dead tree to which the children's father tied the banging branch to deceive them: "dead, dried out" (*dürr*). She is death itself, a female Saturn, devourer of her own children.

Now faith and love put reason in their service. Hansel deceives the witch with the ruse of the stretching a bone out of the cage when the witch asks to feel his finger to see if he is fat enough. Gretel, who before only wept in innocence over the cruel attitudes of others, now claims she does not know how to slide into the oven on the baking board to test the bread, deceives the

---

14. "Der Wind, der Wind, / das himmlische Kind," suggested to the Grimms by Dortchen Wild, 15 Jan. 1815. Cf. Rölleke, *Die Älteste Märchensammlung*, p. 75. She may have gotten it from research suggested by von Arnim into the medieval German of the *Wiener Oswald*: "do machte daz himelische kint, / daz do quam ein gut wint," p. 355. The Grimms would not have hesitated to adopt a phrase which perhaps had not been a remnant of ancient religious faith that had survived in oral folktale, but that could be made into a very close paraphrase of a genuine original which had actually survived by remaining undiscovered in libraries. In German, the phrase also echoes the "Heavenly Child" of the Christmas story, and thus both pagan and Christian mythologies are simultaneously evoked by the children's response.

Hansel and Gretel cannot get home to their father's house, in the Grimm version of the story, because a "broad water" blocks their way. The river Kinzig runs directly along the back of the Grimms' house in Steinau, and is most likely the imaginative model for that part of the story. Wilhelm and Jacob used to play near this spot where there was an area called the "bee garden." When I took the photograph for this drawing, a duck came along and enchanted me, but I didn't try to cross. The two peaks in the background are the roof of their father's house. Drawing by Laurence Selim, from a photo by the author.

witch into showing her how to do it, shoves the would-be killer into her own oven, and shuts the door. No wonder the dove led them here, they fell to temptation, but through their love and unselfish care for each other found ways to free themselves from their cages, put reason and logic to saving, if deceptive, use. Wilhelm debated putting in a line about God giving Gretel the idea of shoving the witch into the oven, but by the final version seems to have thought the better of it. The dove, it seems, had finished its work by leading Hansel and Gretel from the tree to the garden to let love triumph over selfishness. But this is not the case, as we shall soon see.

Originally the Grimm version in manuscript and in the first printing ended here with two simple sentences: "They found the whole little house full of jewels and filled all their pockets with them and brought them to their father, who became a rich man; the mother had died." Indeed the mother had made herself an ugly witch by not loving her children, evil being seen as a disfigurement of beauty, and, as Bettelheim pointed out, it was the mother who had died in the oven. I would add that the amoral attitude, "who says A must say B," arithmetical logic applied where love should control the situation, is dead. The children have come to religious awareness, apparently saved by their own attitudes and efforts alone. Are they home? Wilhelm must have thought about this, and the strong whiff of Pelagianism in the ending must have disturbed him for he amplified the conclusion by the addition of the river that had to be crossed. The children's "good works"—their success in overcoming the evil disfigurement of the witch and in overcoming selfish cravings—do not get them "home." No one, in any form of Christian belief, attains salvation by one's own efforts alone, but rather by the grace of the Holy Spirit. The complete insufficiency of human good works in enabling salvation and the need for a Savior is the crux of Luther's oft-repeated theological cry that salvation is accomplished "by God alone, by Christ alone, by faith alone" (*solo Deo, solo Christo, sola fide*). This theological attitude charts the path through the woods and the world for Lutherans and is the unequivocal soteriology of the Calvinist Reformed church. Theology suggests strongly that there was a religious need for the river scene.

There was no river[15] to cross on the way into the woods, and thus the river

---

15. There is a mention of a river in an Alsatian version of the tale in which "lo ptiat pousset" on first hearing of his father's plans goes down to a river bank to gather pebbles:"*Lo ptiat pousset, qu' èvò hoyï so pére, s'leuveò dvaint lo jo, a s'en alleò dsi lo bord d'le r'vire* [*rivière*], *a rèmasseu tot pien de biancs cayïoux.*" There is no further mention of a river in the tale. The Grimms mention this version in their notes. It is called "Fiaoue ['fable'] ou Conte Lorrain" in Jeremias Jacob Oberlin's, *Essai sur le patois lorrain des environs du comté du Ban de la Roche, fief d'Alsace* (Strasbourg: Stein, 1775), pp. 161–64. This volume is in the rare book section of Princeton University's Firestone Library. It is a retelling in dialect of the Perrault version with eleven children, the debtor who repays his debt, the mother who is the parent who does not want to do what she agrees to, and it is the father who takes the children into the woods—the second time *sans rien dire* (p. 163).

shows the need to return, like the Magi, by a different route into one's own country. To go home the children must pass through the water. The symbolic nature of the water is made clear by the fact that it cannot be crossed by natural means. The children notice immediately that there is "no footbridge, no bridge, no boat"—it is not that kind of water. As in the Exodus narrative, the two carry with them the riches of the despoiled forces of their captivity, and their exodus across the "Red Sea" to their promised land cannot be made by "bridge" or "ferry boat." But the "great water" can be crossed with the help of a magic bird. The white dove appears again, but this time in the form of a duck.[16] The white bird first bade them goodbye from their premoral condition and ate up the bread crumbs that would have helped them return to that state, then led them to the Garden of Eden's gingerbread house to see if they would pass the test of eating and being eaten. Now the bird will lead them through the third stage for arriving at their ultimate destination.

Bettelheim has noted quite correctly, I believe, "Having to cross [an expanse of water] on their return symbolizes a transition, and a new beginning on a higher level of existence (as in baptism)."[17] The duck has "two natures" in one magic entity, it is at home both in the air and in the water. It is the bird of two natures who brings the children through the waters to the other side, where home is. This is clearly baptism, and the duck is the Spirit of Christ who in the liturgy of baptism is called upon to come down on the waters of the baptismal font and to wash the candidate clean of all sin. The sin which is referred to is the original sin of eating what was forbidden in the Garden of Eden—what the children did when they saw the house. Baptism also celebrates the divine adoption of the candidates, welcoming them into living their lives within the kingdom of God. It celebrates their adoption by God the Father, their loving relationship with Jesus Christ, and acknowledges the origin of religious feelings and faith as the Holy Spirit. This is precisely the sentiment which Wilhelm underlined in his German Bible's introduction, and which he repeatedly underlined in the sections on the Holy Spirit and on love in his Greek New Testament.

Bettelheim sees Gretel's concern about not overloading the duck's back with two travelers as a sign of her growing unselfishness, her psychological maturity. Religiously seen, baptism, the initiation into religious awareness, can also be received only one person at a time. The candidates, if not infants,

16. The duck and the river crossing was introduced in the second edition, in 1819. By the final edition Gretel had her rhyming spell in which to address the duck, which Wilhelm seems to have borrowed from Stöber's dialect version in his *Elsässisches Volksbüchlein,* which appeared in 1842. Stöber in turn, in my opinion, must have borrowed the river and duck idea from the Grimms' edition of 1819. See Rolf Hagen, "Perraults Märchen und die Brüder Grimm," in *Zeitschrift für deutsche Philologie,* 74 (1955), pp. 392–410.

17. Bettelheim, *The Uses of Enchantment,* p. 164.

must have arrived at sufficient spiritual maturity to hold their own faith. No one can believe for you, just as, in eating, no one can be moderate or gluttonous for you. Even if it is in the arms of godparents, one is ferried across individually into the realm of spiritual life, and on the back of the one, divine and human, who bore all sinners on his back during the three days of his Exodus. And so the one child waits as the other is borne across the water.

The children, despite their former treatment, can think of nowhere to go but to their father's house. "Love one another, do good to those who hate you." Their riches, gained by their harrowing and hallowing experience, they share. They cling to their father, hang on his neck, for they have come to realize what it is that makes life truly rich, and so has he. After that, they pour their riches out of their pockets so that jewels and pearls are running all over the living room floor. The jewels stand here for the spiritual treasure that Hansel and Gretel have become: mature people tested in their love, sure of what is important to them. The have found the precious pearl of knowing the importance of love and of cleverness, and they have found that they know how to have them work together in harmony. In his final version of the story Wilhelm alludes to a passage from the Sermon on the Mount on spiritual wealth: "Give and it will be given to you: a good measure, pressed down and shaken, overflowing, will be poured into the fold [lap] of your garment" (Lk 6:38) by changing the simple "the children filled all their pockets" to: Hansel filled his pockets, but Gretel filled up her apron ("füllte sich sein Schürchen voll"). Hansel makes the comment: "These are even better than pebbles." The children have acquired a wealth of spiritual life that so exceeds that of their parents that they can now be givers of life. "Now all their worries were over and they lived together in pure happiness."

The story of Hansel and Gretel, in the Grimms' final version, is a story of initiation into the world of spiritual values, freedom from captivity to an inherited materialist sense of human worth. When the children are held in captivity by the very wealthy witch, the children experience that their love for each other is not based on, nor corrupted by, how much food the one gets and how little the other receives. Hansel gets "the best food" and Gretel is given only "crab shells," and yet they do not reassess their value to one another on the basis of food income. They remain something much more important and spiritual: brother and sister, loving and caring for each other, unchanged from the first frightening night when they heard their parents' intentions. They have passed the test of this love. They continue to be worth more to each other than a pessimist would have predicted from the witch's exacerbating test: see if materialism can separate them from mutual spiritual love by segregating them on a food scale at the two extremes—the one will feast, the other fast. It worked with the parents, but it does not work with the children. It is as though Wilhelm were attempting to describe the Christian realization that one does not live on bread alone, or, as St. Paul put it in his letter to the Romans, "The kingdom of God is not eating and drinking, but righteousness, peace and happiness within the Holy Spirit."

The reader may feel that the father of Hansel and Gretel is not worthy of such attention at the end of the tale, but in Wilhelm's eyes he would be. The father had missed the children and was ashamed of himself. That, to a medievalist who loved the epic of *Parzival* as much as Wilhelm Grimm did, is high praise. It is the whole thrust of Wolfram von Eschenbach's *Parzival* that Parzival will never arrive at the Holy Grail until he naturally and spontaneously feels shame for what he has done or, more correctly, shame for what he failed to feel and do. The father, the repentant sinner who realized what his children meant to him at least after they were lost, is saved, but the mother, being without any such human feelings, is nonmoral, incapable of sin and incapable of repentance, and is therefore spiritually nonexistent. The mother's impoverished feelings, the wealth of a witch, are dead branches on the tree of life.

Five

LITTLE RED RIDING HOOD

Through all the editions of the Grimms' tales, this story remains relatively unchanged over the years. Wilhelm seems to have been very much satisfied with the first version as printed in 1812 and reproduced here in Appendix B. We do not have a prior Grimm manuscript of the tale that could show us an earlier version. The very brief commentary made on the story in the first edition is also significant: "Rather surprisingly, outside of our oral saga, we have come across this tale nowhere except in Perrault (*chaperon rouge*) from which comes Tieck's version."[1] In the 2nd edition, 1822, the commentary is little changed and equally obscure: "From the region around the Main river. In Perrault, chaperon rouge, from which comes Tieck's lively reworking of the tale.[2]" The sources of the story are therefore to be found in the oral versions told to the brothers, and in their knowledge of Perrault's and Tieck's versions of *Red Riding Hood*. Neither Perrault's version nor Tieck's can in any way be called religious poetry of the type that Wilhelm thought he found in the old tales. The version which must have been told to the brothers by Jeanette Hassenpflug and her sister must be the source for the inspiration of the Grimms' *Red Riding Hood* even if, as a Huguenot, French-speaking family, their ultimate source was the same Perrault whose original version the brothers must have already known from their reading and perhaps even from

---

1. "Dieses Märchen haben wir außer unserer mündlichen Sage, was zu wundern ist, nirgends angetroffen, als bei Perrault (*chaperon rouge*) wonach Tiecks Bearbeitung." This is in the Grimms' appendix, p. xxii. I am indebted to the staff of the Beinecke Library of Yale University for their graciousness to me in giving me access to their copy of the two volumes of the first edition.

2. "Aus den Maingegenden. Bei Perrault *chaperon rouge*, wornach Tieks [*sic*] lebendige Bearbeitung."(III, 49). I am indebted to the staff of the rare book room of Princeton University's Firestone Library for their continual courtesy to me in giving me access to the three volumes of the second edition of the *Kinder- und Hausmärchen*. The very rare third volume of the second edition, which contains the comments of the brothers Grimm on the sources and variants of the fairy tales was printed in a run of only 500 copies. The printer thought there would be little interest.

their French lessons! The spirituality of the Grimms' *Red Riding Hood* can come only, therefore, from Wilhelm Grimm's reworking of the Hassenpflug version. The second ending to the story, in which the wolf does not eat Red Riding Hood, but instead is tricked by her and her grandmother into slipping off the roof into the trough of sausage water, was published by Wilhelm as an alternative ending. He made no effort to work it into the tale. Rölleke's solution to the juxtaposed presence of the two versions (endings) is ingenious. He believes that the first version (in the belly of the wolf) comes from Jeanette and the second (in which the wolf drowns in the trough) comes from her sister Marie Hassenpflug.[3] I would suggest, however, that the first ending comes from Wilhelm's complete reworking of a Hassenpflug (cum Perrault and Tieck) version, and that the second ending comes from the sisters, perhaps in the tradition of Basile, without any reworking. The second ending, in which Red Riding Hood and her grandmother escape from the wolf by using her own wits, occasions the same theological problem, Pelagianism, that Wilhelm had with Hansel and Gretel's escape from the witch solely by their own wits. That impasse called for balance by the addition of the unbridged river and supernatural transport across the water, and, in *Red Riding Hood*, the rescuing hunter. Wilhelm's Christian spirituality, mystical but quite orthodox, ultimately required the introduction of outside spiritual agency to escape from the mortality caused by the Fall.

In order to see the great difference in spirit between the Perrault/Tieck versions of *Red Riding Hood* and that of the Grimms, we will look at both versions first.

Perrault's version shows such close verbal similarity to the Grimm version that it immediately betrays itself as a source, both direct and indirect, for the brothers:

> There was once a little village girl, the prettiest you ever saw. Her mother doted on her and her grandmother even more so. This good lady had a little red cloak made for her, which suited her so well that everyone called her Little Red Riding Hood.
>
> One day her mother made some bread and said to her, "Go and see how your grandmother is, for I hear she's been ill. Take her a loaf [*galette*] and this little pot of butter."
>
> Little Red Riding Hood left straightaway to go and visit her grandmother, who lived in another village. On her way though the wood, she met a wolf, who quite fancied eating her but did not dare, because of the woodcutters who were working in the forest.

The first paragraph strikes one by its very close identity to Grimm version, but then the differences begin. A good reason, self-protection, is given for the

3. In the *Jubiläumsausgabe*, III, 454.

wolf's not eating Red Riding Hood on the spot, and where in the Perrault version the young girl is carrying the solidly ordinary gift of bread and butter, in the Grimm version it is the more intriguing gift of cake and wine.

> He asked her where she was going. The poor child, who did not know that it is dangerous to stop and chat with wolves, said to him, "I'm going to see my grandmother, to take her a loaf with a little pot of butter that my mother has sent."
> "Does she live very far away?" asked the wolf. "Oh, yes," said Little Red Riding Hood. "It's beyond that mill you can see over there, the first house in the village."

In other words, the fatal meeting between the wolf and the little girl will be of the sort that occurs in town, at the first house in an ordinary village, a house you can see with your own eyes, right there, so to speak, just beyond the mill. In the Grimm version, however, as in the case of *Hansel and Gretel*, the meeting will be of another type, the kind that can occur only at an unusual house, rather difficult for ordinary eyes to see because of the hazel bushes, and because it is so "deep in the forest."

> "Well," said the wolf, "I want to go and see her too. I'll go by this road and you by that one, and we'll see who gets there first." The wolf started to run as fast as he could by the shortcut, and the little girl took the longer path, dawdling to pick some hazel-nuts, chase after butterflies and make little bunches of wayside flowers.

What in the Grimm's version is a temptation to disobedience is here nothing of the sort—just a simple children's challenge about who gets there first. If Red Riding Hood makes a mistake it is simply the very human "mistake" of accepting the challenge and of dawdling and enjoying the day, becoming forgetful for a while of her mission.

> The wolf soon arrived at the grandmother's house. He knocked: Rat! Tat! "Who's there?" "It's your granddaughter, Little Red Riding Hood," said the wolf, disguising his voice. "I've brought you a loaf and a little pot of butter that my mother has sent you." The kindly grandmother, who was in bed as she wasn't well, called out to him, "Pull the handle, the latch will give." The wolf pulled the handle and the door opened. He flung himself on the good woman and gobbled her up, for it was more than three days since he had eaten. Then he closed the door and tucked himself up in the grandmother's bed to wait for Little Red Riding Hood, who, shortly afterward, came and knocked at the door: Rat! Tat! "Who's there?"
> When Little Red Riding Hood heard the wolf's hoarse voice she was afraid at first, but, thinking that her grandmother must have a cold, she replied, "It's

your granddaughter, Little Red Riding Hood. I've brought you a loaf and a little pot of butter that my mother has sent you." The wolf called out, softening
his voice a little, "Pull the handle, the latch will give." Little Red Riding Hood
pulled the handle and the door opened. When the wolf saw her come in, he
hid under the blankets and said, "Put the loaf and the little pot of butter in the
bread bin and come and get into bed with me."

That is the fourth and last mention of bread and butter; they are put in a
bread box, and that is the end of their role in the story. Reasoning helps Red
Riding Hood excuse the dangerously deep voice of the wolf, and she accepts
the invitation to bed. Bettelheim's sexual reading of the story is justifiably
based on Perrault's version and its explicit invitation to get into bed with the
wolf. Red Riding Hood does not get undressed and jump into bed with the
wolf in the Grimms' version, thus parrying a sexual reading but losing some
of the justification for the young girl's shocked dialogue with the wolf. The
Grimm version omits remarks about the size of the wolf's "arms" and "legs"
from the in-bed observations of Perrault's heroine, to steer the reader toward an out-of-bed interpretation based on the Grimms' view of fairy tales
as fragments of religious poetry which they were restoring to their original
effectiveness. Perrault:

> Little Red Riding Hood got undressed and climbed into bed, where she was
> most surprised to see what her grandmother was like with nothing on. She
> said, "Grandmother! What big arms you have!" "All the better to hug you
> with, my dear!" "Grandmother! What big legs you have!" "All the better to
> chase you with, my dear!" "Grandmother! What big ears you have!" "All the
> better to hear you with, my dear!" "Grandmother! What big eyes you have!"
> "All the better to see you with my dear!" "Grandmother! What big teeth you
> have!" "All the better to eat you with!" And with these words, that wicked wolf
> leapt upon Little Red Riding Hood and ate her."

And that is the end of the story. I have heard that French children often cry
when they hear the story, since they identify with the little girl who is so suddenly gone. For those who began with the Grimms' version, it is always a little unnerving to think that a children's story, even a cautionary tale like this
one, could end with such chilling abruptness. Perrault, of course, smiles at
the adult audience and follows his tale with a moral that makes the meaning
of the story even less ambiguous:

> Young girls, as we clearly see,
> Pretty girls, especially,
> Innocent of all life's dangers,
> Shouldn't stop and chat with strangers.

If this simple advice beats them,
It's no surprise if a wolf eats them.
And this warning take, I beg:
Not every wolf runs on four legs.
The smooth tongue of a smooth-skinned creature
May mask a rough wolfish nature . . .[4]

Ludwig Tieck's lively spin-off on the Perrault version, *The Life and Death of Little Red Riding Hood, A Tragedy* (*Leben und Tod des kleinen Rotkäppchens. Eine Tragödie*)[5] is delightfully humorous by reason of the introduction of so much unexpected realism into the fairy-tale world. In the first scene of Tieck's "tragedy," Red Riding Hood is already at her grandmother's house, and the two are having a lively discussion about why there is a crowd in church this Sunday and about daddy's drinking problem. In the first case it is because the pastor is sick and the superintendent is going to run the service. Red Riding Hood uses the opportunity to see if she can get a second red cap from her grandmother.

> RED RIDING HOOD: How happy I will be from the bottom of my heart when they let me receive confirmation. Then you will have to give me another red cap.

> GRANDMOTHER: We can't think about that yet, you're not even seven years old yet, and they don't let children like that come to the Lord's Supper, they are too young to understand anything about religion.

This mention of red caps and confirmation may point to a folk custom of wearing red for confirmation in honor of the feast of Pentecost, when confirmation is customarily administered, since red is the liturgical color of the feast. (At Pentecost the Holy Spirit descended upon the apostles in the form of [red] tongues of fire. Acts 2:1–5.) The association of confirmation and Communion in a spiritual matrix of the family past is prominent in both of the brothers' autobiographies, and is I believe woven into the substrate of the Grimm version of *Red Riding Hood*, though only mentioned in Tieck. The grandmother here, however, is not amused, and says she thinks that black is much more properly respectful of God: one shouldn't look dressed for the dance floor in church.

---

4. This translation is taken, as before, from *The Complete Fairy Tales of Charles Perrault*, trans. Neil Philip and Nicoletta Simborowski (New York: Clarion, 1993), pp. 30–34.

5. The playlet is in verse and contains five scenes; it is dated 1800. In *Ludwig Tieck's Schriften*, 2.Bd. (Berlin: Reimer, 1828), pp. 327–62. Reimer was also the publisher of the Grimms' tales. That Wilhelm enjoyed Tieck's version is clear from the differing adjectives he used to characterize it over the years as a reworking that was "lively" and "appealing" (*"lebendige," "anmuthige"*) in the second and final edition of the *Grimms' Fairy Tales*.

GRANDMOTHER: What is your father doing? Why doesn't he come here?

RED RIDING HOOD: His legs hurt him, it's hard for him to walk, one of his knees is badly swollen.

GRANDMOTHER: Then he should have taken some medicine.

RED RIDING HOOD: Well, he has taken all sorts of things, but he says they don't make him feel good. The cantor thinks that that comes from drinking, and that he would have to stop drinking if he takes the medicine; but father does not want to accept that, he says that the cantor irritates him and that the cantor drinks three times as much as he does and doesn't have any leg pains.

GRANDMOTHER: People are bad! Brandy always has to be their pleasure number one.

RED RIDING HOOD: Yes, there have been a lot of arguments; but mother is right when she objects that drinking is causing him to miss a lot of work.

GRANDMOTHER: Be quiet, my daughter, it isn't seemly for children to notice such things or to talk about them.

RED RIDING HOOD: Mother has brought that up to him too: that he ought to be ashamed when he babbles away drunk in front of me at home in the evening, and for no reason starts yelling and arguing.—I brought some pretty flowers for you . . .

Thus the introduction of the flowers picked by Red Riding Hood in the woods on the way to grandmother's house! There is no wolf at all involved in bringing the flowers. Instead there is the legend of why the leaves of the aspen tree tremble (because it did not recognize Christ in human form and did not bow down as did the other trees [cf. the Cherry Tree carol], it will tremble until the Last Day). This legend is a prelude to Red Riding Hood's downfall. She refuses, out of hubris, to heed the warnings given to her by everyone in the play that the wolf awaits. In the second scene she meets the hunter, who tries to kiss her—who's a wolf?—but she refuses, not out of innocence and morality, but because he smells of tobacco! Then the following exchange occurs:

RED RIDING HOOD: You're hunting today?

HUNTER: Yes, I'm after that rascal (*Ja, es gilt dem Rangen*) the wolf, who is here in the forest, and who eats many an innocent little lamb. . . . I've had my sights on him for a long time.

It is from the above passage that Wilhelm Grimm may have adapted the line that he puts into the mouth of the huntsman that he has been "looking for the wolf for a long time." Red Riding Hood then tells the hunter that his clothes don't fit him very well and that he would look much better if he didn't wear green all the time and had something as beautiful and red as her

cap! She finds the color green to be "rather common, like poorer-class people, you can find it everywhere, on every bush and hedge,"[6] and in her quite
self-assured, petty arrogance, she heeds neither the hunter nor even the birds
who warn her of the danger ahead. In the third scene we meet the wolf, an
unsuccessful lover, who is having a friendly conversation with a dog on how
hard it is to work for human beings, since the humans speak of tolerance and
fail to practice it, but especially how hard it is to work for Red Riding Hood's
father as an employer. The dog even mentions a heavy stone that the child
dragged over to him which he keeps trying to move and carry but cannot
budge. This may presage the Grimms' use of heavy stones at the end of their
version of the story to weigh down the wolf at his demise. In the fourth
scene the cuckoo tries to warn Red Riding Hood, using a (terrible) German
pun. The word for cuckoo, *Kuckuck*, sounds like the word for "look!"—*kuck*
said twice. And the bird keeps repeating the sound, "Kuck, kuck, kuck um
dich mehr!" ("Look, look, look around you more!"). Fortunately, the
Grimms did not feel any urgency to borrow the line. In the fifth and final
scene, however, Tieck's version is a bloody mixture of half-eaten body parts
and talking birds, far from both Perrault and the Grimms. As the scene begins, the wolf is already in bed. He explains that the door was open (left so by
Red Riding Hood when she left earlier) and so it was easy for him to get in.
Grandmother, whom he has strangled, lies dead on the floor under the bed.
Red Riding Hood saunters in, bringing boiled chicken—no sacramental mys-
ticism here!—to give her grandmother strength. She adds that her father was
not in a good mood when she left:

RED RIDING HOOD: I ran away fast because he is a beater sometimes.
He doesn't always want me to go to your house and to stand by you in your
troubles.—You are lying in bed, but at the wrong end. Grandmother, what
crazy hands do you have?

WOLF: They are good for holding on tight to things.

RED RIDING HOOD: My parents back home wanted me to stay overnight
with you.

WOLF: My, that's just what I had in mind too.

*The dialogue then continues as expected about the wolf's large ears, eyes, nose and
mouth, she then cries for help, but:*

WOLF: You are screaming in vain, you're already dead! (*The bed curtains close*)

6. Das Grün ist wie geringe Leut,
   Man findet es so allerwege,
   Auf jedem Busch, jedwed Gehege
   Da wächst es; ach du liebe Zeit!
   Doch ist von da zu Roth noch weit.

Red robins now fly in through the window and go flapping and hopping about, looking
for Red Riding Hood. They find her and the wolf behind the bed curtains and begin
crying out, "O tragedy, O horror," spoofing the chorus in a Greek tragedy! At this point
the hunter appears in the window.

HUNTER: Why are you screaming so hideously?

BIRDS: Red Riding Hood—Lord 'a mercy—is dead! The wild wolf has torn
her to pieces and he's eaten part of her!

HUNTER: Lord have mercy! I'll shoot in through the window—(*he shoots*).
Now there lies the wolf, he is dead, that will have to be the penalty for everything, he is swimming in the red of his own blood. You can commit a crime,
but you can never escape the punishment.

This humorously gory final scene, with chattering birds and hunter, with
one corpse under the bed and the other corpse in it, partially eaten, may have
provided the brothers with "lively" entertainment and with the idea of the
hunter, but a treatment like this of the tale excludes any need for a spiritual resurrection scene. And the boiled chicken, entirely forgotten, does nothing to
help the strangled grandmother revive. The tone is, one scarcely need say, entirely different from Wilhelm's use of the tale.

The Grimm version is a story of salvation. The main change, of course, is
the happy ending, but there are subtler changes as well so that the new ending fits the story.

Once upon a time there was a sweet little girl. Everyone who even laid eyes on
her was fond of her, but the one who was fondest of all was her grandmother,
who was always thinking of what she could give to the child. Once, as a present, she gave her a hood of red velvet and since it was so becoming to her and
she wouldn't wear anything else, she was just called Little Red Riding Hood.
One day her mother said to her, "Come here, Red Riding Hood. There you
have a piece of cake and a bottle[7] of wine. Take that out to your grandmother,
she is sick and weak, and it will revive her."

The story begins with love and fondness, a graciousness in mutual giving
that goes over three generations. The hood which has been given by the oldest generation is red, a sign of female sexual maturity in Bettelheim's reading, but also a sign of the moment of spiritual maturity in a Christian reading
of the tale. The color is the color of Pentecost and of the time of confirma-

7. In the first edition this was *"Bouteille,"* perhaps reflecting the actual word used by
Jeanette Hassenpflug in telling the tale. Since there is only a pot of butter in the Perrault version, and no wine, the word *bouteille* does not originate with him. The word may reflect the
influence of the French occupation of Hesse, or be a simple bow in the direction of Jeanette.
In the second edition it was replaced by the German *Flasche.*

Little Red Riding Hood. *Just outside the house, carefully placed in the frame-work of the open doorway, are the three oaks depicted together. Drawing by Laurence Selim from sketches by Ludwig Emil Grimm.*

tion, when a child is deemed ready to be capable of knowing good and evil, ready to become a child of the covenant, sent on the journey of life, into the woods, just as her parallel figure, the grandmother, may be getting ready to finish it. She is given the bread and wine to carry to her grandmother to strengthen her for her journey, a *viaticum*. The German phrase for "it will revive her" ("*sie wird sich daran laben*") is significant, as is perhaps best revealed by the Grimms' dictionary of the German language:

> **Laben**: verb. *reficere* [refresh, remake], the sense practically coincides with that of *erquicken* [revive] which originally as a much stronger concept referred to the bringing back to life of dead life-spirits.

> The idea of physical nourishment recedes completely whenever *laben* is used in reference to Communion in the Lord's Supper: *di gelabet werden von dem lichamen und von dem blûte Jhesu Christi* [they are revived by the body and blood of Jesus Christ].[8]

By changing Perrault's everyday bread and butter to the bread and wine which can revive the sick, the Grimms have shifted the meaning of the story. Into the hands of the new, confirmed generation the bread and wine has been placed. But, as in the liturgy of confirmation, there is a warning given that the newly confirmed will be tempted to go astray, and the warning comes from the mother: "Get up and go now before it gets hot, and when you get out there walk nice and properly and don't go off the path, otherwise you will fall and break the glass, and grandmother will get nothing."

The warning, "don't go off the path, otherwise you will fall" tells the reader that the story will deal once again, as in the case of *Hansel and Gretel*, with the Fall. The woods will be the Garden of the book of Genesis, and Grandmother's house will be the place where the ancient battle is joined between good and evil, between life and death by being eaten, as in the witch's house. Eve's temptation and fall does not occur only in the case of the generation of old, the grandmother's—the mother knows of it and warns her child, and Red Riding Hood will undergo it for the present generation. But the warning about consequences is too strong. Red Riding Hood will indeed go off the path and "fall," but the glass will remain unbroken, and the wine will retain its power to revive, as the condition of original sin is passed from generation to generation. The Grimms' tale continues: "Red Riding Hood promised to be very obedient [1812 version], but grandmother lived out in the woods, a half hour from the village. As Red Riding Hood came into the woods, the wolf met her. Red Riding Hood, however, did not know what a bad animal he was and was not afraid of him."

---

8. *Deutsches Wörterbuch*, V, 6.

In the Grimms' context this is a statement of prelapsarian innocence, the theological speculations about which Wilhelm had read.[9] To enter the woods, however, is another matter. To enter the woods is to enter one's grandparents' and parents' world, the continuum of the ancient awareness of right and wrong by becoming capable of doing good and doing wrong. "The wolf met her." Walking the path is treading the primeval course of time; "meeting the wolf" is arrival at the ominous age of moral awareness. Where Perrault treats premoral innocence as rather unlikely and as a socially amusing conceit, for the Grimms (and for Tieck) it is a serious personal entrance into the world of religion and religious myth. Psychologically and spiritually the sentence "as she came into the woods, the wolf met her" is ominous indeed, but it is time. After pleasantries are exchanged, the wolf gets down to business: "Red Riding Hood, what are you carrying under your apron?" The question is understood as one of inquiry into sexual maturity by Bettelheim; it is at the same time a question of spiritual maturity, as the answer makes resounding clear: "Cake[10] and wine."

This is a long way from Perrault's "bread and a pot of butter" and Tieck's "boiled chicken"! The little girl is no longer little in a spiritual way and is now old enough to be both tempted to disobedience to her mother and to be entrusted by her mother with carrying the Bread and Wine to strengthen the sick and the weak. The word "cake" is used by the brothers in the sense in which it is defined in the Grimms' German dictionary, quite close to *galette* as noted above, but with an added level of meaning:

> *Placenta, tortus panis* [pie-shaped bread]. From a historical point of view of principal importance is the word *brotkuchen* [breadcake], cake made from bread dough. This is why historically *kuchen* [cake] can mean anything baked, but with the idea of "bread" remaining in the foreground. . . . Luther used the image of a bakery in the highest, most serious sense as an image of the internal, essential union with God and Christ in the sacrament of Communion in the Lord's Supper: "Even if I have sinned, this body of Christ which I now eat has not sinned. . . . I am now one cake with Christ.'[11]

> [*Placenta, tortus panis*, geschichtlich wichtig ist vor allem der brotkuchen, kuchen aus brotteig. . . . so begreift sich geschichtlich kuchen für gebäck

9. He was curious about how Adam and Eve made love before the Fall. He noted with obvious approval the suggestion made by one author that they did it by looking at each other with their eyes. He made a note there that he was reminded of Tristan and Isolde's visual lovemaking on the boat.

10. "Cake" (*Kuchen*), probably a translation of the word "galette" in the French of Perrault's version. A *galette* is a round, flat loaf of bread, well illustrated by Gustave Doré in his depiction of Red Riding Hood's meeting of the wolf. See *Contes de ma mère l'Oye, Illustrations de Gustave Doré* (Paris: Gallimard, 1983), p. 45. The idea is parallel to "hardtack" or "ship's biscuit": flat bread designed to last.

11. *Deutsches Wörterbuch*, V, 2496.

überhaupt, doch so dasz der gedanke an brot im vordergrunde steht. . . .
Luther brauchte diesz backhausbild auch im höchsten, ernstesten sinne als bild
der innern, wesenhaften einigung mit gott und Christo im sakrament des
abendmahls: 'hab ich gesündigt, so hat dieser leib (Christi, den ich jetzt esse)
nicht gesündigt. . . . ich bin nu ein kuche mit Christo.']

The wolf sees the opportunity and wants to get to grandmother before the
girl with the bread and wine arrives. He is the jaws of death, desiring to make
his claim and thwart any prevention. This may be the clue to what Wilhelm
Grimm may have seen as a fragment of ancient religious poetry in this story.
Fenrir in Germanic mythology is the great wolf whose enormous jaws stretch
from one end of the cosmos to the other. At the end of time, at Ragnarok,
when the worlds are collapsing in fire and heat and cold, as the world serpent
arises to kill the god Thor (and be killed by Thor's hammer at the same time)
the great wolf Fenrir will advance on Woden himself, open the enormous
jaws, and swallow the great god of consciousness and feelings. Fenrir's gaping
jaws seem to be a stand-in for cosmic space and its vast unconscious, unfeeling
extent, the very incorporation of Northern Europeans' fear of death—not
just the death of the individual person or god, here or there, but absolute
death, the time when all conscious being would no longer exist, when consciousness itself would have perished, replaced only with the dark jaws of cold
space. Here, where the wolf is the Germanic equivalent for the serpent in the
Garden, he remains in some ways a figure more devouring, even more repre-
sentative of *nihil* than Satan or the serpent. And, like Fenrir of old, he is not just
plotting how to eat you, so to speak, but your roots and origins as well, your
grandmother. When Red Riding Hood says to the wolf, "O, grandmother,
what an enormous mouth you have!" it is, as Wilhelm surely must have
thought, a remnant of a powerful religious feeling thousands of years old.

The wolf is a compound symbol since the Grimms also were aware of the
Germanic-Christian use of wolf as a form of the devil, something they
traced back as far as the ninth-century *Heliand* in their materials for the *German Dictionary*. While the brothers never got as far as the letter "W" in their
efforts to complete the dictionary, their method and materials were used to
finish it. In the Grimms' German dictionary we find that the entry under
"uses of the word" states that "wolf," under biblical influence, has primarily
been used as an image of Satan since he is a *seelenräuber*, a rapacious devourer of souls. The entry cites Luther's remark in his *Table Talk* about sinners' preference for the howling of wolves to the songs of the angels, and
adds an example from a sixteenth-century preacher, quite appropriate to the
Grimms' *Red Riding Hood*: "(Christ) has ripped the sheep out of the jaws of
the wolf, that is, the devil."[12]

---

12. "*(Christus) hatt die schaf dem wolff, das ist dem teuffell, ausz dem rachen gerissen.*" *Deutsches
Wörterbuch*, Jacob Grimm und Wilhelm Grimm (Leipzig: Hinzel, 1873), XIV/II, 1244.

Where does Grandmother live? Like the wolf, Grandmother's house is a harmonized version of Germanic and biblical symbol. She does not live in "the first house in the village" as in Perrault's urbane version, but deep in the woods of Eden. Her house, where the ancient encounter occurs, is not at any geographic distance; it is a "time distance" away—only a quarter of an hour from being met by the wolf, "just around the corner" from entering the woods of personal maturity. Red Riding Hood is now quite capable of reminding the wolf how to get back to the place of origin, the Garden: "Red Riding Hood, where does your grandmother live?" "A good quarter of an hour farther in the woods, her house is under the three great oak trees, underneath them are the hazel-nut hedges which I am sure you know."

The oak is sacramental in Germanic mythology, along with the ash and the evergreen, it is the place of sacrifice to the god Woden. It is thus associated with the god whose great and fatal adversary is, appropriately for Red Riding Hood, the cosmic wolf. Wilhelm Grimm seems not so much to have found this ancient remnant of Germanic religion in the story but to have deliberately added it in order to restore the story's antiquity as indicated to him by the presence of the wolf. But Wilhelm has harmonized the Germanic tree symbol for its highest god with the triune God of Christianity. He locates the house as being not under a single oak, but under "the three great oak trees," three divine trees of one single oaken nature—the Christian Trinity expressed in Germanic image.

The hazel-nut hedge marks off sacred space in Germanic mythology, hazel sticks being placed in a circle to create the sacred space required for a judicial assembly with divine sanction in ancient times. Thus the hazel image is that of a place of contest and divine judgment. Red Riding Hood tells the wolf that he is certainly familiar with the hazel-nut hedges. This cannot be because wolves eat the nuts; they are, in mythology at least, solely carnivores. The reason seems to lie in folklore and in folk etymology based on a belief, found here in an old gloss, that the Latin word for nut, *nux*, comes from the verb *noceo*, which means "to do harm," and that the harmful hazel stands in eternal conflict with the godlike oak tree." From the Grimms' dictionary:

> Nut-hedge (hazel bushes; nut tree). . . . A nut tree is called a *nux* and that comes from the word *noceo*. . . . The ancients write that the hazel-nut tree will not tolerate an oak tree around it, and conversely, that the oak trees will not tolerate a hazel-nut tree, the two being eternally antagonistic to one another.

> Nuszhecken (haselstrauch; nuszbaum). . . . Nuszbaum, nux haizt ain nuzpaum und kümt von dem wort noceo [Dief.]. . . . es schreiben die alten, das der nuszbaum kein eichbaum umb sich dulde, und herwiderumb das die eichen kein nuszbaum leiden, seiend einander ewig zuwider. (VII, 1015)

The Grimms have told the reader in very ancient language that there is an eternal conflict waged in Grandmother's house between God and Satan, and they have said it in a stunning harmony of biblical and Germanic religious imagery. The Garden of Eden has two forbidden trees, the tree of the knowledge of good and evil, and the tree of life, and there is a snake waiting to tempt Eve away from eating from the tree of life into eating from the tree of the knowledge of good and evil, in which the red apple hangs. Said in the Grimms' re-creation of the language of the forest: there are two types of trees in eternal conflict around the primal human house: the live oak spreading above, and the noxious hazel below, and the wolf is in league with the hazel, as Red Riding Hood well knows, and is deadly.

The temptation begins. As in Genesis where Eve saw that "the fruit of the tree was beautiful to look at," the wolf points out to Red Riding Hood that she is not appreciating the beauty that lies off the path: "Red Riding Hood, look at the beautiful flowers, they are all around, why don't you take a look around? I believe you don't even hear how beautifully the little birds are singing! You are just walking straight ahead as if you were going to school, and it is so beautiful out in the woods."

The poet in Wilhelm has induced him to make this passage quite parallel to the dangerous dialogue that will soon follow at the bedside. It is the wolf who uses his big eyes the better to see his prey, his big ears the better to hear it, and he now encourages his prey to do as he does, to be wolf-like, and she falls into his trap. What in Perrault was a contest is here a deception and an irresistible temptation for the young girl:

> Red Riding Hood opened her eyes, and as she saw how the sun's rays were dancing back and forth through the trees, and that beautiful flowers were everywhere, she thought, "If I bring a bouquet of fresh flowers to grandmother it will make her happy, and really it is so early in the day that I will still get there early enough." She walked off the path into the woods and looked for flowers.

She does open her eyes, not that they have been closed up to this point, but they have been on the path. She has been looking, but she has not seen. Now she lifts up her eyes to the beauty all around her, something truly good about the temptation, but what she sees is beautiful enough to overcome her intention to obey her mother's wishes. She is not mature enough to realize that she must both see the beauty of the world and stay on the path. This realization will come to her in the last line of the story. Now, however, she is misled by beauty into straying from the path, and having reached the age of reason, she is even able to begin rationalizing her move: "I will get there early enough." The Fall has occurred. The book of Genesis uses the same image of "opening the eyes:"

The woman said to the serpent, "we may eat fruit from the trees in the garden, but God did say, 'You must not eat fruit from the tree that is in the middle of the garden, and you must not touch it, or you will die.'" "You surely will not die, the serpent said to the woman. For God knows that when you eat of it *your eyes will be opened* and you will be like God, knowing good and evil." When the woman saw that the fruit of the tree was good for food and *pleasing to the eye*, and also desirable for gaining wisdom, she took some and ate it. She also gave some to her husband, who was with her, and he ate it. Then, *the eyes of both of them were opened*, and they realized they were naked.

The eyes of both are opened; they see beauty and now realize that they are naked human beings. One could almost expect the traditional dialogue to begin about "What big limbs you have." Wilhelm Grimm has sewn the religious poetry of Genesis and Germanic myth together. So well has he done this that one cannot tell to what degree any medieval forbears of the *Red Riding Hood* tale might have been thinking of Genesis and composed the tale in this vein, and if Wilhelm has plausibly restored what the medieval poetic force of the fairy tale might have been, or if, as seems to be the case, he has brilliantly created it himself in a full medieval spirit.

When Red Riding Hood finally arrives at the house, and the dialogue with the wolf in the bed has ended with "Grandmother, what a horrendously huge mouth you have!," he jumps out of the bed and swallows her. When the hunter comes by, he comes in the house only because he has heard snoring, and is careful and observant enough to know that the old lady generally doesn't make a noise like that. He finds the wolf in the bed and says, "Do I find you here, you old sinner. I have been looking for you for a long time." Though the second of these two sentences is borrowed from Tieck, "you old sinner" is not. The ancient sinner and adversary has been found by the hunter sent to rid the forest of him. The hunter, like the duck in *Hansel and Gretel*, represents the outside force necessary to complete the exodus and arrive at a new life. This hunter, as opposed to the one in Tieck, does not shoot and kill the wolf. He is afraid of harming those whom the wolf has swallowed into his darkness. Instead, he takes a shears and cuts open, to use a medieval expression, the belly of the beast.

After he had made a few cuts he saw the red hood shining, after a couple more cuts the little girl jumped out and cried, "Oh, was I terrified! How dark it was inside the wolf's body!" Then the old grandmother came out, still alive, and could scarcely breathe. Red Riding Hood then went quickly and got large stones and filled up the body of the wolf with them. When he woke up, he wanted to leap away but the stones were so heavy that he immediately plunged and fell down dead.

The hunter who had long sought the ancient wolf has cut open the dark belly of the beast and saved not just Red Riding Hood, but her ancestral mother as well. Eve too can breathe the spirit once more. What the cake and wine have been sent to do, to revivify the old woman, has been done by the hunter. The hunter's identity as the Savior, as Christ, is shown in the resurrection of the two women, ancient and new, from the death which comes through succumbing to temptation, sin. The wolf is not killed by the hunter, by Christ; he drops dead by the heaviness of the material things which he seeks to have in his belly. Without any spirituality, he dies of the weight of the material world which he makes his prey. Even after he deceives good persons with his accurate promise of eyes open to the beauty of this world, their souls still shine with the red glow of their gifted spiritual light even in the darkness of his belly, until Christ comes and descends into the darkness of their death and performs, here with a simple pair of shears, one of the favorite mysteries of medieval Christianity, the harrowing of hell.

The unusual action that follows after Red Riding Hood and her grandmother jump out of the wolf's body, the substitution of stones in the belly of wolf to take the place of the rescued heroines, is not from Germanic or Christian mythology. It echoes instead ancient Greek religious tales. Wilhelm Grimm showed his awareness of this congruity with classical myth in a note[13] he made in the margin of a parallel fairy tale, *The Wolf and the Seven Little Kids*. In one of oldest of Greek stories,[14] Cronos devours his own children, as is related in Hesiod[15] and Appolodorus.[16] In Appolodorus' somewhat fuller version, Cronos (Time), son of Sky and Earth, was married to Rhea (Flow). In order to foil a prophesy that one of his children would one day usurp him, as each one of the children of himself and Rhea were born in the course of time, Cronos devoured them one by one (as Time does, an ancient Greek might note, with everything to which it has given birth). Rhea, his sister and wife, became very angry as each year as she lost another one of her children: Hestia, Demeter, Hera, Hades, and Poseidon. When her time came to deliver her sixth child, Zeus ("the one who lives"), she hid the child as soon as he was born and took a large stone wrapped

13. The reference is to the story of the avenging wolf sent by Psamanthe to devour Peleus and Thetis. The wolf, however, devours so many cattle en route that his stomach is dragging on the ground, and he is scarcely able to pounce. Thetis in any case fixes him with a deadly look, sticking her tongue out, and the wolf is turned to stone. Wilhelm's note gives his source as J. P. Nitsch, *Neues Mythologisches Wörterbuch*. (Cf. Rölleke, *Die älteste Märchensammlung*, p. 352.) The story is also in Robert Graves, *The Greek Myths*, I, 271–72. Though this tale has a wolf, no humans are eaten to rise again, nor is the stone a substitute for a human in the belly. Hesiod's myth therefore, *pace* Wilhelm, may be closer to the ending of *Red Riding Hood*.

14. Cf. Robert Graves, *The Greek Myths* (New York: Braziller, 1957), I, 39–51.

15. Hesiod, *Theogony* (Baltimore: Penguin, 1973), 38–39.

16. Appolodorus, *The Library*, trans. Sir James Frazer (Cambridge: Harvard, 1939), p. 9.

in swaddling clothes, and gave it to Cronos to swallow—which he did, not noticing that he had been tricked. Later when Zeus grew up, he arranged for his father to swallow an emetic mixed in with his drink. Cronos took a deep draft of the mixture and vomited up first the stone that had been substituted for Zeus and then the other five brothers and sisters, all of whom sprang forth unhurt from the belly of their father. This ancient tale of the awareness of the contest between life (and the other children of time), and being devoured by their very begetter, is a relic of religious poetry emerging from the dark belly of time to shine again in the final scene of *Red Riding Hood*.

In the Grimm version, Fenrir, the cosmic wolf of night, blends with Cronos, god of time, and Christ puts on the clothes of a hunter and performs the task of Zeus to overcome time and the belly of the beast, not to save fellow gods, however, but to save the red-capped human soul. Human weakness is urged to open its mortal eyes, not just to see the beauty of the flowers, but to hope that the red glow of its faith, hope, and love is being watched by the rescuer of the spirit.

Faith in the ultimate survival of life, and hope of personal resurrection from the dead, despite leaving the path, despite the wolf and time, has thus been expressed by Wilhelm Grimm in a beautifully harmonized version of three ancient religious mythologies, that of the Dove, the Raven and the Owl. The story ends with a charming coda: "Then all three were satisfied. The hunter skinned the wolf and went home with the pelt. The Grandmother ate the cake and drank the wine which Red Riding Hood had brought and was revived, and Red Riding Hood thought, 'As long as you live, you are never going to run off the path by yourself into the forest again if your mother has said no to it.' "

The hunter gets the wolf's pelt, the reward of the victor, and, as he disappears into the woods to remain vigilant as before, Grandmother is coming back to life and health by eating the cake and drinking the wine, the eucharistic symbols of her communion with Christ's own descent into the darkness of death, his harrowing of hell, and his Resurrection back into the light. This story as told by Wilhelm Grimm is a story of the path, the temptation and fall, the resultant death, and the salvation by the hunter of the souls of the fallen. The bread which Perrault in his story forgot, the Grimms in theirs united with the bottle of wine, which never broke, and which remained to strengthen the living who had been through death. And Red Riding Hood has come to the realization, so ends the story, that it is better not to walk off the path by yourself when your mother has forbidden it.

A last thought. Who is the mother then, who gives instruction on how to walk the path to the place where the three oaks are, and who gives the sojourners the bread and wine to revive them should their mortality afflict them on the journey? Is she not, in ancient terms, the protective spirit of the home, secretly related to the protective spirit of the hunter? And is she not as well, in medieval terms, the spiritual hunter's wife and consort, *ecclesia*, the church? And is she not also the mother of the brothers Grimm, whom Wilhelm was so moved to watch as she approached the altar in the Reformed church in Steinau to receive the bread and wine of the Lord's Supper?

Six

CINDERELLA

The brothers commented in the first and subsequent editions of the *Kinder-und Hausmärchen* that the tale of Cinderella is one of the best known of the fairy tales and is told and retold everywhere. The story was even told in ancient Egypt. Strabo, writing in the first century B.C., records in his *Geographikon* that the Egyptians of his day still told a curious story of a seventh-century B.C. Greek slave girl and courtesan named Rhodopis, "Rosy Cheeks," and says that the Egyptians connect her with one of the lesser pyramids.

> A story is told of her, that when she was bathing an eagle snatched one of her sandals from the hands of her female attendant and carried it to Memphis; the eagle soaring over the head of the pharaoh, who was administering justice at the time, let the sandal fall into his lap. The king, struck with the shape of the sandal, and the singularity of the incident, sent over the country to discover the woman to whom it belonged. She was found in the city of Naucratis, and brought to the king and made his wife. At her death she was honored with the above-mentioned tomb.[1]

The Grimms mention Strabo[2] prominently in their commentary in the first (1812) edition of their fairy tales but under the category of one of the historical "witnesses" to the general existence and usefulness of fables and children's stories. Curiously, they fail to indicate to the reader any awareness

---

1. *The Geography of Strabo*, trans. H. C. Hamilton and W. Falconer (London: Bell and Sons, 1916), III, 250–52. Naucratis was a small trading enclave for foreigners (Greeks) in the Nile Delta, Memphis was the capital of Egypt. Herodotus, c. 440 B.C., also mentions the same Rhodopis as living at the time of Sappho (c. 600 B.C.) and being a fellow slave for a time with Aesop, but Herodotus does not mention anything about the story of the sandal and the Pharaoh.

2. Strabo is mentioned first, along with only Luther, Johannes Mueller, Sir Walter Scott, and Eloi Johanneau in the first edition. In later editions the list of witnesses was much expanded. For the expanded list of thirty-seven "testimonials" see the *Jubiäumsausgabe*, vol. 3, *"Zeugnisse,"* 271–82.

of Strabo's ancient Greek-Egyptian version of the *Cinderella* story, an omission that seems rather strange. Either they had not read all of the *Geographikon* or they were trying so hard to see uniqueness in their own *Cinderella* that they chose to eliminate mention of Strabo's Rhodopis and the tale's ancient origins. Even in commentaries on the tale in their later editions they remain silent on Strabo's version.

Less strange is the Grimms' apparent unawareness of the more recent ninth-century A.D. Chinese version of a warlord's search for the girl whose foot would fit into a slipper so small that "it was an inch too small to fit the one among them with the smallest feet."[3]

In some versions of the Cinderella story the hero of the tale is as often a boy mistreated by his brothers as it is a girl mistreated by her sisters—the important element in the plot being that the humiliated sibling later becomes exalted. Their own written version, the Grimms comment, is based on three stories from Hessia (*nach drei Erzählungen aus Hessen*).[4] The story was first told to Wilhelm by an unknown woman living in the Elizabeth hospital, the poorhouse, in Marburg in 1810. It was later combined with two other Hessian versions of the story, one of which came from Frau Viehmann in Zwehrn. This combined version told of the discovery of a fountain of blood behind a forbidden door (Bettelheim's interpretive preference is for this version), and included an attempt by an evil sister to replace Cinderella in the bed in which she has given birth. This plot variant is remarked in the brothers' annotations, but their tale does not incorporate either the fountain or the birth incident. Other versions of the tale in Germany use dogs instead of doves to make the prince aware that he is riding off with the wrong (or right) bride-to-be. The third Hessian contribution is probably that of the Huguenot Hassenpflug family, which could explain the close correspondences between the narrative details in the texts of the Grimms' first version (1812) of *Cinderella* and that of Perrault. Wilhelm had a multitude of choices to make among the variants, and if he had to choose between dogs and doves for his version, then doves would certainly have been his preference. In other German variants noted by the brothers it is church that Cinderella cannot attend, rather than a ball, because she has no proper clothes. In another variation, a woman is on her knees in the back of a church and is shedding tears of religious devotion, and as the bishop catches sight of her, a dove comes, picks up the tears and flies away with them. A fourth Hessian contribution from Frankfurt is the incident with the hazel branch brushing the father's hat, and there are still more versions the brothers are aware of from North Germany, Poland, and elsewhere.[5]

---

3. Taken from the brief retelling of the story by Marina Warner in her *From the Beast to the Blonde*, p. 202.

4. Rölleke, *Jubiläumsausgabe*, III, 46.

5. Rölleke, *Jubiläumsausgabe*, III, 46–51; *Synopse*, 315–7, 387–8.

The influence of Perrault is acknowledged in the first edition in the judgmental style not altogether uncommon from the pen of the brothers: "Perrault's '*Cendrillon* or the little glass slipper' does not belong among his better told tales; the countess d'Aulnoy's *Finette Cendron*, despite being even worse from the point of view of form, has many particular details of its own that are richer. In the second volume we will note what must be said about the incomparably more beautiful *Cennerentola* (Pentamerone I, 6)."[6] For this tale there were a plethora of versions for the Grimms to use singly or in combination, and yet the Grimm tale is in the end distinctively their own and perhaps the richest of all.

Grimms' Version

The following is the Grimms' final version of *Cinderella* in my translation, given here in full, since the more familiar story with the pumpkin and the clock striking midnight at the ball is that of Perrault.

> Once there was a rich man whose wife became sick, and when she felt that her end was approaching she called her little daughter, her only child, to her bedside and said, "Dear child, remain good and devout and God will always stand by you and I will look down on you from heaven and I will be close to you." At that, she closed her eyes and died. The little girl went out every day to the grave of her mother and cried, and she remained devout and good. When winter came, the snow put a little white blanket on the grave, and when the sun of springtime had taken it away, the husband took another wife.
>
> The woman brought two daughters with her into the household. They had faces that were beautiful and white, but their hearts were ugly and black. That was the beginning of a hard time for the poor stepdaughter. "Is that dumb goose supposed to sit with us in the living room?," they said. "He who wishes to eat his bread has to earn it—out of here with the kitchen maid!" They took her beautiful clothes away from her and put a gray housecoat on her and gave her wooden shoes to wear. "Now look at the beautiful princess, what beautiful attire!" they cried out with laughter and led her to the kitchen. There she had to do hard labor from morning till evening. She had to get up early before dawn, fetch water, light the fire, do the cooking and the wash. Above all, the sisters did everything imaginable to hurt her feelings, they mocked her, and tossed the peas and lentils into the ashes so that she had to sit there and pick them all out again. In the evening when she was exhausted from work, she did not get to sleep in a bed but had to lay down in the ashes next to the fireplace.

6. "Perraults *Cendrillon* ou le [*sic*; it is not only Homer who nods] petite pantoufle de verre gehört nicht unter seine am besten erzählten Märchen, der Gräfin d'Aulnoy *Finette Cendron* wiewohl noch geringer der Form nach, enthält manche eigenthümliche und reichere Nebenumstände. Wir werden davon im zweiten Band zu dem unvergleichbar schöneren Mährchen *Cennerentola* (*Pentamerone* I, 6) das Nöthige anmerken."

And therefore, since she always looked dirty from the cinders and ashes, they called her *Cinderella*.

It happened that the father wanted to go to a fair, and so he asked the two stepdaughters what they would like him to bring back for them. "Beautiful clothes," said the one; "pearls and jewels," said the other. "How about you, Cinderella," he said, "what would you like to have?" "Father, the first twig that hits your hat on the way home, break it off for me." He bought beautiful clothes, pearls, and jewels for the two stepsisters, and on the way back as he was riding through an area of greenwood, a hazel twig brushed against him and knocked his hat off. He broke the twig off and took it with him. And when he got home he gave his stepdaughters what they had asked for and to Cinderella he gave the twig from the hazel bush. She thanked him, went to her mother's grave, and planted the twig on it. She cried so hard that her tears fell down on it and watered it. It grew and became a beautiful tree. Cinderella went to stand under it three times every day, there she cried and prayed, and each time a little white bird came and landed on the tree, and whenever she made a wish the little white bird would throw down to her whatever she had wished for.

It came to pass at that time that the king gave a feast. This feast was to last three days and all the beautiful young ladies in the land had been invited so that the king's son, the prince, would be able to select a bride. When the two stepsisters learned that they too were to appear at the feast they were simply delighted and called Cinderella and said, "Comb our hair, brush our shoes, and fasten our buckles—we're going to the wedding at the king's castle." Cinderella obeyed, but she cried because she also would have liked to go to the dance and asked the stepmother for her permission to go. "Cinderella," she said, "you are full of dust and dirt and you want to go to a wedding? You don't have any clothes or shoes and you want to dance!" However when Cinderella continued to plead with her, she finally said, "There, I've tossed a bowlful of lentils into the ashes, if you have separated out the lentils in two hours time then you can come with us."

The girl went out the backdoor into the garden and called out, "Tame doves and turtle-doves, and all of you birds under heaven, come and help me sort

> the good ones into the little pot
> the bad ones into the tummy."

At that, two white doves flew in through the kitchen window, then came the turtle-doves and finally all the birds under heaven flew in, crowding and flapping and landing among the ashes. And the doves nodded their little heads and began to peck, peck, peck, peck, and then the others too began to peck, peck, peck, peck, and they sorted all the good lentils out and put them into the bowl. Hardly had an hour gone by and they were all done and they all flew back out again. Then the girl brought the bowl to her stepmother, happy with the thought that now she would be allowed to go to the wedding feast. Her stepmother said, however, "No, Cinderella, you don't have any clothes and you can't dance, you will be a laughingstock." When she heard this, she began to cry and so her stepmother said, "If you can sort out two bowlfuls of lentils from the ashes for me in an hour's time, then you can go with us," but she was thinking, "She will never be able to do that."

After the stepmother had thrown two bowls of lentils into the ashes, the girl went out the backdoor into the garden and called out, "Tame doves and turtle-doves, and all of you birds under heaven, come and help me sort

> the good ones into the little pot
> the bad ones into the tummy."

At that, two white doves flew in through the kitchen window, then came the turtle-doves and finally all the birds under heaven flew in, crowding and flapping and landing among the ashes. And the doves nodded their little heads and began to peck, peck, peck, peck, and then the others too began to peck, peck, peck, and they sorted all the good lentils out and put them into the bowls. And before a half hour had gone by, they were all done and flew back out again. Then the girl brought the bowls to her stepmother, happy with the thought that now she would be allowed to go to the wedding feast. But her stepmother said, "None of this is going to help you a bit, you are not coming with us because you have no clothes and you can't dance. We would be ashamed of you." Whereupon she turned her back on Cinderella and hurried off with her two haughty daughters.

Since no one was now in the house, Cinderella went to her mother's grave under the hazel tree and called out,

> "Shudder and shake, my little tree,
> Throw gold and silver down on me!"

Then the bird threw down a dress of gold and silver to her with slippers stitched in silk and silver. As fast as she could, she put the dress on and went to the wedding feast. Her sisters, however, and her stepmother did not recognize her and thought she must be a foreign princess since she looked so beautiful in the golden dress. They never even thought of Cinderella and assumed that she was at home sitting in the dirt and sorting the lentils from the ashes. The king's son approached her, took her by the hand, and danced with her. He would dance with no one else. He wouldn't let go of her hand, and when someone else come to request a dance of her he said, "She is my dancing partner."

She danced until evening came and then she wanted to go home. But the prince, the king's son, said, "I'll come with you, I'll accompany you," because he wanted to know to whom the beautiful girl belonged. She slipped away from him, however, and jumped up into the dove house. The prince waited until her father came and told him that the unknown girl had jumped up into the dove house. The old man thought, "Could it be Cinderella?" He sent for his axe and pick so that he could smash the dove house apart, but there was no one in it. And when they came into the house, there was Cinderella in her dirty clothes lying in the ashes, and a dim little oil lamp was burning in the hearth. Cinderella had quickly jumped down from the back of the dove house and had to run to the hazel tree. There she had taken off the beautiful clothes and laid them on the grave, and the bird had taken them away. Then she had sat down in the kitchen ashes again, wearing her little gray housecoat.

On the next day, when the feast started up again and her parents and stepsisters were out of the house, Cinderella went to the hazel tree once more and said,

> "Shudder and shake, my little tree,
> throw gold and silver down on me."

At that, the bird threw a dress down that was even more elegant then the one from the previous day. And when she appeared at the wedding feast in this dress, everyone was amazed at her beauty. The king's son, who had been waiting for her arrival, took her by the hand and danced only with her. Whenever anyone else came up to ask her for a dance, he said, "She is my dancing partner."

When evening came she wanted to leave, and the prince followed her in order to see in which house she lived, but she slipped away from him into the garden behind the house. In the garden there was a great and beautiful tree on which the most magnificent pears were hanging. She climbed among the branches as nimbly as a squirrel, and the king's son could not figure out where she had gone. He waited until the father came and said to him, "That unknown girl has slipped away from me, and I think she jumped up into the pear tree." "The father thought, "Could it be Cinderella?" He sent for his pick and axe and chopped the tree down, but no one was in it. When they came into the kitchen, Cinderella was lying there as usual in her place in the ashes. She had jumped down from the other side of the tree, brought the beautiful clothes back to the bird in the little hazel tree, and put on her gray housecoat.

On the third day, when her parents and sisters were out of the house, Cinderella went again to her mother's grave and spoke to the tree,

> "Shudder and shake, my little tree,
> Throw gold and silver down on me."

This time the bird threw down to her a dress that was so magnificent and radiant that she had never had anything like it, and the slippers were completely made of gold. When she came to the wedding feast in that dress everyone was speechless in amazement. The prince danced only with her, and when anyone else asked to dance with her, he said, "She is my dancing partner."

When evening came, Cinderella wanted to leave and the king's son wanted to accompany her, but she darted off from him so quickly that he was not able to follow her. The prince, however, had thought of a trick and had had the whole staircase smeared with pitch, and it was there, as she ran down the stairs, that the girl's left slipper remained stuck. The prince picked it up. It was small, elegant, and completely golden. The next day he went with it to the man and said to him, "No other shall be my bride except the one whose foot this golden shoe fits." Both of the sisters were happy at that since they both had beautiful feet. The eldest sister took the shoe into her bedroom to try it on with her mother standing there, but she couldn't get her large toe into the shoe. The shoe was too small for her, and so her mother handed her a knife and said, "Cut your toe off, when you are queen you won't need to go on foot anymore." The girl cut her toe off, forced her foot into the shoe, made herself ignore the pain, and went back out to the king's son. He then took her as his bride, lifted her up onto his horse and rode away. They had to pass by the grave on their way, however, and there sat the two doves in the little hazel tree and they called out,

> "Coo, coo; coo, coo,
> there's blood in the shoe,
> the shoe is too small
> the right bride she isn't at all."

Then he looked at her foot and saw how the blood was oozing out of it. He turned his horse around, brought the false bride back home, and said that she was not the right one and that the other sister should try the shoe on.

The second sister went into the bedroom and happily was able to get her toes into the shoe, but her heel was too big. Her mother handed her the knife and said, "Cut a slice of your heel off, when you are queen you won't have to go on foot anymore." The girl cut off a slice of her heel, forced her foot into the shoe, swallowed the pain, and went out to the prince. He took her for his bride, lifted her up onto his horse and rode off with her. When they passed by the little hazel tree, the two doves perched in it called out,

> "Coo, coo; coo, coo,
> there's blood in the shoe,
> the shoe is too small
> the right bride she isn't at all."

He looked down at her foot and saw how the blood was seeping out of the shoe and that a bright red color was making its way up her white stockings. He turned his horse around and brought the false bride back home. "She is not the right one, either," he said. "Have you no other daughter?" "No, said the man, "there is only the little stunted and retarded Cinderella there from my dead wife, she couldn't possibly be the bride." The prince said that he was to send for her immediately, but the mother answered, "Oh no, she is much too dirty, it would be improper, she cannot be seen." The king's son insisted that that was what he wanted, and Cinderella had to be sent for.

Cinderella first washed her hands and face, then she entered and bowed before the prince, who handed her the golden shoe. She sat down on a footstool, removed her foot from the heavy wooden shoe, and placed it in the slipper which fitted like a glove. And as she arose and the prince looked her in the face, he recognized the beautiful girl who had danced with him and said, "This is the right bride!" The stepmother and the two sisters were shocked and turned pale out of sheer vexation. The king's son lifted Cinderella onto his horse and rode off with her. When they came by the hazel tree, the two white doves called,

"Coo, coo; coo, coo,
no blood in the shoe!
The right bride he's taking home,
the right bride is now his own."

And as they said that, both birds came flying down and seated themselves on Cinderella's shoulders, one on the right side, and the other on the left, and that is where they remained.

When the time came for the marriage of the king's son to be held, both of the false sisters came and tried to ingratiate themselves so as to get a share of Cinderella's good fortune. As the bridal couple went to the church, the eldest sister was on the right side, the youngest was on the left. At that moment, the doves pecked out one of the eyes of each of them. Afterward when they were leaving, the eldest was on the left and the youngest was on the right. The doves pecked out the other eye of each of them. And thus for their cruelty and falsity they were punished with blindness all the days of their lives.

Perrault's Version

Now let us turn to Perrault's version, since it is a source for the Grimms, to see by contrast just how uniquely rich in spirituality the Grimm version of *Cinderella* is. Then we look at the version they so admired—the Neapolitan dialect version of Giambattista Basile—which they had intended to translate for their collection but then yielded to the constraints of time and their priority of printing German versions first. Since Walt Disney chose to adapt Perrault's version of *Cinderella* rather than the Grimms', most of us became familiar in childhood with the French version:

There was once a man who took for his second wife the most haughty, stuck-up woman you ever saw. She had two daughters of her own, just like her in everything. The husband for his part had a young daughter, but she was sweet-natured, taking after her mother, who had been the best person in the world.

The wedding was barely over when the stepmother let her temper show; she couldn't bear the young girl's goodness, for it made her own daughters seem even more hateful. She gave her the vilest household chores: it was she who cleaned the dishes and the stairs, who scrubbed Madam's chamber, and the chambers of those little madams, her stepsisters; she slept at the top of the house in an attic on a shabby mattress, while her sisters had luxurious boudoirs, with beds of the latest fashion, and mirrors in which they could study themselves from head to toe. The poor girl suffered it all patiently and didn't dare complain to her father, who would have scolded her, because he was completely under the woman's sway.

When she had done her work, she would retire to the chimney corner and sit in the cinders, so that they commonly called her Cinderbutt [*Cucendron*], though the younger sister, who wasn't quite so rude as the elder, called her Cinderella [*Cendrillon*]. And despite everything, Cinderella in her rags was still a hundred times prettier than her sisters, for all their sumptuous clothes.

The opening of the story in Perrault completely eschews any explanation or description of the demise of the first wife. In the Grimms' version, the separation caused by the death of the mother is the emotional matrix and the key to the symbolism of the story. This is so even in the first version (1812), printed only four years after the death of the Grimms' own mother, in which the dying mother tells Cinderella, "My dear child, I will have to leave you." There is no provision in Perrault for a mystical communion between mother and child after the mother has passed on to the next world. The magic in Perrault's version is independent of the grave. Basile, on the other hand, goes into great detail on the disappearance of the first wife, as we shall see, since the opening of the story in his version is her murder by her daughter. To return to Perrault:

> It happened that the king's son gave a ball, to which he asked all the quality; our two misses were also asked, as they cut quite a dash in the district. They were thrilled, and kept themselves very busy choosing the clothes and hairstyles which would show them off best—a new worry for Cinderella because it was she who ironed her sisters' petticoats and pleated their ruffles. They couldn't talk of anything but clothes. [Cinderella then helps and advises because she has such good taste and offers to do their hair.] But while she combed, they said to her, "Cinderella, wouldn't you like to go to the ball?" Cinderella sighed. "You're making fun of me, ladies, that's not my place." "You're right. People would have a good laugh to see a Cinderbutt at the ball." Anyone else but Cinderella would have tangled their hair, but she was good, and she styled it to perfection. The sisters went nearly two days without eating, they were so excited and they broke more than a dozen corset laces pulling them tight to get a wasp waist, and they were always at the mirror.
> At last the happy day arrived, and they set off. Cinderella stared after them as long as she could, and when she could no longer see them, she began to cry. Her godmother, who saw her weeping, asked her what she wanted. "I want . . . I want . . . " She cried so hard she couldn't finish. Her godmother, who was a fairy, said, "You want to go to the ball, isn't that it?" "Yes," sighed Cinderella.

And so begins the magic which we all know. The fairy godmother is, much in the style of a Grimm fairy tale, a harmonized figure who is capable of magic through two traditions. She is a godparent, and therefore responsible for the child's human and religious welfare from the moment of baptism, and she is a fairy, a spiritual figure possessing the power to bestow gifts, who comes from the pre-Christian world of pagan Celtic religion. Cinderella brings her a pumpkin from the garden. Her godmother, practical as well as magical, first scoops it out and only then taps it with her magic wand, and it becomes a beautiful gilded carriage. Six mice from the mousetrap are changed into six horses as each receives a touch of the wand. A rat is tapped into being a coachman, six garden lizards are transformed by the wand into footmen in full livery. There is no hazel branch, no grave, no mystical tree in the story, nor are there any lentils to be sifted from the ashes with the help of doves. Finally, the magic wand changes Cinderella's clothes to cloth of gold and silver, and she gets a pair of glass slippers, "the prettiest in the world." Then comes the famous warning from the fairy godmother not to stay a moment after midnight, for if she does, "everything will return to what it was." At the ball the prince is completely taken with her (and "even the king, ancient as he was, couldn't stop looking at her," Perrault notes in an aside to the adults). Cinderella sits near her sisters and shares the prince's gifts of oranges and lemons with them, but they see only beautiful hair and clothes, not who she is. At a quarter of twelve she flees the ball. On the second night, all goes as before, but in running "like a doe" she drops one of her glass slippers.

The third part of the story begins with the infatuated prince's search for the girl whose foot fit the slipper.

> He started by trying all the princesses, then the duchesses, and all the court, but it was no use. The slipper was brought to the two sisters, who tried everything to force their feet into the slipper, but they couldn't manage it. Cinderella, who was watching, and who recognized her own slipper, laughed and said, "Let me see if it fits me." Her sisters burst out laughing, and jeered at her. The gentleman in charge of the slipper looked closely at Cinderella, and finding her extremely attractive, said she was right, because he'd been told to try all the girls. He made Cinderella sit down, and putting the slipper on her tiny foot, he saw how it slipped on, and fitted as perfectly as if it were made of wax. The sisters were astonished, but even more so when Cinderella took the other slipper from her pocket and put it on her foot. Then the godmother came and touched Cinderella's clothes with her wand, making them turn into garments even more stunning than all the others.

Because the Grimm tale involves cutting the feet, the slippers could not be made of glass, for then the bloody toe stump would have shown, and thus the change to a golden slipper. Of greater importance is Perrault's use of goodness as being "transparent" to those who have eyes to see. In his version, the sisters do not recognize their own sister because their eyes do not see beyond the external, clothes and cinders. Cinderella, however, in Perrault's ending of the story, graciously pardons them: "So the sisters recognized her as the beautiful lady they had seen at the ball. They threw themselves at her feet and asked forgiveness for all the harsh treatment they had made her suffer. Cinderella raised them up, and kissed them, and forgave them with all her heart, and asked them to love her always."

Cinderella remains true to her good self, and the story arrives at a very Christian ending, full of forgiveness and the prevention of future jealousy by finding husbands at court for the two sisters. "Cinderella who was as good as she was beautiful, took her sisters to live in the palace, and married them the same day to two great lords of the court." Perrault, it seems, feels that beauty in a person is not enough; goodness must also be present to create charm. Both pagan and Christian virtues in harmony characterize a person of charming graciousness. His moral:

> Beauty in a woman is a very rare treasure:
> Of it we can never tire.
> But what's worth more, a priceless treasure,
> Is charm [bonne grâce] which we all admire.
> Ladies, better than teased up hair, is:
> To win a heart, and conquer a ball.
> Charm is the true gift of fairies;
> Without it you've nothing; with it, all.

This ending contrasts very much with that of Wilhelm Grimm, who ended his first version with the prince riding off with the right bride to the approving chant of the doves, but who added that he knew of a further ending (S. einen weiteren Schluß.).[7] In that ending the birds peck out the eyes of the sisters, which takes the conclusion out of the hands of Cinderella's goodness and beauty and pushes the outcome into the realm of the natural spiritual world.

Basile's Version

Giambattista Basile published his version in Neapolitan dialect in 1634, preceding Perrault by sixty-three years, in a collection of fifty folktales that soon came to be called Il Pentamerone. In tone and content, Basile's version of Cinderella is also that of a courtier and is an exposé in fairy-tale form of Neapolitan high society's origins in criminal behavior, social climbing, and the deceptive manipulation of affection. The tale charms by its marinade of gruesome content in a light and appealing tone. The story begins with murder, and does not end with the perpetrator condemned, but, with the help of the spirits, exalted. The perpetrator is Cinderella herself. Basile's title creates an initial wariness, La Gatta Cennerentola—"The Cinder Cat." Her magic combination of humility and the help of the spirits results in a person who is con-

7. Rölleke, Synopse, p. 313.

Cinderella is helped by the doves. The background is a gothic doorway centered on the grave of her mother, which is marked by the cross and the tree growing at its head. This is the tree from which the dove watches over Cinderella. Drawing by Laurence Selim after Ludwig Emil Grimm.

foundingly free of conscience, strikingly amoral, and quite successful in adversity, a cold murderess who is unfairly deceived and then vindicated. This is not the type of tale one would imagine that the Grimms would enjoy, but in fact they did, perhaps as they enjoyed Tieck's version of *Red Riding Hood*, and this phenomenon shows how broad could be their definition of, and delight in, *Mährchen*.

Basile's story begins with its moral:

> In the sea of malignity it is always envy which, in return for the gift of an inflated bladder-float, gives yours a rupture; and when envy even thinks that someone else might have drowned in the sea, it sees itself as being underwater, or thrown against a rock. . . . Once upon a time there lived a prince who was a widower and he possessed an only daughter, so dear to him that he saw everything through her eyes, and the princess had a governess, who taught her all kinds of fancy work, and educated her in many other feminine endowments.[8]

The plot then begins with the widowed prince taking a new wife, who turns out to be arrogant and haughty and looks down on her new stepdaughter and treats her with contempt. One day the girl said to her governess, "Oh God, I wish that you had been my mother, you love me and are always caressing me." The girl continued this singsong so long that one day the governess lent a pleased ear to it and told the girl, "If you do as I say, I will become your mother, and you will be as dear to me as the pupils of my eyes." Zezolla (the girl) asks to be told what to do and assures the governess succinctly that she will carry it out: "You write, I'll sign" (*tu scrive, io firmo*). The governess tells her to wait until her father is away and then to ask her stepmother to let her wear one of the older dresses stored away in the big trunk. "And," the sly governess adds, "since your stepmother loves to see you in rags, she will do it. When you are in the storage room, and she tells you to hold up the lid of the trunk for her and begins rummaging around the tattered rags inside, then let the lid fall and break her neck."[9] This Zezolla does, and kills her mother. Afterward, manipulating her father's feelings for her as instructed by her governess (the governess assured her that "from you, your father would take counterfeit money"), Zezolla persuades him to marry the clever governess, Carmosina (the name might be rendered "Blood Red"). Eventually the father does as his daughter asks.[10]

8. For my retelling here of *La Gatta Cennerentola* I am using Basile's Neapolitan original and Burton's antique-style English translation: Giambattista Basile, *Lo Cunto de Li Cunti*, a cura di Ezio Raimondi (Milano-Napoli: 1960), pp. 18–31. *Il Pentamerone*, trans. Sir Richard Burton (New York: Liveright, [1893], 1943), pp. 45–51.

9. Basile's use of the lid of a trunk to perform the murder of family member is also found in the Grimms' Low German tale *Von dem Machandelboom* (*The Juniper Tree*).

10. The initial part of the story with Cinderella's murder of her mother is often left out of translations. Cf. *Old Neapolitan Stories*, which is aimed at small children.

At the wedding all are merry. A dove comes, settles on a low wall outside and says to Zezolla, "Whenever you desire to have something, send a message to the dove of the fairies on the island of Sardinia (*la palomma de le fate a l'isola de Sardegna*), and it will arrive immediately."

The dove in Basile's version is there to acknowledge and reward Zezolla for her recent murderous actions and comes, therefore, not from heaven, nor surely from her mother's grave. Rather, with a Neapolitan sense of humor, Basile has the dove come from Sardinia, immediately casting the behavior and reputation of the people of that island in a bad light. The dove with its promise of reward seems to be the spirit of despicable, but successful, criminal behavior.

As the story continues with its twists and turns, the deceiver becomes the deceived as Zezolla meets the six daughters whom the governess had kept concealed and now ingratiates completely with Zezolla's father. He, in turn, gradually forgets his daughter Zezolla, and she is sent down "from the chamber to the kitchen, from the throne's canopy to the hearth's chimney, from cloth of gold and silk to sackcloth and burlap, from the scepter to the spit." And it is then that her name too makes the descent from Zezolla to "The Cinder Cat" (*la gatta cennerentola*).

One day the father has to go on an official mission to Sardinia and asks what presents each of the daughters would like him to bring back. The six ask for fine presents and robes, and the Cinder Cat asks only that he recommend her to the dove of the Sardinian fairies. After initially forgetting his own daughter's request, and being magically punished in the harbor by not being able to move his ship forward or back, the father remembers, goes to the fairies of the island, and is given a gift by them to bring back to Cinder Cat: a date tree. The tree is accompanied by the gift of a mattock to cultivate the soil, a golden bucket with which to water it, and a silken cloth with which to wipe its leaves. When Zezolla had planted and cared for her gift for four days a fairy comes out of the tree just as the tree had reached the stature of a woman, a spirit no doubt bearing a startling resemblance to herself, and asks her, "What do you wish?"

The Grimms seem to have been impressed by Basile's pointed delineation of the reprehensible character of a father who is careful only about bringing back presents to his stepdaughters, and incorporated his behavior into their version. In any case, thus begins the magic part of the story for Cinder Cat. She is taught a magic rhyme by the fairy to say to the tree, the last line of which is *Spoglia a te, e vieste a me!* (Take off your clothes and give them to me!) When she recites this spell for the first time, the tree gives her the raiment of a queen, puts her on a fine horse followed by twelve pages "all dressed with luxury and taste," and off she goes to celebrate a festival to which her well-dressed stepsisters were invited. At the feast she so impresses the king that he tells a courtier his "mouth was watering" for "that delightful dove" (*sta penta palomma*). The story does not hesitate thereby to suggest a rather intimate connection between the dove and the Cinder Cat. Since the "dove" is Cinder Cat, then one can interpret the dove that appeared to Zezolla after her calculated murder of her mother as her own spirit, revealed as "Sardinian," a predatory catlike part of her self which she now cultivates, waters, and polishes, and which she calls upon to "clothe her." This is not the spirit of Perrault's graciously self-effacing heroine, nor is this the way in which the dove in the tree is interpreted by Wilhelm Grimm, but it may be the incident that appealed to him for a reply: to re-imagine the meaning of Zezolla's dove in a more transcendental way. When a servant is ordered to follow Cinder Cat and find where she lives, she distracts him by throwing money on the ground. When he bends over to gather it up, she is gone.

The second time there is a festival, the same is repeated, except that Cinder Cat comes even more splendidly attired. As she escapes the attention of the king on this occasion she tosses pearls and jewels at the servant sent to follow her. The king is even angrier at her escape and informs the unfortunate servant that if he doesn't find out who she is next time, he will get as many strokes and kicks in the rear as he has hairs in his beard!

For the third festival, the date tree outdoes itself, and Cinder Cat comes "in a golden carriage accompanied by so many servants that she looked like a prostitute arrested on a public thoroughfare surrounded by policemen." This surprising comparison, omitted often in English translation, says a great deal about Basile's critical distance from his heroine and from her behavior. On this occasion Cinder Cat races away in the carriage at such a violent speed that her slipper flies out the coach window and into the hands of the pursuing servant of the king. In the final part of the story the king admires the slipper, and as he gazes at it he says, "If the foundation is so beautiful, what must the house be like?" and "If I cannot have the tree[!], I worship the root." The latter thought once again suggests a connection between Cinder Cat and the Sardinian spirit of the tree.

The king invites all the women in the land to try on the slipper. When all the women have tried on the shoe in vain, the king issues a further command that no woman is to be left out. At this point Cinder Cat's father admits that he still has a daughter at home, "but she is not worthy." "Let her be at the head of the list," says the king. When she arrives, he recognizes her but pretends he does not. When the slipper comes to Zezolla, it flies to her foot "like iron to a magnet." Zezolla is embraced and crowned queen of the land. The father of Cinder Cat plays no further role, but the six stepsisters are livid with jealousy (*livide d'invidia*) and have no stomach to see any more. They leave the place and walk home dejectedly to their mother's house, resigned however, despite themselves, that "only a madman opposes what is in the stars" (*ca pazzo è, chi contrasta co le stelle*).

The fatalism that ends the story is used to discourage the vice of envy on the classical Greco-Roman religious basis of its ultimate futility—one cannot fight fate. What is in the stars will come to pass in any case, and it will happen even if it is in league with criminal vanity and on the side of a murderess. With the stars' help the Neapolitan Cinderella goes from rags to riches, backed by the help of the "dove" of Sardinia.

The Spiritual Transformation of Cinderella

Wilhelm Grimm certainly admired the well-done tripartite form of Basile's plot, with its satirical explanation of how one becomes queen in Naples, but what relic of ancient religion would he have found here to admire? Evil rewarded? I think it more likely to be the presence of a spirit of a person in a tree, and the triumph of fate whether for good or ill. The word for "fairy" in Basile's version is *fata*, and thus reading the story in the original as the Grimms did, it is the "Sardinian fate" that is in league with Cinder Cat. The satiric story is so well told from the point of view of form that it is easy to overlook its embodiment of the ancient Classical (and Indo-European) belief in fate, its inevitability and, in its blindness, its moral neutrality. For Wilhelm, Basile's version of the story would have contained a relic of classical religious belief, an echo of the feelings of the ancient Greek world of Athena's owl. The ancient past is still present, quietly concealed on the fringes of a modern story, just as the ancient religion of fatalism and the blind parcae are still present in the modern Italian phrase: *che sarà, sarà,* "what will be will be."

The Grimms' version of the tale has an entirely different slant. Fate is still present in the Grimms' version as Cinderella's predestination, the tree and the dove are there together with the rise from rags to riches, but how the story is held together is transformed by the magic of the communion of saints, the most encompassing bond of faithful love in Wilhelm's Trinitarian Christianity. The communion of saints is found in the Apostles' Creed, a statement of common belief formulated initially in the second century, added to over several centuries, and now used by all Christian denominations. Its final phrases are "(I believe in) . . . the communion of saints, the forgiveness of sins, the resurrection of the body and life everlasting." A useful description of the communion of saints as helpful communication between the "saints"—that is, among those who are good, whether still living on earth or already in the next world—might be the following: "As everyone knows, the communion of saints is nothing else but a mutual sharing in help, satisfaction, prayer and other good works, a mutual communication among all the faithful, whether those who have reached heaven . . . , or who are still pilgrims on the way in this world" (*Mirae Caritatis*, ency. Leo XIII, May 28, 1902).

In a more medieval vein, Aquinas stated in his exposition on the Apostles'

Creed, "The benefit of Christ is communicated to all Christians . . . , and this communication is realized through the sacraments of the church. [This benefit which Christ communicates is chiefly] the *Holy Spirit*, who *through the unity of love* communicates the blessings of Christ's members *one with another*"[11] (emphasis mine).

John Calvin's Reformed theology is even more explicit about the nonsleeping state of the soul's continuing consciousness after the death of the body: "For the Anabaptists and some Lutherans the soul sleeps—free from pain but also free from consciousness. For the followers of Calvin the soul rests, but fully aware of being in the presence of the divine. . . . The soul rests but does not sleep."[12] In a very strong polemic,[13] Calvin argued for the soul's continuing consciousness, something that could easily have prompted the Grimms' insertion of the mother's promise to look after her child after death, and justifying the depiction of the mother's abiding awareness of her daughter in the symbolic tree growing above the grave.

This makes sense of the dying mother's admonition to Cinderella in the Grimms' version, that she will continue to look down on her daughter and help her, but Cinderella must remain "good and devout"—that is, she too must remain a part of the communion of saints, if this is to happen. The Holy Spirit as the giver of gifts and the enabler of *the unity of love* in the communion is represented as the dove in the tree over the grave. The reading of the fairy tale then breaks down into three parts:

1. The communion of saints obtains between mother and daughter, through the tears which Cinderella sheds as a sign of love. The father, stepsisters, and stepmother do not weep and are not a part of the supernatural communion.

2. The communion is extended to nature. The doves come to help Cinderella sort the good lentils from the bad. The natural is in league with the supernatural in the ability to discern what is good from what is bad, the knowledge of good and evil. Even animals select the good and reject the bad, not only in the realm of seeds and food but in the realm of people, and thus they help Cinderella.

3. The communion is extended to the head of the communion of saints: the King's Son and his Father. They too know how to pick the good and reject the bad, thus they reject the two stepsisters and bring Cinderella into their glory.

11. *Summa Theologica*, 3, 82.6 ad 3.

12. *Heaven, A History*, Colleen McDannell and Bernhard Lang (New Haven: Yale, 1988), p. 184.

13. *Psychopannychia: or, the Refutation of the Error Entertained by some Unskillful Persons, Who Ignorantly Imagine that in the Interval between Death and Judgment the Soul Sleeps* (Corpus Reformatorum 33:188), in *Tracts and Treatises in Defense of the Reformed Faith* (Grand Rapids: Eerdmans, 1958), p. 432.

In addition, "Blessed are the poor in spirit, for theirs is the kingdom of Heaven," could almost be given as a subtitle for the Grimms' *Cinderella* since it begins with a death-transcending alliance of dying mother and surviving daughter, one of them about to go to "the kingdom of heaven," the other soon to be relegated by a non-feeling family to the humiliation of the "poor in spirit," to make her bed among the ashes. Cinderella's promise to be "good and pious," the condition which enables the two who are separated by time and the grave to be united in a communion of saints, is a union that contains its own source of magical wealth: the dove in the tree over the grave. In the Grimms' religious reworking of *Cinderella*, the heroine remains good and devout despite all mockery, the tree of Sardinia becomes a magical hazel tree identified with the still-living love of the dead for the living, the mother for her daughter. The tree motif, moreover, is intensified by its repetition in the story in the form of two added trees, one an elevated dove-house and one a tree with pears, to function as a refuge for the fleeing heroine. The three religions are thus entwined again, the Germanic hazel, the Christian dove tree, and the Classical "golden apples," all attempting to help the good and humble Cinderella. The element of enviousness in the story is changed from the sisters' simple envy (in Perrault) to that of a colder "blindness" of the heart, a lack of appropriate love (in Grimm), thus accusing the father almost more strongly than the two sisters and the wicked stepmother. The stepsisters will not be forgiven for their jealousy, as in Perrault, but symbolically punished in order to reveal their spiritual blindness. The enabling spirit for the plot is neither the "fairy godmother" nor the "spirit of Sardinia" but the tree of Cinderella's mother's spirit with the dove of the Holy Spirit in its branches. No pumpkin is changed to a carriage nor will the ominous hour at the ball be midnight, but Cinderella leaves the ball earlier at a more biblical time associated with the story of Christ: "And when evening had come . . ." (*Als es nun Abend war . . .*).

In the Grimms' earliest printed version, 1812, the manuscript version of 1810 is missing, the beginning is unmistakably spiritual:

> Once upon a time there was a rich man who lived for a long time in happiness with his wife and they had one child, a daughter. Then the wife became sick, and when she was dying she called her daughter and said, "Dear child, I have to leave you but when I am up in heaven, I will look down on you. Plant a little tree on my grave and whenever you want something shake it and you will have it, and also whenever you are in distress I will send you help, just remain good and devout." After she said that, she closed her eyes and died, but the child cried and planted a little tree on the grave, and she didn't have to bring any water to water it because her tears were enough.
>
> The snow came and put a little white blanket on the mother's grave and

when the sun had taken it off again, and the little tree had become green for its second time, the husband had taken another wife.[14]

The contrast between the child's real and abiding grief, versus the father's pause of a single winter's duration before finding another wife, reveals the determining role of fidelity in Wilhelm's religious view of love as a divine and diachronic reality. Though the daughter exemplifies the Second Beatitude, "Blessed are those who mourn, for they will be comforted," the brief winter of the husband's discontent sadly exposes the one-snowfall's depth of the husband's soon evaporated loving communion with his wife. The Germanic religion's tree of faithfulness and protection does not grow for him, and in Wilhelm's version of *Cinderella* the indifferent and disloyal father attempts to chop it down. There is an echo here of the father of Hansel and Gretel who was a woodcutter and who added the chopped off branch to strike against the dead tree in order to deceive the children into believing that their father's protection was faithfully nearby.

After the first version, Wilhelm added the story line from Basile about the father's going away (but not to Sardinia) and bringing back the requested presents to his two stepdaughters and the "tree" to Cinderella. Wilhelm Grimm's comment in the story that it was not necessary to water the tree since the girl's tears were enough is, I believe, a response to Basile's version where all sorts of implements were brought back to enable Zezolla to cultivate the date tree, which, in any case, is not planted on the grave of her mother whose neck she broke. Wilhelm has the father bring back to Cinderella a hazel twig, not a date tree, from the first branch to knock his hat off, and Cinderella plants it on her mother's grave. Cinderella's request for such a present from him is a reproach. One need not restrict the interpretation of the hazel twig to being a phallic symbol only, for the twig is from a magic tree. It should remind the father of the magic of his natural love for the branch of his own tree: it should knock his hat off, which it does, to make him realize how unnatural a father he is, but alas, he remains blind to his own condition. Thus Wilhelm has incorporated the distant trip of Basile's story into his narrative, but has changed the meaning of the tree to a spiritual one. Placed on the grave, the twig transcends death, and the roots absorb the tears of Cinderella's love; it grows to become a hazel tree filled with the spirit of the wife and mother, a comfort to the one member of her family who mourns her and a reproach to the one who does not.

This curious and moving depiction of resurrection and the continued communion of saints in the form of a protective tree growing from the grave is not just to be found in Wilhelm's storytelling but also in his life. When researching in the Hessian Archives in Marburg, I came across Wilhelm's copy of the me-

14. Rölleke, *Synopse*, p. 299.

dieval German epic the *Ruolandsliet* ("The Song of Roland"), one of the works he taught at the university. On page 131 I found a little sprig of lancet-shaped leaves. On one leaf Wilhelm had carefully written in small and precise letters: *von dem grabe der Kurfürstin am 13 März 1841* [from the grave of the Princess of Hesse-Kassel, on the 13th of March, 1841]. Apparently he had visited the grave of Karoline, the princess who had been so friendly to her lady-in-waiting, his Aunt Zimmer, and had assisted her in supporting and caring for him and his brother after the death of their father in Steinau.[15] While at the cemetery, he must have plucked off a twig from the tree growing above the princess's grave, moved by emotions similar to those he wrote into his version of the story of *Cinderella*. Then he placed the inscribed leaf among the pages of one of the world's most famous stories of loving fidelity in the face of death, the *Song of Roland*. One can only conclude that Wilhelm's personal religious faith in the ultimate triumph of love and resurrection, his love of medieval story, and his rewriting of the fairy tales were all deeply connected.

As the story continues, Cinderella is ridiculed by her stepsisters and made to wear an old gray coat (*einen alten grauen Rock*); they then mock her and call her "Princess." This is a curious passage since the Grimms' library reveals that the brothers had had a long interest in the holy coat of Trier, a relic thought at the time by many to have been Christ's seamless garment, and often described as an old gray coat.[16] This allusion to Christ's own garment is almost too direct, and by the final version of this tale Wilhelm had modified the unmistakably alluding word for coat, *Rock* to the parallel but more humble and indirect *Kittel*, a light coat for indoor work. The meaning of the passage is clear in its context: the real daughter is humiliated by jealous stepsisters, she sits in the ashes of misery as in the sufferings of Job, an old coat is put on her, while she is mocked for her dirty clothing and derisively called "Princess" (which she will soon be), all of which recollects the ridiculing of Christ during the Passion, his being forced to change clothes, to wear a kingly robe while being spat upon and called "King."

They stripped him and put a scarlet robe on him, and after twisting some thorns into a crown, they put it on his head. They put a reed in his right had

15. The grave may also have been that of the later Auguste, also princess of Hesse, and a great friend and patron of the Grimms, including Ludwig Emil. She died on February 19, a month before the inscription. Ludwig Emil had sketched her walking with the Grimms in the garden as late as 1840.

16. The Grimms' library contained six books concerned with the holy coat of Trier (*der heilige Rock zu Trier*). This does not mean, of course, that the brothers were convinced of the relic's authenticity. The fact that the holy coat was a part of local folk religion was enough to justify its symbolic use in the tale. Any relic or remnant, any object still existing in the present time which had been a part of the joys and sufferings of the past, fascinated Wilhelm, such as the window in the castle at Steinau which had known the sorrowful imprisonment of the English princess.

and knelt before him and mocked him, saying, "Hail, king of the Jews!" They spat on him, and took the reed and struck him on the head. After mocking him, they stripped him of the robe and put his own clothes on him. (Mt 27: 27–31)

Wilhelm is also aware that in Classical mythology, the humiliated who sit in ashes may be the very ones destined to be exalted, and thus he refers in his commentary to Homer. Odysseus also sat in ashes, from which he was raised to glory. The ashes of Cinderella's abandonment and subsequent loneliness is a bereavement which Germanic, Christian, and Greek spirituality recognize. In Wilhelm's creative imagination they invite the Spirit of God Himself, as in the Second Beatitude, to come to the thrice-watered roots of the Germanic-Christian tree.

And when he came home, the father gave the stepdaughters what they had asked for and to Cinderella he gave the twig from the hazel bush. Cinderella thanked him, went to her mother's grave and planted the twig on it. She cried so hard that her tears fell down on it and watered it. It grew and became a beautiful tree. Every day Cinderella went to stand under it three times, there she cried and prayed, and each time a little white bird came and landed on the tree, and whenever she made a wish, the little white bird would throw down to her whatever she had wished for.

The second part of the story is the succession of the three days of the ball. The Grimms' final version begins with rhythmic biblical cadences echoing Luther's translation of the parable of the wedding feast:

Es begab sich aber, daß der König ein Fest anstellte, das drei Tage dauern sollte und wozu alle schönen Jungfrauen im Lande eingeladen wurden, damit sich sein Sohn eine Braut aussuchen möchte.

(And it came to pass that a king gave a feast. This feast was to last three days, and all of the beautiful young women of the country had been invited so that the king's son would be able to select a bride.)

It is in Wilhelm's version, not Basile's or Perrault's, that the purpose of the ball is the marriage of the king's son. This was not the case in his earliest version. In the 1812 version the sisters called for Cinderella and said, "Cinderella, come upstairs! Comb our hair, brush our shoes and lace them tight, we are going to the prince's ball!" In the final version there is a slight change, "Comb our hair, brush our shoes, make the lacings tight, we are going to a wedding up at the king's castle!" And thus begins the three-times-repeated encounter with the king's son which is traditional in all versions of *Cinderella*.

When Cinderella asks to go to the ball, her stepmother at first tells her she cannot go. Then she feigns consent and, throwing a bowl of lentils into the ashes on the hearth, tells Cinderella she can go if she can pick out all the lentils in two hours. This Cinderella does with the help of the two doves who fly in to help her. Then her stepmother throws two bowl of lentils into the ashes. Again the two white doves fly in with a whole crowd of birds to assist. Her instruction to them, to know the difference between the good and the bad, every German child (and adult) knows by heart:

> Die guten ins Töpfchen,
> die schlechten ins Kröpfchen.
>
> The good ones into the little pot
> the bad ones into the tummy.

Thus judgment is made, but the stepmother still refuses, turns her back on her stepdaughter's poverty and walks off to the ball with the two haughty stepsisters.

Though the commentary of the brothers Grimm does not state it, this incident ultimately goes back neither to Christian nor Germanic mythology but to Classical Roman storytelling.[17] It is found in Apuleius' story of *Psyche and Cupid*. In that story, the passionate love affair between "the soul" (Psyche) and "erotic love" (Cupid) deeply offends the goddess Venus, the mother of Cupid, who cannot comprehend what her divine son would find attractive in the human "soul." After cursing at "soul" for being pregnant with "love's" child she, "beauty," loses her temper completely, but then arranges a test for "soul"/Psyche:

> After this denunciation she leaped upon Psyche, tore her clothes to shreds, tugged out her hair, shook her by the head, and beat her black and blue. Then taking the wheat, barley, mullet, poppy seed, peas, lentils and beans, and mixing them into a single confused pile, she said: "To my eyes you're such an ugly slut that the only way you're likely to get a lover is by working you're fingers off for him. Separate this promiscuous mass of seeds. Sort out each grain; and collect them all in their original heaps. See to it that you obtain my approval by having the task finished when I return at dusk." . . .
>
> But Psyche did not lift a hand towards the hopelessly confused mound. She sat staring in silent stupefaction at the impossible task. Just then an ant (tiny toiler of the fields), realizing what a monstrous labor had been set on the girl, felt himself revolted with pity for the mighty godling's mate and with anger at the mother-in-law's cruelty. Dashing busily about he summoned the whole

---

17. It is unclear to me why the Grimms did not acknowledge this source. Even if their version's incident of the lentils thrown among the ashes was mediated through one of their "Hessian sources," the brothers would have recognized the source of the incident in *Psyche and Cupid*.

tribe of ants that were at work in the nearby meadows. . . . [the task is accomplished, and when Venus returns:] "Slut," she said, "this is no work of your hands. He did it all, the lad you seduced to the hurt of both of you." Then, casting her a crust of brown bread, she retired to sleep.[18]

By transforming the Classical ants into doves, Wilhelm's version of the story takes on a Christian tone, but by depicting the responding doves as two, parallel overtones of Woden's two conscious ravens are heard. Nature is religious, and it is on the side of the good soul (Psyche). The underlying Roman myth behind the lentils lends more credence to the interpretation that Cinderella represents the soul of the good person, and it is this soul that the king's son seeks for a bride. The child of their marriage, in Apuleius' version, is "Joy."

For the first ball Cinderella goes to her mother's grave under the hazel tree as soon as nobody is home and recites a spell,

> Shudder and shake, my little tree,
> Throw gold and silver down on me!

"And then the bird threw a gold and silver dress down to her with shoes that had been stitched with silk and silver." Now she can go to the wedding, she is clothed in the gifts of the white bird. She wears the spiritual clothes of good-heartedness and faithfulness, the gifts of the Holy Spirit noted by Wilhelm in his Bible. They are far superior to anything worn by the others at the ball, and she is therefore the one who should dance with the king's son. She dances "until evening comes," and when she leaves the ball it is to escape by jumping up into the dove house.[19] Since there is no carriage in the Grimms' version, she slips from the hand of the prince to the place of the dove. Since all that she has is the wealth of her goodness, things that are of the spirit, thrown down by the bird in the tree, this is her appropriate refuge. When the father comes, he sends for his wood axe and pickaxe, and smashes the dove house in two, which is indeed what his lack of love for his wife and daughter has been doing all along. But, she is not there, she is back at the hearth in the ashes—one can see her beautiful raiment only if one has the eyes of the spirit, eyes that can see the richness of a good soul, not if one attempts to destroy her dove house with the blind axe of coldness.

The second time she attends the ball with the help of the white bird and

---

18. Apuleius, *The Golden Ass*, trans. Jack Lindsay (Bloomington: Indiana University Press, 1962), p. 134.

19. *Taubenhaus* in the original. If this word is translated "dovecote" the reader is often at a loss how to visualize it. If it is translated "pigeon coop" too much is lost. Therefore I have kept the translation literal.

stays again "until evening came," the prince tries to see which house she lives in by jumping into "the garden" behind the house. "There was a great and beautiful tree in the garden on which hung the most magnificent pears, and she went from branch to branch with the skill of a squirrel." The tree in the garden again lets us know that we are in a place of testing to determine if we human beings can see. The doves can see, the ants can see, Isaiah says the ox and the ass recognize their owner, but can human beings see the good and the spiritual on the tree of life, the "golden apples" of the classical garden of the Hesperides, and of Eden, and of the Germanic Iduna? The father sees only with his axe, which he again calls for, and chops down the "tree in the garden." She is not there, she, the same beautiful "princess" is wearing a gray old coat, sitting by the fire. Her father does not see her at all, as the pear tree crashes down to earth under his axe.

And "on the third day" all is repeated, except that this time the prince has smeared the stairway with pitch, a tar made from the sap of the evergreen tree, and thus by means of the tree's mediation is able to secure one of her shoes as Cinderella attempts to slip away. But Cinderella is the Psyche whom the prince wants to love and marry, the soul good and devout. When the sisters attempt to put on the shoe that the prince brings around to each of the ladies of his kingdom, each one resorts to something unnatural to make it fit their foot. The one cuts off a part of her heel, the other cuts off a part of her toe. There is no need to see the slipper as a vaginal symbol only.[20] It is clearly a symbol for the fact that one "soul" fits, and fits naturally with the king's son. Attempts to force the toe or heel into a symbol of rightness when the soul of the person doesn't fit are doomed to failure. And nature says so. It is the two white doves sitting in the tree above the grave of the mother who call out the unnaturalness to the prince:

> Coo, coo; coo, coo,
> there's blood in the shoe,
> the shoe is too small
> the right bride she isn't at all!

When the king's son returns to the father with the second stepsister, he asks a question reminiscent of the question put to Jesse[21] by Samuel when he was looking among Jesse's sons for the right one (David) to be king of Israel, "Have you no other son?" The prince says to Cinderella's father, "Have you no other daughter?" "No," he answered, "there is only the little stunted and retarded Cinderella there from my dead wife, she couldn't possibly be the bride." The father's answer is cold, objective, and rational, betraying his lack of paternal, subjective involvement (he echoes the cold rationality of the

20. See Bettelheim, *The Uses of Enchantment*, pp. 265–71.
21. 1 Samuel 16, 1–12.

stepmother in *Hansel and Gretel*: "If you say A, you have to say B").[22] Cinderella's stepmother adds, when the prince asks that she be sent for, "Oh no, she is much too dirty, it would be improper, she cannot be seen."[23] What wise, unknowing words! She cannot be seen, but perhaps it would be proper for the eyes of this particular prince, by him she can be seen. Her association with death is also made by the father by calling her something "retarded and stunted" and associating her with his dead wife. Her name in German, *Aschenputtel*, makes her a creature of the ashes, also associating her with mortality, "Ashes to ashes, dust to dust," and bringing her into ritual relationship with Ash Wednesday and the long ritual fasting-death of Lent which ends with Easter resurrection. Since all of Christendom covers itself in ashes on Ash Wednesday, at least it did in the Middle Ages, as a reminder of the human condition, Cinderella is a stand-in for everyman; everyone can identify with her and feel regret at her living among the ashes of unloving people and rejoice in the three days of her predestined rescue by the love of the king's son.

The father's objective description of his daughter brings a dismaying thought at this late point in the story. Perhaps Cinderella, *pace* Walt Disney, is not pretty. The father is, if nothing else, detached and objective. Perhaps our imaginations should realize that there is a physical reason, in Wilhelm's version, for her father's rejection, for the acknowledged beauty of her stepsisters, and for the fact that it is only her mother, and the king's son, who find her beautiful: the real Cinderella is stunted both physically and mentally. If one cannot see the beauty of her goodness and piety, the assets her mother told her to cultivate, we too as readers would shy away from her and see only a misshapen and retarded child tolerated in the home, allowed to live only near the ashes. Beauty exists in the eye of the beholder. The story at this point puts the adult reader in a quandary as he or she meditates on the question of whether or not the father should be considered right about Cin-

---

22. The word the father uses is crude, *verbuttetes*, "retarded," "stunted," [*butt* and *buttet* are defined by the Grimms in their German dictionary as "stupid, dumb" and "stunted, short and fat"], a vulgar dialect expression that one could not possibly use in describing one's own. Kafka may have been influenced in his depiction of the crudely objective father in *Twelve Sons* by this exposé of the horror of objectivity and distance when used by a father in depicting his own child.

23. "Ach nein, das ist viel zu schmutzig, das darf sich nicht sehen lassen." The grammatically correct neuter pronouns subtly also allow the denigrating suggestion that Cinderella has become a thing; literally translated: "Oh no, she is something much too dirty, it is not proper for something like that to let itself be seen." The original almost makes one think that poor Cinderella is a dirty part of human nature, something proper people would prefer to conceal, something in the family better kept hidden: the longing for a love that does not pass with time, the desire for loving contact to continue with the dead, the hope that the dead live on. This is all something which, despite its expected impropriety in the father's and stepmother's eyes, lies at the heart of the three religions and especially in Christianity's belief in life after death and in the communion of saints. This passage takes Wilhelm's spirituality beyond *Red Riding Hood*.

derella's physical condition, her beauty. If beauty exists in the eye of the beholder, how then does the reader's eye behold? Does it behold as the conventional eyes of the family do, or does it behold Cinderella as the natural-supernatural world would, as the animals in the story do and as do the eyes of the dove, the prince, and the prince's father? The function of the plot from this point on is to continue to steer the reader away from the family's way of looking at Cinderella by exposing their sight as blindness and to direct the reader toward seeing through they eyes of the Trinity of love: the Dove, the Prince, and the King.

The ending of the Grimms' *Cinderella*, despite this, is sometimes dismaying for those raised on Disney's version (taken from Perrault) or on Perrault's own version of the story, but the Grimms' ending fits as well as the shoe. First, the golden shoe itself is obtained by the king using pitch or tar smeared on the steps of the palace. This, however again establishes a hidden connection between the plot and the mother's spirit since pitch is a tarlike, gluey substance obtained from the resin of a tree. Second, it is the prince himself who comes down from the castle bringing the shoe to the house, as did Christ in the Incarnation, and he does not pull back from the dirty hearth maid, but lets her have the shoe as he did the others. This act alone means that he will recognize her since he does not go by wealth or external beauty as the determinant of personal worth. The great beauty and nobility which he saw in her when they danced together were all the gifts of the Dove, the Holy Spirit, in the tree. When the shoe fits and she stands up so that the prince can see her face, he recognizes her as his dancing partner and says, "This is the right bride." God dances with the good. As they ride off, the two white birds in the tree chant that she is indeed the right bride, and then fly down from the hazel tree above her mother's grave and land—one on her right shoulder, the other on her left. Her mother's two gifts passed on to her, goodness and piety, remain with her, making her the right bride for the king's son. With a white bird on each shoulder, she becomes a Germanic religious depiction of a person divinely inspired, as was Woden by Hugin and Munin, the ravens Consciousness and Memory, on each shoulder. Since they are white doves, however, and not black ravens, they are also the Holy Spirit depicted in Germanic form,[24] inspiring her consciousness and her memory of her mother so that she will remain what her mother told her to be: good and devout.

The father now disappears from the story. He is replaced by the Father

---

24. This depiction of the dove(s) on the shoulder(s) may be inspired by the *Heliand's* Germanic-Christian depiction of Christ's baptism in the Jordan. In the *Heliand's* reworking of the scene, the Holy Spirit as a great dove descends upon Christ by alighting on his shoulder, following the iconography of Woden. See *The Heliand, The Saxon Gospel* (New York: Oxford University Press, 1992), p. 35, and note 52. The Grimms were aware of the *Heliand* in manuscript prior to its printing by Schmeller, whose first edition came out in 1830.

known only from the words of the Prince. The earthly, objective father replaced by the subjective, loving heavenly Father, and by the Prince who came to seek a soul of goodness and piety, a person of humility, poor in spirit, to be given the kingdom of heaven. The story does not end here however. The Christian-Germanic twin birds remain on Cinderella-Psyche's shoulder, visible to some perhaps, but surely not to the stepmother and the stepsisters. When the day of the wedding comes, the sisters are present; they do not go away "livid with envy," as they do in Basile's version, but remain in the hope of flattering their way into being a part of their sister's glory. That "glory," the glory of two beautiful souls in communion, is a glory that is not visible to them. It was not seen when Cinderella was in rags at the grave or ashes at the hearth obeying their orders, and it is not something they could see in her now. What it would mean to be a soul betrothed to the King's Son is beyond them, as it was beyond the jealous sisters who envied Psyche's love of the god Cupid. And therefore Wilhelm reinforces the everyday mystical level of the story by having both sisters walk blindly into, and exit blindly from, the place where the king's son weds humble Cinderella: the church.

> Now as the bridal couple went to the church the eldest sister was on the right side, the youngest on the left. The doves pecked out one of the eyes of each one of them. Afterward, when they were leaving, the eldest was on the left and the youngest was on the right. The doves pecked out the other eye of each one of them. And thus for their cruelty and falsity they were punished with blindness all the days of their lives.

So ends the story in the Grimms' version. The two raven/doves of awareness and spirituality continue their job of sifting between the good and the bad and perform the last judgment. They could tell the good lentils from the bad in the ashes; they pecked out the bad and devoured them, and they put the good in the bowl. The king's son is able to sift through the three sisters presented to him, and is able, when he uses the doves' eyes, to see through both cosmetics and ashes, to see which one is good and devout. He recognizes the one who danced with him during the three days to Easter, the one who is fittingly his bride. The materialistic mother and sisters were blind to their relationship to the little girl and to the enormous value of such a relationship in itself. The doves, by blinding them, are merely making their condition visible. Just as in the case of Oedipus, they did not know their own. But, whereas Oedipus realized how blind he had been and gouged out his own eyes in repentance and realization, the sisters chose to feign sight of Cinderella's worth by coming to the wedding while actually remaining in the permanent state of spiritual sightlessness.

The father, whose axe attempted to eliminate the tree and the dove house and cut the roots of his daughter's spiritual ties to him, has no dove/raven of consciousness of his daughter, nor memory of his wife; he is inexcusably blind-hearted. His punishment is perhaps the worst of all. The story can no longer see him. It doesn't even punish him. He disappears from the tale without a mention, for he offended against the dove and the raven, against the great commandment of love, and has been replaced in Cinderella's life with the loving unity of the Father and the Son.[25]

25. This was a very important concept for Wilhelm, and finds expression here. As noted above, it is one of the few passages in his copy of *Parzival* which he underlined for the importance of content.

> got ist mensch unt sins vater wort
> *got ist vater unde suon,*
> sin geist mac groze helfe tuon.

> (God is a human being and his Father's Word
> *God is Father and Son,*
> this Spirit of God can give great help.)

The passage is taken from the young knight's moment of realization on what he must be like to be a chivalrous knight from the inside out, beginning with faithful love and giving the Trinity as the validation and exemplar. His brother's black-and-white mottled skin does not stop Parzival from recognizing his family relationship to him, nor blind him to his brother's greatness. He is the opposite of Cinderella's father. (From the Hessian *Staatsarchiv* in Marburg.)

Seven

SNOW WHITE

In their commentary on the origins of their version of *Snow White*, the
brothers Grimm wrote: "taken from many diverse Hessian stories" (*nach
vielfachen Erzählungen aus Hessen*).[1] They remark on how well known this
story is and on the many varieties in which it is told in the Germanies, including the retention everywhere of a North German version of the heroine's name, Sneewitchen, even if in garbled form, in the High German–
speaking regions of the south. In one of the several German versions of the
story which they describe, a king and queen are riding along in a sleigh, and
as the queen tries to peel an apple she accidentally cuts her finger, causing
blood to spill on the snow. In others, it is a count and a countess in the sleigh.
The countess makes a wish for a baby girl as white as the snow piles, as red as
three pools of blood which they pass, and as black as three ravens who fly
overhead. In still another version, the queen drives Snow White into the forest, has the carriage stop, and suggests that Snow White get out to pick a
bouquet of red roses; as the girl is gathering them the carriage quickly drives
off, abandoning Snow White in the woods. In yet another, the queen takes
Snow White to dwarfs in the forest who kill young girls, but they decide not
to kill her in exchange for her doing household work. In this version, while
with the dwarfs, Snow White had left her pet dog, named "Mirror" (*Spiegel*)
back in the castle. When the queen returns to the castle, she asks the dog:

> Mirror under the bench,
> Look in this land, look in that land,
> Who is the fairest in England?

> (Spiegel unter der Bank,
> sieh in dieses Land, sieh in jenes Land:
> wer ist die schönste in Engelland?)

---

1. Rölleke, *Jubiläumsausgabe*, III, 87. Much of the following review of sources taken from the
Grimms' commentary on the tale which is on pp. 87–90 of this volume.

After hearing the disconcerting answer, the queen plots Snow White's death again as in the other versions. Whoever retold this tale and in retelling decided that the mirror would be better as a pet dog, while implausibly retaining "Mirror" as a canine name, demonstrates a peculiar, if animal-loving, imagination.

Another German source acknowledged by the Grimms' is the much lengthier story of *Richilde* in Musäus's collection of German fairy tales, *Volksmärchen der Deutschen*, published initially in 1782, some thirty years prior to their own first edition. Musäus's style has much of the ironic and even satirical air of Perrault and Basile and seems far more destined to appeal to the rationally and sophisticatedly cynical adult reader than to children. His version begins with an un-Grimm-like lampoon of piety and devotion in the person of the excessively pro-clerical Count of Brabant, Gunderich der Pfaffenfreund (Gunderich the Clergy-friend) who is always at Mass or walking in processions, and who, thus restricted in his time for procreation, has no children. It is intimated that the understandably childless countess of Brabant finally achieves pregnancy only after a very private sacramental confession to one of her husband's esteemed clergyman visitors, renowned Dominican Albertus Magnus. Albertus Magnus in turn, his remarkable interest in the future child noted by court gossip, then fashions a magic mirror through his knowledge of the black arts as a gift for the child. This child is Richilde, who becomes the jealous mother of Blanca,[2] the persecuted heroine. The mother uses the enchanted mirror in the traditional manner to find out who is "the most beautiful in the land of Brabant."[3] The mirror, however, is not capable of magic speech, but answers sensibly by showing an image, as mirrors will do. As Richilde's behavior toward her more beautiful child deteriorates, in a nice touch the mirror darkens and rusts to a degree that its images become faint and useless. The mother attempts three times to poison her daughter, first with a half-poisoned apple (*Granatapfel*, pomegranate), the second time with perfumed soap, and the third time with a loving letter from herself laced with poisonous salts. She has forced the court doctor, Sambul the Jew, to concoct the poisons by bullying and by the offer of money, but each time his conscience gets the better of him and he merely injects a sleeping potion or a strong narcotic into the apple and the soap, and smears only sleep-

2. *Blanca* means white in Spanish, and therefore is partly related to "Snow White." It is almost as though "Snow White," were a combination of the "snow" of *Snae-frið* and the "white" of *Blanca*. Another Spanish curiosity in *Richilde* is the use of *dueña* for the mistress of a castle, perhaps to evoke the time of the Spanish rule of the Lowlands.

3. Wilhelm seems to have seen a connection here to Wolfram's *Parzival*. In his copy of *Parzival* which he used for his lectures in Marburg he underlined the following two lines from the end of the epic: <u>vil liute in Brabant noch sint,</u> / <u>die wol wizzen von in beiden</u> ("there are many people in Brabant who still know about both of them"). He may suspect then that the story of Lohengrin is still remembered, through folktale continuity with epic of the medieval past, as the happy couple of Brabant at the end of the fairy tale *Richilde*.

inducing aromatic salts on the letter. He is punished by Richilde for his lack of success at causing the death of her child by having his beard pulled out and his ears cut off. In contrast to the Grimms, therefore, Musäus eschewed the mystical or magical, made the conscience of the professional doctor the instrument of mercy, and thereby enabled Blanca, "Snow White," to awaken reasonably each time from the casket on her own. By turning her apparent death into a medically induced sleep, Musäus makes the moment of crisis in the narrative fully responsive to reason and avoids any real need for supernatural agency to overcome death. The story's religious content is thus not found in the realm of the spiritual or mystical, but is in the realm of morality and conscience.

The dwarfs are present, but they are demythologized and described as "court dwarfs" presumably kept in the castle for the service and amusement of the nobility. They are, however, honest and helpful. They are not asked to make a glass casket for Blanca, but they insert a little glass window in it above the face of the "corpse" so that they can watch her, and eventually they see the rosy color returning to her face.

The need for rescue by the prince is diminished by the doctor's successful preventive efforts, but it is not done away with entirely. The prince appears when Blanca is lying in her third occasion of sleep. On arrival he applies a papally blessed relic to her heart and, lo, just at that moment the effect of the salts wears off, Blanca awakes and gets her prince, who is neither mythical nor timeless, as Rölleke might have liked it, but rather Gottfried of Ardenne. The ending follows very much in the same spirit of the Enlightenment. The countess, Richilde, is invited to the wedding of her daughter, having been deceived into believing that she herself is to be the bride. After fainting at the shock of seeing Blanca alive and in the bridal veil, she is forced to dance at the wedding feast in glowing hot shoes, but at the end of the dance is discovered to have suffered only burns and blisters to the feet. She is thrown into a tower to give her time to repent. Death is avoided even in her case, with the liberal and enlightened hope that imprisonment will work her eventual rehabilitation. The concluding lines of the story do not serve as the place for the ritual statement about "happiness ever after" for the young couple. In an effective twist, the last lines treat the conscientious Jewish doctor as the real hero, in the style of Lessing, and comment approvingly on his new position as prime minister to the king of Morocco, describing him as being blessed with children and grandchildren, and promising that it is he who will live happily ever after.[4] The Grimm version, in contrast, will reinterpret the fundamental narrative in the style of Romanticism and retain the death of Blanca (and her mother), thus returning the religious level of the story from the moral to the transcendental.

---

4. See Musäus, J.K.A., *Volksmärchen der Deutschen* (Darmstadt: Wissenschaftliche Buchgesellschaft, 1961), pp. 75–117.

Because of its age and provenance, the most remarkable version of *Snow White* to the Grimms was the medieval Norse story of *Snaefrið* in the *Harald-saga* of Snorri Sturluson's *Heimskringla*. Snorri lived from 1179 to 1241, and Harald Fairhair of the saga lived in the ninth and early tenth centuries, thus establishing the great antiquity of the roots of the story.[5] The name *Snaefrið* might be translated "Snow Lover,"[6] and this story bears some remarkable resemblances, as well as differences, to the Grimms' version. I have italicized some significant similarities.

King Harald went *one winter* a-feasting in the Uplands and had a Yule feast made ready for himself in Toftar. On the eve of Yule, Svasi came to the door whilst the king was at the table and he sent a messenger to the king to come out to him. [The king is annoyed but goes out, crosses the stream with the man and goes to his hut.] There *Snaefrid,* Svasi's daughter, stood up, the most beautiful of women, and she offered the king a cup full of mead; he drank it all and also took her hand, and straightway it was as though fire passed through his body, and at once he would lie with her that same night. But Svasi said that it should not be so except by force, unless the king betrothed Snaefrid and wed her according to the law. The king took Snaefrid and wed her, and he loved her so witlessly that he neglected his kingdom and all that was seemly for his kingly honor. [They then have four sons] Afterwards *Snaefrid died,* but *the color of her skin never faded* and *she was as rosy as before when she lived.* The king always *sat over her* and thought that she would come to life again, and thus it went on for three winters that he *sorrowed* over her death and all the people of his land sorrowed over his delusion. And to stop this delusion Torleiv the Wise came to his help, he did it with prudence in that he spoke to him first with soft words, "It is not strange, O king, that thou shouldst remember so bright and noble woman and honor her with down [blankets] and precious coverlets as she bade thee. But thy honor and hers is still less than it seems, in that she has *lain for a long while* in the same clothes, and it is fitter that she should be raised and the clothes changed under her." But as soon as she

5. The Grimms were deeply impressed by the story, even rhapsodizing over it in their commentary as being "almost historical" (*fast historisch*). Despite the age of the story, which delighted the brothers as collectors of folklore, the original ending with its religiously satirical tone received no attention from Wilhelm whatsoever when the religious poet in him re-created the story of *Snow Lover* as *Snow White.*

6. In Old Norse, *snœ* is "snow," *frið* is, as a noun, "peace," "serenity," "friendliness," as an adjective it can mean "beautiful," "friendly," or even "alive." The Grimms' entry in their German dictionary admits to the puzzling nature of *fried* when used as a component of names. As a given name it seems to me to be a parental wish, that the child will be someone who enjoys something—for example, Siegfried "enjoys victory," Winfried "enjoys friends," Godfried "enjoys God," "friend of God." "Snaefrid" could mean "Snow Friend," or perhaps "Snow Beauty." I think it is best understood as someone who will love the snow and share the snow's loveliness. The names Snow White and Snow Lover are, therefore, quite close. In medieval literature, white skin was considered to be very desirable as a sign of great, and aristocratic, beauty.

was raised from the bed, there rose from the body a rotten and loathsome smell and all kinds of evil stink; speedily a funeral bale was then made and she was burned. But before that, all the body waxed blue and out crawled worms and adders, frogs and paddocks and all manner of foul reptiles. So she sank into ashes, and the king came to his wits and cast his folly from his heart and afterwards ruled the kingdom and was strengthened and gladdened by his men, and they by him, and the kingdom by both.[7]

The similarities are as remarkable as the Grimms thought. The location of the story in winter, the closeness of "Snow White" to "Snow Lover," the corpse that maintained its rosy red color and promise of life, the long watch over the body, the hope of resurrection are all there. However, the story is more a clash of religious thought than a harmony. The story stems from the time when Norway was still pagan—"Yule" is repeated twice, but there is no hint of Christmas; the king's love of the queen is not favored by all; his attitude of continuing fidelity to his wife is "witless." When the king sits by her corpse awaiting its resurrection, he is described as being in a state of delusion. Reasonable people have to persuade him to examine the hideous state of the body, and when the body is "raised," there is a rotten and loathsome smell and an exodus of reptiles. Harald then quickly forgets his idling over resurrection and returns to his senses and rules his kingdom as a proper king should. The tale could easily be seen as an attack on those in the North who were dawdling with the new Christian religion's central tenet by exposing belief in resurrection as an intoxicated lover's self-delusion. When he is cured of his Christian-style dreaming, Harald becomes a good and sensible man once again.

In Wilhelm's eyes, however, the story would probably have been seen as striking evidence of religious consciousness from pre-Christian times, a Germanic prayer of hope and waiting for a beloved dead princess to rise, as one waits for spring to rise from beneath the white snow of winter. It is Rölleke's view, based on the Grimms' commentary discussed here, that the German word itself used for the name of the heroine of the story, *Sneewittchen*, was derived by the Grimms from *Snaefrið*,[8] thus they could be confident that they

---

7. Snorri Sturluson, *Heimskringla* or *The Lives of the Norse Kings*, ed. and with notes by Erling Monsen (New York: Dover, 1990), 61–62.

8. *Synopse*, p. 384. Curiously, in their earliest manuscript of the story, 1808, the Grimms entitled the story *Schneeweißchen* and gave the expected *Sneewittchen* merely as a variant along with *Unglückskind* (*Child of Misfortune*). Later, I believe because of the existence of the early medieval Nordic story of *Snaefrið*, they came to prefer and settle on the North German form, *Sneewittchen*, as more geographically suggestive of northern ancestry than the South German *Schneeweißchen*. The Grimms claimed to have encountered both variants everywhere in Germany, but the word, except for "White"(*Blanca*), is inexplicably absent in Musäus' *Richilde*, and the suspicion must arise that they themselves are responsible for the word in its two main forms by translating and combining "Snaefrið" and "Blanca" into "Sneewitt," "Snow White."

were aware of the oldest Germanic form of the story. Wilhelm's "restoration" of the tale of *Snow White* is thus not a return to the pre-medieval original, nor a simple retelling of what they wrote down in 1808 from their Hessian sources, nor a combination of the two. By insertion of the birds, the resurrection, the prince, and the huntsman, and by reinterpreting the dwarfs and the apple, the tale will become a story of salvation told in a harmony of Christian spirituality and Germanic myth with a Classical element as well.

The other older work noted by the Grimms as containing part of the story of *Snow White* is in Basile's *Pentamerone*. In the story, called *"The Kitchen Maid"* by the Grimms and *"The Young Slave"* by Burton, a young girl, Lilla, jumps over a rose bush on a dare. To prove she cleared it completely and thus to get the prize, she deceptively eats the petal of a rose which she had actually touched and knocked to the ground. She becomes pregnant by the rose leaf and gives birth secretly. She sends the baby, Lisa, to the fairies for their help, and when they come to see her, each gives the girl a charm. However, in a twist similar to that of *Sleeping Beauty*, the last fairy to come was running and tripped and fell, painfully spraining her ankle. In her "anguish of pain she cursed the child, saying that when she had reached her seventh year, her mother in combing her hair would forget the comb sticking in the hair on her head, and this would cause her to die." It happens in the seventh year, and in her agony, Lilla, the mother, "ordered seven glass chests one within the other, and had Lisa put within them." The chest was then placed in a distant chamber in the palace, but the mother kept the key, giving it only when death approached to her brother, the baron.

The mother dies. The baron, her brother, takes a wife a year later, gives his wife the key, and begs her above all never to open the room. Being asked not to open the door makes the wife feel suspicious and jealous, which leads to uncontrollable curiosity. In a fit of jealousy (Basile's favorite vice to target), the wife opens the door and finds the glass casket: "She beheld the seven crystal chests, through which she could perceive a beauteous child lying as it were in a deep sleep." Curiously, and conveniently for the beauty of the child, the glass caskets had grown in size as the child grew. In a fit of wild jealous rage, thinking the child to be her husband's and herself cuckolded, the stepmother pulls the child out of the glass chest by her hair in order to beat her black and blue, which she does; but as she pulls Lisa by the hair, the comb falls out, and Lisa comes to life again. After an incident with the traveling father bringing home gifts, including a knife, he eventually realizes through magic that this slave girl is his sister's child, who had been locked in the room! He learns of his wife's abuse of his niece and restores her to health and beauty, and sends the jealous wife home to her family.[9] The story thinly hints at incest, but this the Grimms ignored for other elements.

---

9. Taken from Giambattista Basile, *Il Pentamerone*, pp. 169–73.

What Wilhelm saw here, I think, were elements of a timeless tale: a fated incident, an accidental dislodging of the item causing death-sleep, the overtones of Classical religion, Christianity's fear of the corroding sin of jealousy, and Germanic religion's hope in the casket made of crystal through which the person in the sleep of death could be seen as potentially revivable. The paradox of love is there as well. As in the case of Cinderella what a mother sees as beautiful and to be protected, even in death, an insecure (step)mother can imagine as a living memory of time past and a threat to herself.

The red of the rose petal may have impressed him as analogous in all three tales: the rosy red color of the dead Snaefrid, the red rose petal that Lisa swallowed, the roses that Snow White was sent to pick, the rose color of her cheeks. The spiritual common thread is the deep human helplessness and grief over the death of someone loved, expressed in Norse, Neapolitan, and German versions of these tales. The patient waiting of King Harald for three winters gives forlorn expression to the hope that somehow human love possesses a supernatural vitality that can transform death into a temporary sleep from which one be can awakened by love. It is this fragmentary hope of King Harald that Wilhelm restored to life as he reworked the remnants of ancient religious poetry come down to us as "almost historical" (as he referred to *Snaefridr* [his spelling]).

The very earliest version of this story which the Grimms themselves wrote down is in a manuscript from 1808 taken down by Jacob and sent to Savigny, the main source for which must have been an oral telling of the story by Marie Hassenpflug. The detail of the half-poisoned red and white apple in the manuscript of 1808, which Jacob Grimm took down from her, indicates that she may have known of Musäus's version. There is no Perrault in the background in this case, since he does not have the *Snow White* story. By the final version in 1857, it is the first part of the story and the last which have been most extensively reworked by Wilhelm. The middle part, the events at the house of the seven dwarfs, with the three visits by the jealous queen, has been changed the least. The version of 1808:

> Once upon a time, it was winter and it was snowing down from heaven, a queen was sitting at an ebony window & was sewing. She wanted a child very very much. And while she was thinking about this she poked herself more or less in the finger with the needle, so that several drops of blood fell on the snow. She made a wish and said: Oh if only I had a child as white as this snow, as red-cheeked as this red blood & as black-eyed as this window frame.
>
> Soon after she got a wonderfully beautiful little daughter, as white as snow, as red as blood & black-eyed as ebony & the daughter was called Snow White. My lady the queen was the most beautiful lady in the land, but Snow White was still a hundred thousand times more beautiful & when the queen asked her mirror:

Mirror, Mirror, on the wall,
Which lady in England is fairest of all?

The mirror answered: My lady the queen is the most beautiful, but Snow White is still a hundred thousand times more beautiful.

My lady the queen couldn't stand that a moment longer because she wanted to be the most beautiful in the kingdom. When now my lord the king had journeyed off to war, she had her coach hitched up and gave the order to drive into a dark forest far away & she took Snow White along. In this very same forest there were many very beautiful red roses. Now when she had arrived there with her little daughter she said to her: Oh Snow White, why don't you get out and gather me some of those beautiful roses! And as soon as she had gotten out of the coach to carry out this command, the wheels [turned and] drove off at the greatest speed, but my lady the queen had arranged all of this because she hoped that the wild animals would soon devour the child.

Now Snow White was all alone in the great forest and so she cried very much and kept on walking & kept on walking & and got very tired until she finally came to a little house.

In this first part, compared to the final version, there is no alliterative verse in the first line, it is the mother herself who becomes jealous of the very child she had wished for, the child is driven into the woods with the mother directing the coach, there is no hunter and therefore no request for a sign of the child's death, nor is there any mercy shown. The roses are the ruse for facilitating the abandonment of the child in the woods and speeding off.

In the second part of the manuscript version, Snow White finds the house empty because the seven dwarfs were at the time working in the mine. She goes inside and finds the seven dishes along with the seven spoons, forks, knives, and glasses on the table and the seven beds. She takes a little bit from each plate and a drop from each glass, tests each bed and finds the seventh fits her. When the dwarfs come home, each asks the ritual question, "Who's been eating from my dish, drinking from my mug . . . ?" When they find her in the seventh bed, they have compassion on her and let her stay. The seventh dwarf does as well as he can sharing the bed of the sixth. When she awakes she tells them the story about how her mother the queen drove off and abandoned her in the forest. Out of sympathy for her, the dwarfs invite her to stay and to cook their supper for them, and they warn her to be careful and not let anyone in the house. The queen disguises herself and comes three times to tempt Snow White. The first time as an old peddler woman selling bodice laces, Snow White falls to the temptation to buy them, and the queen laces them up so tight that Snow White collapses and is left for dead. The dwarfs come home, loosen the laces in time, and save her.

The second time, the queen comes with a beautiful comb. Again Snow White falls to the temptation, but is rescued by the returning dwarfs who remove the comb, and at that Snow White comes back to life. The third time, disguised as a farm woman selling apples, she tempts Snow White to bite into the poisoned red half of an apple. The dwarfs are helpless this time. However, "they laid Snow White in a glass casket in which she completely maintained her former appearance, they wrote her name and her ancestry on it, and watched over it carefully day and night." As is clear from this description, there is very little in this part that was later altered or inserted by Wilhelm with the important exception of his insertion of the queen's jealous questioning of the mirror on the wall, repeated in ritual style, marking off her three attempts to destroy Snow White as moral temptations.

The third part of the story, the ending, as related to them by Marie Hassenpflug, quite clearly disappointed Jacob and Wilhelm. In the manuscript they put a long line next to it, which included the entirety of the conclusion, and wrote the following comment in the margin:

(The ending included is not correctly told and is too skimpy. In other versions the dwarfs revive Snow White by striking her 32 times with little magic hammers. I don't know it very well though. Some of the material is in Musäus's Richilde.)

(Das eingeschloßene End ist unrecht erzählt u. zu mangelhaft. Nach andern machen die Zwerge das Schneeweißchen wieder lebendig, indem sie mit kleinen Zauberhämmerchen 32 mal anklopfen ich weiß es aber nicht recht. ein Stück des Stoffs ist auch in Musäus Richilde.)[10]

It is indeed interesting to see that the Grimms judged the quality of the materials told them both from the point of view of narrative form (Does the end flow appropriately from the plot as given?) and whether there is a fullness in the ending that satisfies. These are, of course, aesthetic criteria for "rightness" and, like Cinderella's slipper, the ending must not be artificially forced into place; it must, naturally, fit. The criterion for what "fits" is something that can be different from author to author of the stories, but for the brothers, it seems, it must include above all adequate expression of the ancient spirituality which they find in fragmentary form in the fairy tales, and thus "fulfill" the story. The following is the ending from the 1808 manuscript which the brothers found both incorrectly told and too skimpy:

One day the king, Snow White's father, was returning to his kingdom & had to go through the same forest where the 7 dwarfs lived. When he saw the casket and read its inscription he felt great sadness about the death of his beloved daughter. In his entourage, however, he had with him very experienced physicians who requested and obtained the corpse from the dwarfs, took it and tied a rope to the 4 corners of the room & Snow White came back to life. There-

10. Rölleke, *Synopse*, p. 383.

upon everyone went home, Snow White was married to a handsome prince, & at the wedding a pair of shoes were heated in the fire to glowing which the queen had to put on and in them dance herself to death.

The ending seems vapid indeed. The rope's connection to the corpse is not clear. The revival from death through the efforts of trained physicians and their four ropes seems totally out of place, inappropriate both to the rationalist and the romantic. The princely husband has no connection to any earlier part of the plot and is brought in pro forma. There is no presence of the spiritual, nor does it serve any rescuing function. There are, so to speak, no helpful birds in the ending. The father, to be sure, rescues his own, which must have pleased Wilhelm, but the ending is quick and contrived—the result is flat and does not arouse interest. The glowing shoes seem like an afterthought except for one item, the poignant use of the reflexive verb "dance herself" to show the lonely self-punishment of the jealous.

Let us look now at the Grimms' final version of 1857, a world masterpiece.

Once upon a time in the midst of winter as the snowflakes were falling like feathers from heaven, a queen sat at a window which had an ebony frame and sewed. And as she was sewing, she looked up at the snow and she stabbed herself in the finger with the needle and three drops of blood fell onto the snow. And since the red looked so beautiful in the white snow she thought to herself, "I wish I had a child as white as snow, as red as blood, and as black as the wood of the window frame." Soon thereafter she had a child which was as white as snow, as red as blood, and as black-haired as ebony wood, and therefore was called Snow White. And as the child was born the queen died.

The first thing is, of course, the famous "fairy-tale style" of Wilhelm Grimm. In the German original the lines flow in the measured pace of poetic prose. The almost hypnotic rhythm, with its repeated use of "and" to begin sentences, deliberately creates a biblical and religious feeling around a most everyday occupation, sewing. The first sentence has been rewritten by Wilhelm so that it ushers in the story with alliterative verse, recalling medieval epic poetry as much as does the queen's position, sewing at a castle window. The alliteration of *f* is luckily the same in English as in the original: flakes, falling, feathers; *flocken, fielen, federn*. The single seemingly insignificant action in the scene, a pinprick, occurs by inadvertence. As the queen looks at the falling snow, and wishes for a child sent from heaven, she is distracted and stabs herself with the sewing needle and her blood falls on the snow. The accident causes life to come from a love-wounded person, and thus Wilhelm begins to rework the story into a framework. As the story begins, so will it end, by inadvertence. A servant will stumble and the apple core will fall from Snow White's mouth, and she will live again. What or who controls these accidents? They happen by chance. "Chance" (or, really, "necessity") was revered by the ancient Greeks as the ultimate divine force driven by the fates.

By changing the drops of blood from "several" to "three"—and the brothers did that at a very early date; it had already been changed in the second manuscript version in 1810—the story's beginning contains an allusion to Wolfram von Eschenbach's medieval epic *Parzival*. In one of the central scenes, Parzival is fighting for his life but cannot take his eyes off three drops of blood which have fallen into the snow. They remind him of Condwiramurs, his truly beloved wife, whose name means "love leads," or "love shows the way." Thinking of her, his strength is redoubled, and he is able to fight off his attackers if just to see her again. Bettelheim sees the needle and the blood as suggesting sexual intercourse, which is one thing that it does. But the scene also recalls a need for the fidelity of love and companionship even when distance make it physically, but not spiritually, impossible. Condwiramurs comes "leaping over five countries" to be at his side when Parzival is pressed so hard that he could be killed. Blood dripping in the snow is profoundly ambiguous. It can mean that death is coming, or it can mean life and love is on its way. In the case of Snow White's mother, it meant both.

For Snow White herself, the blood in the snow designates her identity as a person. She will be named Snow White because of those three colors. Wilhelm's revision, however, has removed the possibility of identifying the colors solely with her external beauty as in the 1808 text in which the mother clearly wanted a child who is "red," meaning the color of her cheeks, who is "white as snow," which by combination with the other colors can only refer to her skin, and who is "black" in the sense that she has eyes or hair of black. If "beauty" is "worth" in Wilhelm's revisions of the tales, then he obvious wishes her beauty to be on more levels than the physical alone, and thus he does not specify exactly what part of her body the three colors might refer to. The imagination of the reader is not entirely left without guidance however. The medieval and biblical tone of the opening lines immediately suggest that there are more levels to beauty than skin color alone, and that the visible colors should be interpreted as revealing her invisible internal beauty.

Snow White's mother wishes for a child who will be a beautiful human being, one red as blood: loving and warm; white as snow: innocent and heaven-connected; and black as ebony wood: mortal, at home with the dark earth, living within the familiar framework of the tree. Mortality is the framework of the window through which the queen looks out on her world. She looks up and sees snowflakes falling gently, but falling, to the black earth. By the end of this short paragraph their fate will be hers. "And as the child was born the queen died." The mystery of the story will be: what is the meaning of the life of such a beautiful creature, born at such a cost to life, and made of such beautiful components?

As the story continues, the king takes another wife. The Grimms, under pressure from contemporary criticism that parents should not be depicted so severely, as would be the case if the mother herself became jealous of her daughter, yielded and changed the mother of the Hassenpflug version to a stepmother. On the one hand this is not out of accord with the tradition of Basile, but on the other it does not quite carry the force of acting in an "unnatural" manner as it does when the jealous person is the child's own parent. When the mirror is asked the fatal question, the formulation has been changed in order to give it an air of timelessness and a sense that it is unrestricted to any geography. The queen does not ask who is the fairest in England or in Brabant, but simply, "in the land." The answer allows the reader's fantasy to supply a real or imaginary place:

> My lady the queen, you are the most beautiful woman on the site,
> but a thousand times more beautiful than you is Snow White.

Unlike Musäus's mirror, this one can indeed speak. Being a mirror, and not a paid portrait artist, it always "tells the truth." Wilhelm lets this hidden metaphor justify the magic of the talking mirror in the story, making it unnecessary to resort to the rationalist use of mirror images alone.

Wilhelm then introduces an incident that is not at all in the manuscript. When the queen calls the huntsman to take Snow White out into the woods and kill her, the story verges off in the direction of Classical mythology. When Jocasta the queen, the mother of Oedipus, wanted to get rid of her child, she too ordered one of her herdsmen to take the infant out into the wilderness and to abandon him on a wild mountainside to be devoured by the wild animals. The herdsman, however, took pity on the helpless young child and spared him. The herdsman returns to her and says nothing to the queen about letting the baby go free. Wilhelm Grimm then interweaves another ancient myth with this one. There is no substitution of an animal for the baby in the Oedipus myth. This brief allusion to the Oedipus story is therefore deftly interwoven with the biblical story of Abraham in which an animal is substituted (by the parent) for the child who is spared. In Genesis 22, Abraham lowers his knife and does not kill his son Isaac on the altar but lets his son go free and substitutes a wild ram caught in a nearby thicket for the child. The herdsman in *Snow White* kills a nearby wild young boar in order to bring back its lungs and liver (*Lunge und Leber*—the alliteration helps make the act seem northern and medieval) to Snow White's mother, the queen. Wilhelm then completes the incident by giving it a Germanic twist at the end. In the myth of Sigurd (Siegfried) the Dragon Slayer, the same request is made by the treacherous Regin who shows Sigurd how to kill the dragon by digging a camouflaged pit in the earth and striking up from below. Regin hopes, however that the venomous blood will then pour into the pit and destroy the hero, and the treasure will be his. This is the passage in Padraic Colum's retelling:

Then did Regin, hearing the [death-]scream that let him know that Fafnir was slain, come down to where the battle had been fought. When he saw that Sigurd was alive and unharmed he uttered a cry of fury. For his plan had been to have Sigurd drowned and burnt in the pit with the stream of Fafnir's envenomed blood. But he mastered his fury and showed a pleased countenance to Sigurd. . . . "Fafnir is slain," Sigurd said, "and the triumph over him was not lightly won. Now may I show myself to king Alv and to my mother, and the gold from Fafnir's hoard will make me a great spoil."

"Wait," said Regin cunningly, "you have yet to do something for me. With the sword you have, cut through the Dragon and take out the heart for me. When you have taken it out roast it that I may eat of it and become wiser than I am." Sigurd did what Regin would have him do and cut out the heart of the dragon and he hung it from stakes to roast.[11]

When the equally cunning queen sees the cut-out lungs and liver provided by the hunter, she has them roasted triumphantly as if she were incorporating Snow White's magic beauty into herself, just as Regin wished to incorporate into himself the magic wisdom of the serpent. What the stepmother eats, however, is the life of a pig.

The harmony of the three mythologies under Wilhelm's hand in this passage is a work of art. In David Luke's translation:

So she sent for a huntsman and said: "Take that child out into the forest, I'm sick of the sight of her. You are to kill her and bring me her lungs and liver as proof." The huntsman obeyed and took Show White with him, but when he had drawn his hunting-knife, and was about to thrust it into her innocent heart she began to cry and said: "Oh, dear huntsman, let me live; I will run away into the wild forest and never come home again." And because she was so beautiful the huntsman took pity on her and said: "Run away then, you poor child." The wild beasts will soon have eaten you, he thought, and yet it was as if a stone had been rolled from his heart because he did not have to kill her. And when a young boar happened to come bounding up he slaughtered it, cut out its lungs and liver and took them to the queen as the proof she wanted. The cook was ordered to stew them in salt and the wicked woman devoured them, thinking she had eaten the liver and lungs of Snow White.[12]

---

11. Padraic Colum, *Nordic Gods and Heroes* (New York: Dover, 1996), pp. 227–28. This is the scene where the hero inadvertently (again!) lets a drop of blood from the dragon's heart fall on his finger. When he puts his finger into his mouth to ease the burning pain and tastes the blood he can from that moment understand the speech of birds. This is an episode of which Wilhelm seems to have been very cognizant.

12. *Jacob and Wilhelm Grimm, Selected Tales*, trans. with introduction and notes by David Luke (London & New York: Penguin, 1982), p. 75.

With this ingenious interweaving of the three mythologies Wilhelm ends the first part of the story.

For the middle part of the story we are on familiar ground, the archetypal and mythic place of biblical religious consciousness, the place of the experience of temptation, fall, and salvation: the Garden of Eden, woven together with the garden of Easter, redone as Wilhelm Grimm's forest with the little house which is as old as the hidden room in which the queen concocts her poison, and into which Hansel and Gretel, Red Riding Hood, and now Snow White are destined to enter. The satanic role of the tempting serpent, played by the witch in *Hansel and Gretel* and by the wolf in *Red Riding Hood,* both of whom wish to devour the little hero and heroines, is played in *Snow White* by the wicked queen and stepmother, who also was interested in devouring the lungs and liver of Snow White. Because she covets being the most beautiful of all, Wilhelm constantly associates her with evil and wickedness, uses the colors green and yellow of her (in contrast to Snow White's red, white and black) to describe her as the stunningly beautiful embodiment of jealousy, absolutely incapable of tolerating any rival—not even one for whom she should feel love.—She is, in other words, Lucifer. Wilhelm's close approximation of the character of the (step)mother to the character of the angel Lucifer ("light-bearer"), second only to God in beauty, rests upon the cause of his fall in the biblical myth because of his infatuation with his own beauty and his refusal to accept that anyone else was "the most beautiful in the land."

In church preaching tradition it is often taught that Lucifer tempts human beings out of jealousy and that he always tempts with some form of the same temptation to self-infatuation to which he himself succumbed. "You will be like God," and "You will be as beautiful as God" are the poisonous and deadly apple. Wilhelm's retention of the hellish fire-heated shoes at the end and his placing of the apple temptation in the third and climactic position in the narrative reinforce the image of the queen as the consummately beautiful, jealously ruthless Lucifer. She is loveless but beautiful, and Wilhelm refers to her true identity when he calls her "godless." To the little house she comes disguised as someone plain-looking and of no great consequence, and is that not a wry description of the camouflaged nature of Wilhelm's reworked tale?

What of the temptations themselves? I believe that Bettelheim's reading, that the three temptations are all attempts to deceive Snow White into accepting her mother's concept of the nature of personal beauty, is correct. If she becomes like her (step)mother, she will be dead, her very great personal beauty will wither. Lucifer baits with each of the three gifts: "You will become like me." Snow White's soul, seen through the eyes of her real mother and through the eyes of the owl, the raven, and the dove, is a thousand times more beautiful than the most beautiful person in the land. Her personality, her very soul, is red: loving and warm, white: innocent and faithful, and black: mortal. But those colors can also be seen through her stepmother's eyes. If Snow White can be tempted to exchange her spiritual sense of what about her is worthwhile, to adopt material criteria only, she will lose her personal beauty, she will die. The tighter, in other words, she tightens the bodice strings for the sake of her figure, the closer she comes to asphyxiating her self. The more intently she lets the queen properly fashion her hair with the black comb, the more its poison takes effect on her person.

The colors too warn of the mortal danger of externalizing the nature of beauty / worth. Snow White's soul is beautiful because it is "white"; to tempt her to buy the bodice lacings and to tighten them provocatively in order to let more of her skin show is to tempt her to embrace the queen's interpretation of the beauty of "white." Snow White's "redness," her warmth and loving nature, are very attractive and will appeal to a prince. Can she be tempted to interpret the attractiveness of her self as "red" as a reference to her mouth's apple color? Snow White's real beauty is also "black." If she can be made to act as if that color refers primarily to her hair rather than to her mortality, her ultimate vulnerability, she will cease to value what makes her ultimately attractive to God. If she were to accept such an un-magical mirror's notion of beauty, then, should even the prince most beautiful come down from his father's castle at the time when the snowflakes fall like feathers from heaven, she would find him plain-looking and uninteresting. Each Lucifer-like deception is a threat to her soul because each one leads her further away from spiritual awareness of what about her person makes her a thousand times more beautiful than the most beautiful person in the land.

Each temptation enables her to rationalize her way out of heeding the sound advice of the dwarfs, and in some sense it shows an innocent "lack of faith" on Snow White's part that the magic mirror is telling the truth—something the queen knows to be the case. Each time she submits—to the bodice strings, to the comb, and to the apple—she is showing a lack of faith in the message of the magic mirror. If Snow White is already, naturally, "a thousand times" more beautiful than the stepmother, then there is no need whatsoever to put faith in the artificially created improvements of lacings and combs, nor for eating (suspiciously like her stepmother's attempt to eat beauty) the beautiful apple. Snow White, like Cinderella, is the most beautiful person in her family regardless of her appearance.

She does eat the apple, however, as did Eve in the Garden. The good dwarfs are able to rescue her from the consequences of the laces and the comb, but not from the consequences of eating the apple. "She was dead and she remained dead" (*das liebe Kind war tot und blieb tot*). Wilhelm certainly put this line into the text to distinguish himself from Musäus's heroine's narcotic-induced sleep. The good dwarfs and, presumably, the adept physicians, were Wilhelm to have allowed them into his tale, are now quite helpless.

Just who are these dwarfs who can do so much rescuing but cannot save from death? Their house, as we have seen, is the place of religious experience and of testing. Wilhelm makes this point again when in addition to the seven forks, and plates, and cups of the seven dwarfs, he mentions that when they come home at night they light their seven little lamps. The seven lamps recall the menorah in the temple and the seven lamps of the seven Christian churches. Immediately before the lamp lighting Snow White got into the seventh or Sabbath bed and "commended herself to God." The dwarfs offer her protection and kindness, asking only that she do her part in the daily work. They themselves live a life of goodness and labor in the mines. All of this Bettelheim treats unusually, seeing only the "working in the mine shafts" and their small stature as identifying characteristics:

> So dwarfs are eminently male, but males who are stunted in their develop-
> ment. These "little men" with their stunted bodies and their mining opera-
> tion—they skillfully penetrate into dark holes—all suggest phallic connota-
> tions. They are certainly not men in any sexual sense—their way of life, their
> interest in material goods to the exclusion of love, suggest a pre-oedipal
> existence.[13]

I suggest that pre-Freudian thoughts might be possible in the context of Wilhelm Grimm's mind-set as well. Dwarfs are characters from Germanic religious thought and story, and very often they are associated with both magic and the ability to make the greatest of swords and rings and armor. They are always associated with fine and magical workmanship, but they are not gods, and they do not always have a fine disposition. The seven of this tale are a mixture of Germanic workers and Christian disposition. The fact that they are celibate, carry the seven lamps, give the heroine good advice on the intent and persistence of the Lucifer-like queen, rescue her twice from death at the queen's hands, point to the familiar mix of Germanic and Christian. In some senses, their daily working is not unlike that of medieval Bene-dictine monks whose motto was, and is, *ora et labora*, pray and work! To see them only as stunted "little men" is to look at them through the eyes of Cin-derella's father—or Snow White's stepmother! More importantly the reason for the appearance of the prince on the scene is not by accident but is con-nected with the presence of the dwarfs. In the Grimm version the third part of the story, the ending with the prince, is introduced rather solemnly: "And it came to pass that a prince was traveling through the forest and he came to the house of the dwarfs[14] in order to stay there overnight" (*Es geschah aber, daß ein Königssohn in den Wald geriet und zu dem Zwergenhaus kam, um dort zu übernachten*). In other words, the prince is acquainted with the house of the

---

13. Bettelheim, *The Uses of Enchantment*, p. 210.

14. There is a connection suggested between the helpful doves and the helpful dwarfs. It is indicated by the similarity of the compounds used in the German for both places where the heroines take refuge, Cinderella in the *Taubenhaus*, Snow White in the *Zwergenhaus*.

Snow White in her glass casket on a little mountain top, surrounded by the stars, rocks, and trees. One of the seven dwarfs is keeping vigil. Alert and waiting are the owl at one end of the casket, the raven at the other, and the dove perched directly above Snow White. Drawing by Laurence Selim after the print by Ludwig Emil for the 1825 "Little Edition."

dwarfs and feels it is a place where he can stay overnight, perhaps not unlike a monastery, a place of refuge for the soul. What the king's son finds is the body of Snow White, which the dwarfs had washed "with water and wine," but which they did not wish to "sink into the black earth." It is curious how that passage evokes both Christian myth and ritual with water and wine, and also, combined with the "black" earth, the three colors of Snow White's personality. As in the Passion, which the scene has now evoked, there were three days in which all stopped work and kept watch over the body.

It is in this context that we come to the glass casket. Not the small window above the face of *Richilde's* Blanca, not the expanding glass cases of Basile, nor even the open air bier of King Harald's Snaefrid, but the dwarfs love Snow White so much that "they had a glass casket made, so that she could be seen from all sides, they laid her in it and wrote her name on it in golden letters and said that she was the daughter of a king." They not only refuse to bury her, but one of them is constantly on vigil where she is, and they place the casket on top of a mountain, so that all the world and God above can see the one whom they love so much. There are three glass objects in this tale associated with seeing, only two of which are transparent and transitive, the other is reflexive. The first to be encountered is the window, through which Snow White's mother can look and admire the beauty of the world and nature's falling snow, the transparency of the glass giving her sight of the beauty of the outside world and suggesting the tragic wonder of the world coming to be within her. The second is the non-transparent glass of the mirror into which the queen can look, continually observing how beautiful she is, or appears to be. She prefers the mirror, glass rendered opaque, to the appreciation of anything beyond the castle window, reflecting only her admired light image back to herself. The third is something that is an appeal to heaven: a casket of glass placed on a mountain, so designed as to not impede being looked into, a transparent display of human mortality and its beauty, an appeal and an invitation to the provident eye of God and a benevolent nature to look upon the black ebony frame of mortal goodness. The glass casket is an invitation to those who love the beauty of a good soul to be moved as was King Harald centuries ago, to hope that the red and white of life will come back to her. "Blessed are those who mourn, for they will be comforted." The glass of the casket is the second beatitude turned into an appeal, a prayer like the one she said before she laid herself down to sleep when she first found the spiritual house in the forest: "she commended herself to God," as now does the transparency of the coffin.

And who comes to stand watch and to see if this very open appeal of a glass casket on a mountain is answered? The answer is, I think, one of Wilhelm Grimm's finest, and in it he reveals in slightly veiled form the heart of the magic of his fairy tales: "And the animals came too, and cried over Snow White, first an owl, then a raven, last a little dove (*Und die Tiere kamen auch und beweinten Schneewittchen, erst eine Eule, dann ein Rabe, zuletzt ein Täubchen*).

Nature, which always recognized her as one of her own, now cries over her loss. Only those who did not love do not mourn. Cinderella knew that, even pets and animals know that. But of all the animals of the forest (Disney will have many more), why these three? For millennia the three religions have accompanied the good human being with hope for rescue for as far as they can go, up to the grave. The Classical, the Germanic, and the Christian religions can now only mourn, keep watch over the body as they have always done, and hope. Where do these spirits of hope come from? Where in the forest is their real place of origin? Their colors tell much. The owl is reddish brown, the raven is black, the dove is white. They are the colors of Snow White's soul, her person itself, and it is from the soul of the good person that religion's spirit originates, from its red loving warmth, from its white loyal innocence, and from its humbling, black and earthlike, mortality. The three birds are the soul of mankind keeping watch over the body to see if it can come to life again, to see if there is a "resurrection of the body and life everlasting," to see if death is a sleep. As they keep their long vigil over her, the owl dreams of her rescue by some provident accident, the raven dreams of her rescue by a tree, and the dove dreams that one day the king's son will come for her.

And the king's son does come, and when he looks through the glass casket and sees her he realizes why he came into the woods, he cannot live without her. Faith, hope, and love write the ending. The prince is surely the Christ figure of Wilhelm's many readings in the New Testament on the Resurrection. Christ is the friend of the Germanic religious dwarfs, and he sees the beauty of the dead Snow White. Wilhelm seems almost to be thinking of St. Paul's famous equation of death with sleep as the prince asks if he can take her with him: "But we do not want you to be uninformed, brothers and sisters, about those who have fallen asleep, so that you may not grieve as others do who have no hope. For since we believe that Jesus died and rose again, even so, through Jesus, God will bring with him those who have fallen asleep"[15] (1 Thes 4:13–15).

As the prince is about to bring her with him and has the servants lift up the casket to carry it, one of them—by chance—stumbles over a shrub and the bit of poisoned apple flies from Snow White's throat. All three birds of the spirit must be happy, since it is the Spirit of God over time that guided them, the good human spirit, to this point. Each now contemplates its prescribed role in the raising of Snow White. As the bearers of the glass casket stumble, Athena's owl sees the event as one fated to happen "by accident." Woden's raven fixes its gaze upon the cause of the accident, a small "tree." Christ's dove contemplates the loving arrival of the prince, whose love, with

15. Unfortunately, in modern translations the poignant metaphor of sleep is often ignored and the Greek original "those sleeping" and "those having fallen asleep" (*koimonenon* and *koimethentas*) are bluntly rendered "the dead."

the help of a tree and an accident, caused Eden's poisoned apple to be spit out. As Snow White opens her eyes, lifts the lid of the casket and sits upright, she says, "Oh God, where am I?" The answer which Wilhelm wrote is Christ's, the answer hoped for for millennia, "the king's son says, 'You are with me,'" and he tells her that he loves her more than anything in the world and immediately invites her to follow him into the eternal world of the Father. "Come with me into my father's castle, you will be my wife." The story comes to a mystical Trinitarian ending as the good soul, led by the Spirit in the owl, the raven, and the dove, is brought to a meeting with the Son, who conducts the person in love beyond death to his Father's house.

The last lines of the story do not end with this promise of eternal life in the heaven from which the snowflakes were falling at the beginning of the tale, in a sort of Christmas to Easter sequence, but rather with the punishment of the evil queen. Her first shock, taken from Musäus's version, is the sight of Snow White alive and in the bridal veil. Her second is to realize that she is not among the blest invited to the wedding feast of the king's son. The shoes are made glowing hot for her and, instead of just getting a few blisters, she is made to dance until she falls down dead. This quick introduction of a second death in the story, the queen's, suggests the Christian concept that there is nothing for the good person to fear from "the first death," rather it is the second death that is serious. The death of the unloving queen-mother is another kind of death. It is the death of the red and white aspect of the personality, an ignoring of the humility suggested by the black framework, in sum, the spiritual consequence of her preference of the mirror to the window. The queen's misuse of her mirror nourishes a corrosive envy of the beauty of others, creates a poisonous apple in the secret chamber of her soul, and maintains a closed circuit of reflection that excludes the love of neighbor and precludes any real interest in the coming of the King's Son.

Eight

SLEEPING BEAUTY

There is a poetic continuity acknowledged by the Grimms between the sleep
motif in *Snow White* and in *Sleeping Beauty*. In the story of *Snow White* it was
one person whose death was a sleep of waiting, in *Sleeping Beauty* it is the sleep
of the whole family. In *Sleeping Beauty* the black ebony-wood framework that
surrounded the life of Snow White and her mother becomes the thorny hedge
of a hundred years that surrounds everyone who lives in the castle. When the
right King's Son comes through the hedge of thorns at the appointed moment
in time he awakens not just one person held within its time-created frame but
all who live (sleep) there. The hedge itself exists as a result of the wish of the
old woman who sits and spins thread, a figure of deep mystery from the ancient religious past, known by many names: the Parcae, the Norns, the weird
sisters, the fates, or less mythically, the passage of time.[1]

When Bruno Bettelheim published his admirable analysis and interpretation of this tale he focused on what in it fascinated him most, the adolescence of the heroine and the 100 years of time. He equated the two and
thereby initiated a rich and fascinating reading of *Snow White*.

> Adolescence is a period of great and rapid change, characterized by periods of
> utter passivity and lethargy. . . . During the months before the first men-
> struation, and often for some time immediately following it, girls are passive,
> seem sleepy, and withdraw into themselves. While no equally noticeable state
> heralds the coming of sexual maturity in boys, many of them experience a

---

1. The Parcae, as three bizarrely dressed, ugly old women, are present in the Grimms' tales
in a funnier form in the story *The Three Spinners* (*Die drei Spinnerinnen*). There, from their millennia of spinning the thread of time, one of them has developed a hanging lower lip from lick-
ing the thread, one has an enlarged flat foot from the spinning-wheel treadle, and the third has
acquired an overdeveloped thumb from twisting the thread. They help the poor princess do her
required spinning, under the very significant condition that she not be ashamed of them nor
fail to invite them, as relatives, to her wedding. She does not fail, and at the royal wedding, be
the rite ever so Christian, the three spinners have their appropriate and allotted places at the
table.

period of lassitude and of turning inward during puberty which equals the female experience. It is thus understandable that a fairy story in which a long period of sleep begins at the start of puberty has been very popular for a long time among girls and boys. . . . Those fairy tales which, like "The Sleeping Beauty," have the period of passivity for their central topic, permit the budding adolescent not to worry during his inactive period: he learns that things continue to evolve. The happy ending assures the child that he will not remain permanently stuck in seemingly doing nothing, even if at the moment it seems as if this period of quietude will last for a hundred years.[2]

A little further on, Bettelheim also refers to this same time period as suggesting a period of spiritual development. He calls it a period of "contemplation," a period of "concentration on the self," a time when this "period of deathlike passivity" at the end of childhood is a time of "preparation, from which the child will awaken mature, ready for sexual union," which "it must be stressed" is in fairy tales "as much one of the minds and souls of two partners as it is one of sexual fulfillment."[3] Bettelheim's complaint about the Grimms' version of *Sleeping Beauty* is that the malevolent fairy is not punished. This curious observation is a natural consequence of his interpretation of the story, including the old woman's spinning activity in the tower as exclusively psycho-sexual and centered on the onset of menstruation. Underlying the phenomenon of menstruation, however, even philologically, lies the calendrical "month," the phenomenon of the moon's marking of the passage of time. Bettelheim complains that the thirteenth wise woman, the fairy of the lunar year who gave the child "the curse," is not punished at the end of the story. He feels strongly that this is a distinct flaw in composition on the part of the brothers Grimm. One may certainly object to this criticism, however, if the thirteenth fairy in reality merely curses the heroine with an advance awareness of "mortality," with becoming aware of her growing up and being "timed." If the thirteenth wise woman and the woman at the spinning wheel are one—namely, age, the passage of time, with its ultimate consequence of death and the need to provide for reproduction—then how would one imagine that such an entity is to be punished?

Seeing the 100 years of sleep as a time of personal growth in preparation for sexual love is nonetheless a thought-provoking and rewarding reading of the story, and it is made only richer when also seen in the overall light of aging, time-in-us, as a preparation of the mind and souls for another love, a rescuing and transtemporal loving union that will pierce the natural hedge of time. After all, adolescence is a preparation for the love of becoming a spouse and a parent. Soon after the lethargy period is over, looking at the newborn child, the adolescent is invited to a higher state of self-awareness: the adolescent-become-parent will also one day duly pass away and be re-

2. Bettelheim, *The Uses of Enchantment,* p. 225.
3. Bettelheim, p. 232.

placed by those who follow just as happened with Snow White's mother. The baby will one day be there and will take the parent's place—something that the mothers in the fairy tales accept with love, and the stepmothers, the queen-mother with the mirror in *Snow White*, resent. A futile and sinful resentment, one might say, poison to the soul. The Grimms' version suggests there may be more to the time of love than its passing. But to punish the spinner of mortality is beyond the reach of the brothers Grimm. The wicked queen can be punished if she kills, she is a moral entity, capable of good and of sin. The Parca, the Norn, the woman who spins the thread of time, is of another realm and of another religious awareness; she is quite beyond good and evil, gods and men.

The name of the story deserves a comment. Perrault called it *La Belle au bois dormant*, a magically ambiguous title in which the enchanted sleep can hover in meaning between referring to the girl or to the forest: "The Beautiful [Girl] in the Sleeping Forest" or "The Beautiful [Girl] Asleep in the Forest." It is from the latter that the unambiguous English "Sleeping Beauty" is taken. In German, on the other hand, the girl is associated with the forest itself, since she and the story are called *Dornröschen*, "Little Hedge Rose," "Little Briar Rose," or, literally, "Little Thorn Rose." The Grimms' title suggests the wild, uncultivated roses that can be seen in country areas growing in long tangled vines along old fences. This common wild rose, or briar rose, is quite diminutive compared with the hothouse, cultivated variety to which we have become accustomed. The thickness of its stems, the relative density and size of the thorns, the obscuring proliferation and thick "forest" of leaves and the smallness of the flowers, the entanglement of the hedge, make the roses quite difficult to get at. It is a common experience to get one's hand painfully scratched in trying to reach through the impeding web of stems and leaves to pluck a wild rose. It is to this experience that the name of the story, and the fate of the princes in it, allude in the German. The Grimms seem to have borrowed the name "Little Thorn Rose" directly from the German translation of Hamilton's *L'Histoire de Fleur d'épine*, not at all impeded by their disapproval of a tale that they regarded as having no roots in the past and being an entirely ahistorical concoction of the author. It appeared in 1731.[4] Their choice of this name, despite their dislike of its origin, shows its importance and relevance for the story. Calling the story "Little Thorn Rose" instead of "Sleeping Beauty" shifts the identity of the heroine. Instead of being identified by name with the 100-year sleep, in the Grimms' version the secret of the heroine's identity lies in the mysterious and mythic nature of the thorn hedge.

The first written version from the brothers Grimm comes from the manuscript of 1810. It is in Jacob's handwriting. Jacob appears to have taken it down as told by Marie Hassenpflug. The reactions of the two brothers to the

4. See Rölleke, *Synopse*, p. 359.

story are quite different and very much in accord with their personalities. Jacob made the disconcertingly direct and sober comment: "This seems to be completely [or 'taken'] from Perrault's *Sleeping Beauty*" ("Dies scheint gz[5] aus Perrault's Belle au bois dormant"). Not only is the truth of this comment more than evident, but it could well have been the kiss of death for final inclusion of *Sleeping Beauty* in the Grimms' collection, as indeed it was eventually for *Bluebeard* and several others. The Grimms' tales were supposed (initially at least) to be versions from good German stock which showed some distinct difference from the French versions. Jacob saw exactly what the story was. Wilhelm, however, thought he saw a remnant of ancient Germanic myth in it.

> The virgin who is sleeping in the castle surrounded by the wall of thorns until freed by the king's son is analogous to Brynhild who is surrounded by a wall of flames through which Sigurd penetrates.

> (Die Jungfrau, die im Schloß mit Dornenwall umgeben schläft, bis sie der Königsohn erlöst, ist mit der schlafenden Brynhild, die ein Flammenwall umgiebt, durch den Sigurd dringt, insofern identisch.)[6]

Thus it was perhaps that the tale was saved for inclusion in the Grimms' collection. It is impossible to say by what Nordic route Wilhelm would have thought the tale of Brynhild's rescue came through to Perrault and then to Marie Hassenpflug, but he was quite aware of the Germanic ethnicity of the Frankish tribes of France, and he saw evidence of Germanic religious myth in the tale. In addition, as they note in their commentary of 1822, structurally the version from Marie Hassenpflug, at least as taken down by Jacob, does not have the extended ending the brothers found in the Italian and French versions.

In order to bracket them from consideration here, it is necessary to take a look at the excluded endings of the French and Italian versions. The extended endings of both introduce turmoil into the story. They re-channel the thrust of the plot from one of enchanted sleep to one that culminates in rape, jealousy, and intended cannibalism. These narrative elements were never integrated into the Grimms' version. In Perrault, after the happy episode of Sleeping Beauty's awakening on time (no kiss!) from her long sleep and her marriage to the prince, she finds herself as princess in the clutches of a queen mother-in-law who is an ogress. The queen is just barely deceived by a kindly cook into eating a lamb, a goat, and a deer as a substitute for devouring Sleeping Beauty and her two children. When the good chef is found out and ordered under pain of death to cook Sleeping Beauty in

---

5. Rölleke, *Synopse*. The abbreviation could stand for *ganz* or *gezogen*.

6. Rölleke, *Synopse*, p. III. This is Wilhelm's remark from the first printed version. Jacob's remark is only to be found written on the manuscript.

a piquant sauce, he worries himself over a culinary problem he will have to solve: "The young queen was past twenty, not to mention the hundred years she had slept, and her flesh was rather tough, however beautiful and white." Luckily he finds a tough deer which he substitutes. When the ogress finally realizes that she has been the victim of a venison deception, she orders a vat with serpents prepared into which Sleeping Beauty is to be thrown. Luckily, the king rides in at that very moment, and the wicked old queen in frustration jumps into the snake vat herself.

In Basile's ending, a king happens to ride by the castle where Talia, the heroine, is in her long sleep. He finds her within, admires her beauty, and has intercourse with her without her awareness while she is asleep. She later gives birth to two children in her sleep, not quite knowing how such a thing could have happened. She only wakes up (and this is the part whose ingenuity the Grimms admired) when one of the babies looking for a nipple sucks on her finger and thus pulls out the sleep-causing splinter of flax from under the nail. When the king's wife finds out about her husband's dalliance, she, like some other queens having a taste for a good human meal, attempts to have the two children cooked and served to him for supper and to have Talia burned alive. She is deceived by a kindly cook who prepares a meal of goats instead. When she learns of the deception by overhearing the hidden children, she threatens the cook and forces him to yield, but before the cannibalistic tragedy can occur, the king arrives home just in time and his wicked wife is burned in the fire she had intended for Talia. The Grimms apparently enjoyed the subtle differences between the endings of Perrault's and Basile's versions, but kept their distance from them and maintained an air of *admirandum sed non imitandum*.

The Grimms' commentary of 1822 on their own version of *Snow White*:

> From Hesse. The virgin who is sleeping in the castle surrounded by the wall of thorns until saved ["*erlöst*"] by the right prince before whom the thorns give way, is the sleeping Brunhild of the old nordic saga who is surrounded by a wall of flames through which only Sigurd can penetrate, who awakens her. The spindle with which she stabs herself and which causes her to fall asleep is the thorn of sleep with which Odin stabs Brunhild; cf. Edda Sämundar 2, 186. In the Pentamerone (5,5) it is a splinter of flax. In Perrault, la belle au bois dormant. Snow White's sleep is similar.[7] [There follow comments on the differences between Basile's and Perrault's versions, with reference to the extended ending absent in the German version.]

Perrault's version begins with a king and queen who want to have a child, and when one comes, invite seven fairies to come to stand as godmothers. The number seven was not carried over into the Hassenpflug version, nor

---

7. Rölleke, *Jubiläumsausgabe*, III, 85 [97].

was the delightful idea that pagan spirits, the fairies, are being invited to act as godparents at a christening. This must have been regarded by Perrault as a lovely illogical juxtaposition, sure to cause theological discomfort or enlightened amusement, but to Wilhelm it would have signaled the Christian element, the relationship between birth and death and the sacrament of baptism. Baptism appears, however, not to have been in the German version told by Marie, which had twelve good fairies as well as the unfortunate thirteenth, who were attending a birth celebration rather than a christening. Wilhelm finesses the situation by making the celebration be a celebration of the birth of the child, with the baptismal background hinted at. The king, to return to Perrault, has seven golden caskets made containing the golden utensils for the use of each of the seven fairy godmothers at the feast:

> But, as each one took her place at table an old fairy was seen coming in. No one had invited her because she had been shut up in her tower for more than fifty years and everyone thought she was dead or else spellbound. . . . The old fairy thought they were insulting her and muttered a few threats through gritted teeth. . . . Next the fairies gave their gifts to the princess. The youngest gave her the gift that she would be the most beautiful person in the world, the next that she would have the wit of an angel, the third that she would move with enchanting grace, the fourth that she would dance to perfection, the fifth that she would sing like a nightingale, the sixth that she would play every musical instrument. The old fairy's turn came, and, her head shaking more from spite than from age, she said that the princess would prick her finger with a spindle and die.

The gifts are the gifts of an accomplished lady of the seventeenth-century court, and are different in the Grimm version, but essentially the good gifts and the curse are both present. When the last fairy to speak appears from behind a tapestry she gives not a death curse, but says the princess will sleep 100 years—without specifying the age at which the accident will befall the princess—and promises that a prince will awaken her. The king makes the effort to prevent anyone from using a spindle, but the princess goes one day to the top of a tower "to a little garret where an old lady sat alone, spinning her wheel." After the princess pricks her finger and falls down in a faint, Perrault enjoys depicting a futile courtly attempt to revive her. "They threw water in the princess's face and unlaced her stays, they chafed her hands, they rubbed her temples with eau-de-cologne . . ." The princess remains in her 100-year sleep, but Perrault makes sure to add, "Her eyes were closed, but you could hear her breathing softly, which showed that she was not dead." No mystical connection of sleep and death here!

There is also no concomitant falling asleep of the others. Their sleep happens because the good fairy (summoned from 12,000 leagues away by a dwarf wearing seven-league boots!), arriving in a dragon-pulled, blazing chariot of fire, is concerned that the princess might feel ill at ease all alone in the castle when she awakes, and so she touches everything in the castle and puts it to sleep—almost everything, with the important exception of the king and queen! Perrault maintains mock deference to sovereigns who must always, even in fairy tales, be seen to remain awake to provide good government to their countries. With charm and grace he displays his complete skepticism about the existence of the otherworldly creatures of myth with their flaming chariots and seven-league boots. The mystical connection of spirit between generations of the present and those of the past is not for Perrault as it is for the Grimms. With all but the sovereigns asleep, the trees and brambles, bushes and thorns then grow around the castle, so that a person could not even see the turrets, "unless you were very far away." As deliberately misplaced naturalism alternates with irony, Perrault follows the prince after he has passed through the wall of brambles and trees.

> He was surprised that none of his companions had been able to follow him, since the trees had closed in on him again as soon as he had passed. But he did not falter; a young prince in love is always brave.
>
> He entered the castle and found himself in a great courtyard, where all that he set eyes on was enough to freeze him with terror. There was a dreadful silence, and the image of death was everywhere. The bodies of men and animals lay scattered on the ground, apparently lifeless. However he soon realized from the glowing noses and ruddy faces of the guards that they were merely sleeping, and the dregs of wine in their glasses showed that they had been drinking when they dozed off . . . rifles on their shoulders, snoring fit to burst. . . .
>
> On the bed was a princess, a young girl of fifteen or sixteen, whose untarnished beauty seemed to shine with an unearthly radiance. He approached in trembling adoration and fell on his knees before her. And so, as the spell had now been broken, the princess woke. Looking at him with eyes so tender and loving that you would never believe he was a stranger, she said, "Is it really you, my prince? You certainly took your time." . . . In all they talked to each other for about four hours and still had not said half the things they wanted to say to each other.

As the story continues in ironic-naturalistic style, the rest of the castle awakens and they all discover, since they aren't all in love, that they are starving, and everyone heads for the food. The prince helps the princess up and is a true French gentleman: "She was fully dressed in magnificent style, but he was very careful not to tell her that she was dressed like his grandmother, because she was no less beautiful for being out of fashion." The couple are married after supper by the chaplain, "and the lady-in-waiting drew the curtains round their bed," though the princess really didn't feel drowsy. The second ending now begins with the two children, Dawn and Day, and the cannibalistic and vengeful queen mother-in-law takes over. As mentioned above, the Grimms stopped their tale here, as did presumably their first source Marie Hassenpflug. Wilhelm then completely reworked and altered the tone to heighten the suggestion of the ancient mythical elements which he found in the tale.

The relevant incidents at the beginning of Basile's *The Face* (*Lo Caro*), and at the beginning of *Sun, Moon and Talia*, which the Grimms noted as parallel to their *Sleeping Beauty*, is the use of a bone in the one, and a splinter of flax in the other, in the place of the spindle. Neither of Basile's stories begins with water, neither as a baptismal feast, nor as the queen bathing and wishing for a child. *The Face* begins with a king asking all the wizards of his kingdom to divine his daughter's fortune, and they tell him that "a bone will cause her to unstop the channel of her life." To prevent the presumed tragedy which this saying indicates, the king builds a great tower in which to shut up his daughter, and gives her twelve ladies-in-waiting and a governess to watch after her therein. They have orders under pain of death to give her only meat without bones. A beautiful Romeo appears under the window one day, and, after exchanging mock baroque flowery compliments, she, Renza, determines to escape. The guard dog by chance brings in a bone to chew on, and no one notices it. This bone the heroine cleverly uses as a mason's tool to remove the mortar around a large stone in the tower, and she slips out . . . thus "unstopping the channel of her life" in a sense different from that in which the king understood the phrase. At this point the story is already on a very divergent path from that of the Grimms, which is where we will leave it.

Basile's *Sun, Moon, and Talia* begins with the same assembly of wise men and seers to forecast the future of a great lord's newly born daughter. They prophesy that she will come to great danger from a small splinter of flax. The king immediately forbids that any flax should ever come into his house. The heroine, however, because of this decree, has never seen a spindle or distaff, and so, when she sees an old woman pass by her window spinning, is overcome with curiosity. She then asks to play with the spindle, but she is unfamiliar with spinning flax and gets a splinter under her fingernail and falls down dead. Later a king happens to pass by the castle where she has been left and "on fire with love, he carried her to a couch and, having gathered the fruits of love, left her lying there."[8] In good classical fatalistic style, Basile so conceives the tales that the very attempts made by the father in both tales to prevent a prophesied fate from occurring, the presence of a guard dog and the absence of flax, become the means by which it occurs. Classical fatalism is also present in the Grimm version, but it is made milder by the presence of the good fairy and a rescuing prince.

More important by far is the connection seen by Wilhelm to the ancient Germanic religious myth of Sigurd's ride through the flames to rescue Bryn-

---

8. *The Pentamerone of Giambattista Basile*, trans. N. M. Penzer (London: John Lane the Bodley Head), II, 130.

hild. Brynhild was a Valkyrie ("chooser of the fallen"), one of the divine beings who rode onto the battlefield, choosing who will win and lose, live or die, and then choosing among the fallen those who will be taken to heaven to be their husbands. They often took the shape of the raven, since the raven could often be seen after a battle among the fallen, feeding. Brynhild had aroused Woden's anger by letting herself come under the power of a human, who had stolen her "feather coat" while she was bathing and refused to return it until she promised to give him victory against his enemy Hjalmgunnar. She agreed to his terms. Hjalmgunnar happened to be a favorite of Woden, a favorite to whom he had just promised a victory in battle, only to find his divine will frustrated by the disobedience of Brynhild. He punished her with having to lead an earthly life by pricking her with the magic thorn from the tree of sleep, which immediately sent her into a deep slumber. Woden then took advantage of the thorn's effect to lock her up in a castle surrounded by flames. She now could have no husband except the one that would be so daring as to ride through the wall of flames. That hero was Sigurd ("Victory-fated," in German, "Siegfried.") The Volsung saga then tells the story:

Heimir said that her hall was only a short distance away and that he believed she would want to marry only that man who rode through the blazing fire surrounding it. They found the hall and the fire, and there they saw a golden-roofed fortress [mark of a temple] with fire burning around the outside. Gunnar spurred his horse toward the fire, but he shied away. Sigurd said: "Why are you drawing back, Gunnar?" He answered: "The horse does not want to leap this fire," and he asked Sigurd to lend him Grani [Sigurd's horse].

"He is at your disposal," said Sigurd. Gunnar now rode at the fire, but Grani did not want to go. . . . Then Sigurd rode with his sword, Gram, in his hand and on his feet he bound golden spurs. When the horse felt the spurs, he rode forward toward the fire. There was a deafening roar as the fire swelled and the earth began to tremble. The flames rose to the heavens. No one had dared do this before. It was as if he rode into pitch-darkness. Then the fire subsided. Sigurd dismounted and went into the hall.

Thus it is said:

> The fire began to flare
> And the earth to shudder
> And high flames
> To heaven towered.
> Few of the king's men
> Had courage enough
> To ride into the flames
> Or to leap across them
> Sigurd with his sword

Spurred Grani on.
The flames expired
Before the prince,
The fire all fell back
Before the fame-hungry one.
The harness was radiant
Which Regin had owned.

And when Sigurd got past the flames, he found a beautiful dwelling and inside it sat Brynhild. She asked who the man was. He called himself Gunnar [he
is Sigurd, however, deceiving her on his friend's behalf], "and with the consent
of your father [Odin] and your foster father, you are my intended wife, provided I ride your wavering flame and if you should so decide." [Brynhild then
warns him that she is a warrior and that he had better be ready to kill her suit-
ors and to surpass every other man in courage, and he reminds her that he
crossed the fire. She acknowledges this and . . .] he stayed there for three
nights, and they slept in one bed, the sword Gram he placed unsheathed
between them.[9]

Again, without arguing with Wilhelm Grimm about how to establish a line
of connection between this medieval Norse tale and the story he was told by
Marie Hassenpflug, the main point for his re-creation of *Sleeping Beauty* is
that he saw a remnant of Germanic religious myth in it and thus regarded
the story as a fragment of ancient religious belief, worthy of expansion and
restoration to emotional effectiveness. The following is the oral tale as first
taken down in manuscript by Jacob Grimm from Marie.

A king & a queen had no children. One day the queen was bathing, a crab
crawled out of the water and onto the land & said: you will soon get a daughter. And it happened too, and the king in his joy held a great feast & in the
country there were thirteen fairies, but he only had twelve golden plates and
therefore couldn't invite the thirteen. The fairies gave her gifts of all virtues
and beauties [this sentence added in the margin]. Now when the feast was almost over, the thirteenth fairy came & said: you didn't invite me & I announce
to you that your daughter, in her fifteenth year, will prick herself in the finger
with a spindle & will die of it. The other fairies wanted to fix this as well as
they were able & said: she will only fall asleep for a hundred years.
    The king sent out an order that all spindles in the entire realm should be
gotten rid of, which happened, & when the king's daughter was fifteen years
old, & one day when the parents had gone out, she walked around in the castle
& finally came to an old tower. A narrow stairway led into the tower and there
she came to a little door in which there was a yellow key, which she turned &
came into a little room in which an old woman was spinning her flax. And she

9. *The Saga of the Volsungs, The Norse Epic of Sigurd the Dragon Slayer,* trans. Jesse L. Byock
(Berkeley: University of California Press, 1990), pp. 80–81.

Little Thorn Rose, Sleeping Beauty, sleeps her hundred-year sleep as angels built into the ceiling vaults look down. The light in the room comes through a gothic church window, suggesting the real nature of the castle in which she awaits her prince. Between the bed and the wall is the deadly spinning wheel with the flaxen thread on its armature which blends into the thorn hedge outside the window. Drawing by Laurence Selim after the print by Ludwig Emil for the 1825 "Little Edition."

joked with the woman and wanted to spin too. Then she pricked herself with the spindle & fell immediately into a deep sleep. Since at that moment the king and the court had come back, everyone in the castle began to sleep, including the flies on the wall. And around the castle a thorn hedge grew up so nothing of it was seen.

After a long, long time a king's son came into the land to whom an old man told the story which he remembered having heard from his grandfather, & that many had already tried to go through the thorns but all of them had remained hanging in them. When this prince came near the thorn hedge all the thorns opened up before him & in front of him they seemed to be flowers & behind him they became thorns again. Now when he came into the castle, he kissed the sleeping princess and everyone woke up from being asleep & the two got married and if they have not died, then they are still alive. "Orally"[10]

The almost stenographic synopsis of the story made here by Jacob does indeed seem to be a skeletal outline in German of the bare narrative (without Perrault's humor—the king, for example, also falls asleep) of the first part of Perrault's story. Since Wilhelm saw more here than Jacob, it is his own poetic rewriting over the years which will supply a warmth and fullness completely lacking in the manuscript above, re-imparting spiritual enchantment to the magic sleep, the thorn hedge, and the arrival of the king's son.[11]

Wilhelm's final version of the tale of *Sleeping Beauty*, or *Little Thorn Rose*, begins with an animal change from a crustacean to an amphibian, from the crab to a frog.

A long time ago there was a king and a queen who said every day, "If only we had a child," but they never got one. Now it happened one day as the queen was seated bathing [lit.: "seated in the bath"] that a frog crept out of the water onto the land and said to her, "Your wish will be fulfilled, before a year passes you will bring a daughter into the world." What the frog said came to pass and the queen gave birth to a girl who was so beautiful that the king couldn't contain himself for sheer joy and held a great feast.

Because the scene at first suggests a bathtub, but then "crawled . . . onto the land" suggests a river bank, it is helpful to consult the Grimms' German dictionary to find their definition of "bath:"

---

10. Rölleke, *Synopse*, pp. 106, 108. The added word "orally" indicates that Jacob took the story down from an oral telling of it by Marie. This is also where he has his comment that the tale seems completely taken from Perrault.

11. In the manuscript the words *Prinz* ("prince") and *Königssohn* ("king's son") are used interchangeably. By the final version, the far more richly ambiguous "king's son" is the only word for "prince" used in the story, suggesting Christian emotion in the finished tale.

The root seems to go back to the Sanskrit bâd, vad 'lavare' [to wash] and to be related to βαθυσ [deep] . . . just as tief [deep] is to taufen [to baptize] . . . the concept of the bath originated from cooling off, washing, in the river. . . . [The Grimms then give the following as the first meaning of the word "bath":] 1) to sprinkle the newborn child, to wash, to bathe. In a spiritual sense, the bath of baptism, of rebirth. Titus 3:5.

(Die wurzel scheint auf das skr. bad, vad lavare zurückzukehren . . . bathys . . . so wie tief zu taufen. . . . der begriff des bades ausgieng vom abkühlen, waschen im flusz. . . . 1. Das neugeborene kind besprengen, waschen, baden. in geistlichem sinn das bad der taufe, der wiedergeburt. Tit.3,5.)[12]

In other words, the scene, whether imagined in the household tub or not, was intended to evoke a primal scene: washing by the riverbank, with "the bath's" ancient origin in cooling off and cleansing, and its spiritual meaning of baptism's cleansing and rebirth. Where Perrault is quite explicit that the feast which begins the story is a baptismal celebration, the Grimms' much more richly ambiguous use of "bathing" carries "baptism," or christening, only as one connotation, and not the first. The waters first seem to connote the passage or "flow" of time.[13] The queen is thus seated both in the pre-Christian waters of time and the spirit-indwelling waters of baptism. It is theologically interesting that there is an association of the word "bath" with "baptism" in the Grimms' dictionary and that baptism there is not described just as a washing from original sin, but also as the removal of its mortal consequence. The Grimms call the bath of baptism a "rebirth" and cite from the letter of Paul in the New Testament as a part of the dictionary definition. In other words, we have once again a weaving of Germanic and Christian symbolism in the water of the initial scene.

The crab of the manuscript version is a water creature of one nature and primarily of one world only. The Grimms' frog which emerges from this ambiguous water of pagan "time flow" and Christian rebirth, is a amphibious "double-natured" being. Like the duck in *Hansel and Gretel*, a frog is at home crossing the boundaries between two worlds, and at helping people in the stories to do the same. The duck is at home in the sky and on the water, the

---

12. From the entry under *"Bad," Deutsches Wörterbuch,*I, 1069. The citation from the letter to Titus is: "He saved us, not because of any works of righteousness that we had done, but according to his mercy, through the water of rebirth and renewal by the Holy Spirit." The German word for river, *Fluß,* is the equivalent to the English "flow," and thus suggests passage, and here the passage of time, even more directly than "river."

13. Perrault does have "the waters" in his opening scene in the sense that the childless king and queen were going every where "taking the waters" to try to find a cure for their sterility. *"Ils allèrent à toutes les eaux du monde, voeux, pèlerinages, menues dévotions . . . , et rien n'y faisait."* This is possibly the origin of the queen who "was in bathing," *"war im Bad,"* in Jacob's manuscript of Marie Hassenpflug's oral version of the story. Cf. Perrault, p. 21.

frog is at home in the water, and walks just as confidently upon the land. He is a creature of spirit like the birds in Wilhelm's world, with the resulting non-restriction to one realm of material existence. The frog swims in the sea and then walks on the land crossing the dangerous barrier between worlds without threat to his life just as the "right prince" will do at the thorn hedge, while others, either the fish of the sea or the predecessors of the right prince, will die on the shore or in the thorns if they try it. The frog is directly associated with the prince, something seen in another tale as well![14] The talking two-natured frog also knows the future and informs the queen that she too will soon make a transition from one state of life to another, from wife to mother, and that a new person will go across from non-existence into being. The frog is Germanic and Christian, he is both magic and Christ's holy Spirit who lives in, and can rise out of, the flow of the water, be it of time, the womb, or of baptism, the Spirit who crosses from heaven to appear in nature on earth announcing a birth, the new life of a human being emerging from the sacrament of the waters.

When the king in his happiness invites the twelve fairies, the "wise women," to give his daughter every gift of nature, Wilhelm changed the first gift. In Perrault it is beauty, in the Grimms' version it is virtue. Goodness is, as in all the other Grimm tales, the spiritual characteristic that makes "beauty" a reality. Only three gifts are named in the Grimm version—virtue, beauty, and wealth—the accomplishments of a court lady being of less interest, before the thirteenth old wise woman arrives. She arrives uninvited. Who would ever invite the gift of "aging" to come to a birth celebration? But she is always there, nonetheless, at every celebration of a birth or a birthday, as inevitably as the question put to the guest of honor: "How old are you?" The king can ban her spinning wheel all he wants, but she is always there, concealed in the deepest part of his own castle, turning her wheel, measuring and cutting thread. She is as uninvited as she was in the biblical story of creation, when, as God was busy speaking, inviting light, the heavens and the earth to come into being, she quietly arrived, unbidden: "evening came, and morning came." The tale of *Sleeping Beauty*, with its appeal to the three stories of Sigurd, of Theseus, and, above all, of Christ, is the place where a spiritual watershed is reached concerning her, the old woman. The soul is tugged in two opposed directions: between the religious tradition's perennial hope that the faithful spirit of love will perform the ultimate rescue of the soul,

14. The transformation of the frog into a prince in *The Frog Prince* (*Der Froschkönig*) by throwing the ugly creature at a wall is a scene rooted in medieval German humor. In the *Nibelungenlied* of the early thirteenth century, the rather unappealing Gunther is in bed having trouble wooing Brunhild. She throws him out of bed, and when he persists in his unwanted advances, she hangs him up on the wall for the night. He then arranges to be replaced in his marital bed the following night by his friend Siegfried and, lo, Brunhild's "frog" is transformed into a hero.

and the religious tradition's equally ancient fear that the impersonal uninvited guest, time, will have the final say. Wilhelm Grimm with his asthma and dangerous heart condition was told by his doctors that he would only have a chance to live if he slept upright in his chair all night long. He suffered attacks of terror and fear of death every time he had an episode of tachycardia paroxysmalis in which his heart began to race and pound uncontrollably. He stayed in the chair all night, sleep and death nearby, and waited for his neighbor's pet quail to announce the dawn.

The princess will fall into a sleep of 100 years, says the twelfth wise woman, modifying the curse laid upon the princess by the thirteenth wise woman, who dictated that the princess would prick herself with a spindle and fall down dead. The twelve good wise women are quite parallel to the seven dwarfs. They are earthly people who are also spiritual personifications. The dwarfs were able to remove the comb and to loosen the bodice laces, but once Snow White was dead of the poison in the apple, she was dead. The twelve fairies are able also to modify the sentence of death, but they cannot remove it entirely. Like the twelve apostles, they are able to impart their ameliorating magical wisdom to the reader, but they too must wait. Death will be a sleep of 100 years. The twelfth wise woman is not able to arrange for the king's son to come and love the sleeper of a hundred years, that is beyond her power. As it is in *Hansel and Gretel*, the goodness intrinsic in human nature can frustrate some of the lethal designs of the witch, but is unable to get itself across the very broad body of water between here and the father's house. For that the duck had to be enchanted into coming. None of this was too far removed from the everyday world of the Grimms. Their father's house where they grew up in Steinau constituted a sizable part of the city wall adjacent to the principal gate to the town, and the little river Kinzig flowed along the back wall of their home. There are ducks in it to this day, and from outside the wall returning home, the Grimms as little children had to cross "a broad water." This childhood experience they seem to have made into a theological metaphor, found throughout the tales. Thus the twelfth fairy can grant the limited sleep, but not the arrival "home."

The father's attempts to prevent the tragedy of the death sleep by burning all the spindles are as every reader immediately knows doomed to fail. He performs the same futile effort to frustrate fate which is done by the fathers in Basile's versions of the story and with the same result. This effort from classical mythology echoes once more the futile efforts of the father of Oedipus to prevent the murderous destiny of which he has been forewarned from taking place. Because all the spindles in the realm have been destroyed at the father's command however, the daughter is all the more fascinated when she sees one. Bettelheim's reading of this episode, that the attempts by parents to prevent their children from discovering sex are doomed to failure, is a good one. It is improved, I believe, if one sees the spindle also as the spindle of time, and the destroying of the spindles as an attempt by adults to prevent children from learning about their future death. It is futile therefore to attempt to prevent adolescents from coming upon the mortality which sex and reproduction are designed to forestall, and from discovering the importance of love and hope for one another which sex and love arouse. Thus we arrive at the ancient dilemma faced by religious consciousness.

The father's efforts, as much as sex, are evidence of the lengths to which love will go to secure the safety and salvation of the one loved. And that is what the story is also about. Love now confronts the old woman herself. She is old because she represents the duration that is characteristic of time, she lives deep in the central tower of the castle because she is something so intrinsic to being human that any parental attempt to ban her spindle, her thread, and her spinning wheel from the human realm is as laughable as it is laudable. The key to her room is not yellow, as in Perrault, but rusty, because ancient, and it is a key because the young girl is opening the door to the answer, she is looking into a magic mirror, and seeing, perhaps with the first moments of her adolescence, that time happens inside. When she says hello to the old woman in the tower she says it in very familiar and neighborly German, "Good Morning, dear old mother" (*Guten Morgen, altes Mütterchen*). She is looking at an old friend, the hidden origin of all, her future one day, and her past. She sees, and knows instinctively that she has now become a part of the spinning of the wheel; she immediately asks if she too can spin the thread, become a mother of another generation. As Sleeping Beauty leans down to pick up the spindle, she inadvertently pricks herself, just as did Snow White's mother before her with the needle in the snow, and falls down in the sleep of death.

In the Grimms' version, the sleep immediately happens to everyone, it spreads, by itself, (*verbreitete sich*) over the whole castle. The whole of the family, like the whole of creation, is treated as being in a mystical communion, as if all were in a sleep of death, held in the framework of the spinning of time. The king and the queen, the horses in the stables, the dogs, the flies on the wall, the birds on the roof, the fire on the hearth. Everything and everyone goes into a state of suspended animation. Finally at the end, "on the trees in front of the castle not a leaf was stirring. . . ." and, quoting from the miracle of the calming of the storm in the New Testament, Wilhelm writes, "Und der Wind legte sich" (And the wind grew calm). The storm is over, the bad thing predicted as necessary destiny has come to pass. What can the princess do now to help herself across the waters? Nothing, except perhaps to possess two very potent religious charms: be beautiful and wait.

The thorn hedge is another harmonized creation from the three religious traditions. Like the classical labyrinth of the Minotaur, it is a maze through which the rescuing hero must find his way. Like the Germanic tree Yggdrasil at Ragnarok which opens to save the children, the hedge opens up of itself at the right time and then closes protectively behind. Finally the circular wall of thorns around the castle is like the crown of thorns with which Jesus passed painfully through his time from Good Friday to Easter. As Sleeping Beauty sleeps on, this thrice-mystical thorn hedge grows ever higher and older around the castle. Spinning and weaving, the old woman is in the tower, creating an impenetrable web of time around the sleeping rose within the maze. As the years wear on and the thorn hedge grows higher and higher, the castle can no longer be seen, but the turning of the wheel is just bringing the day closer for the coming of the king's son. Sleeping Beauty becomes an object of many princes' desire. Many would like to come and rescue her, but it is not "the fullness of time" and Yggdrasil does not open for them, the maze confuses them, and they do not wear the thorns as a crown. They cannot penetrate to the castle tower. The many "wrong" princes are like the false messiahs of many sects who themselves have come and gone, impaled and left hanging by the passage of time. With them die the hopes they aroused of overcoming the spindle of the old woman in the tower. None of them was the right king's son.

Sleeping Beauty is the obverse of *Cinderella*. In *Cinderella*, the spiritual problem was: which of the sisters is the "right" bride? Which human being is the right human being for the love of the King's Son? Whom does the slipper fit? Neither of the two sisters who cut off portions of their feet by their own deed to make the shoe fit, is the right bride, though the shoe did then fit, and the birds of the natural world said why. Finally the prince had found the right bride. "Many are called, but few are chosen," and salvation is by faith alone, by beauty, not by deeds. The dominance of the idea of only certain souls being the "right" ones to be the brides of Christ, and the punishment of the others may reflect a Calvinist emphasis on predestination from the Grimms' Reformed upbringing. In *Sleeping Beauty*, however, the question is turned around: which prince is the right prince? Which suitor is the right suitor? The interwoven criteria from the poetry of the three religions are simple enough: he will be the one who comes in the fullness of time, 100 years, he will find his own way through the maze of thorns, and nature will recognize and make way for him, as the birds did for Cinderella. The deadly thorn hedge will open up of itself.

When the right king's son comes to the castle in the Grimms' version it is like the coming of Sigurd, before whom the wall of "wavering flames" died down of itself to let him pass. When the right king's son comes it is like the coming of Theseus, the prince of Athens who went across the water to Crete to enter the maze of the labyrinth and there to find and kill the Minotaur. This he did in order to free Ariadne and to cancel the tribute of Athenian slaves sent every year to the island. In her love, Ariadne gave Theseus a ball of thread which he was to unravel as he made his way through the labyrinth, so that he would be able to make his way out again. He made his way into the maze, killed the Minotaur, and came out again, led by Ariadne's thread. He took her back to Athens, and they were married there and ruled as king and queen. The Greek myth contains the thread and the maze and the rescue as in *Sleeping Beauty,* and the heroine assists with the thread. The coming of the right king's son to Sleeping Beauty points most of all to the descent into death and the Resurrection of Christ. Wilhelm's spirituality turns upon the Resurrection of Christ, divine providence, and the mystical union of love and life from John's Gospel.

In writing done so softly as to suggest that the king's son is performing the harrowing of hell, the king's son passes through the crown of thorns woven around the castle which had stopped all other "messiahs" but which he is able to survive and pass through. As he goes on through the rooms of the castle all is in a Sheol-like state of limbo. One hundred years having passed is not enough of itself to reawaken the silence of Sleeping Beauty and all her family and all her world. The king's son passes quietly[15] by all the sleepers,

> Then he kept on going and everything was so quiet that you could hear your-self breathing, and finally he came to the tower and opened the door to a little room in which Little Thorn Rose was sleeping. She was lying there and was so beautiful that he couldn't turn his eyes away, and he bent over and gave her a kiss. As he touched her with his kiss Little Thorn Rose opened her eyes, woke up, and looked at him in a very friendly way. Then they went down together and the king woke up and the queen and the entire court and they looked at each other with wide-open eyes.

This beautiful scene with its unusually loving revocation of fate by a kiss, *"he touched her* with his kiss" has a magic about it that may go back as far as the *Heliand* for its inspiration. In the parallel scene in that early medieval version of the gospel story, Jesus raises the son of the dead widow of Naim, nullifying, as in *Snow White,* the decision of fate, the thirteenth fairy, by a loving act of touching the unfortunate person:

> They were carrying the body out of the hill-fort's gate on a stretcher, it was a very young man. The mother was walking behind the corpse, her heart was grief-stricken. . . . it was her only child. She was a widow, she had no more

15. The surprisingly effective use of quietness throughout this scene may have been inspired by a sermon of Herder on the raising of the widow of Naim's son. Herder concentrates throughout on how quietly and effectively Christ comes to the widow's bier, as softly as spring-time awakening the tree and the seed: *"Leise war die Hülfe Jesu aber schnell und wirksam . . .[wie der] Frühling . . ., der den Baum und die Saat erweckt, wird auch deine Gebeine beleben."* "Homilie über die Geschichte der Auferweckung des Jünglings zu Nain, Lukä vii, 11–17" in *Herder's Werke, ausgewählte Werke in einem Band* (Stuttgart and Tübingen: Cotta, 1844), pp. 1382–1385. The first sermon in this section deals with Christ as "life and light" (p.1335), another connection to Wilhelm Grimm's spirituality.

In German, and especially in the German New Testament, to "raise" a dead person is to "awaken" them, and thus the clearer similarity in the Grimms'text between the activity of the Christ and that of the prince.

joy except for this one son, he was all that was left to her of happiness and delight—until fate took him from her, the great Measurer's doings.[16] The Son of God became filled with compassion and spoke to the mother. He told the widow to stop crying. . . . "There is no need for you to mourn over the life-spirit of your boy." Then he walked up to the stretcher, and the Chieftain's Son touched him with holy hands, and spoke to the hero, telling the young man to get up, to rise up from his resting place. . . . The mother fell at Christ's feet and praised the people's Chieftain[17] before the crowd, because He had pro-tected a life-spirit so dear to her against the workings of the Measurer.[18]

What follows in Sleeping Beauty's castle is almost an alleluia of waking up on the part of all creation. The horses get up and shake themselves, the dogs jump up and wag their tails, the doves on the roof pull their heads out from under their wings, the flies creep on the walls, the fire waves its arms in the air . . . and then the great marriage feast is held for Sleeping Beauty and the king's son. The narrative thus follows the spirit of Christian story more strongly in this tale than in any other. In the story of Sigurd, Brynhild was captive but not asleep and she first offers the rescuer a challenge to fight rather than love. In the story of Theseus, the maze is indeed there and the hero does penetrate it, but there is no feeling of time, more of a feeling of space, and in that space, the heroine Ariadne waits outside for the hero to emerge. In Wilhelm's final version of *Sleeping Beauty*, the wall is clearly a crown of thorns that has to be gone through and that turns to flowers, the beautiful person is saved by a kiss of love from the savior-prince (very far in-deed from the sleeping rape that occurs in Basile and Perrault). The frog of the bath is revealed to be the king's son whose love brings about a general re-birth, as the allusions to baptism and the amphibious spirit in the water sug-gested, not only for the right sleeping person alone, but a rebirth which spreads to the whole communion of those who love the sleeping beauty of a good soul. The good king is the first to receive reawakening to new life, not because of his rank primarily, but because he was a caring father whose love drove him to try, even if in vain, to protect his daughter from the conse-quences of the curse. In this he is the stand-in for all the fathers in the classi-cal religious myths who made the same effort. If the enchanted sleep is inter-preted only as adolescent lassitude, that, I believe, does not do justice to the

16. *metodigisceftie* "[god] the Measurer's doings." Fate is made responsible for the timing of the young man's death. The author of the *Heliand* acknowledges the active power of fate's thread in this world, but wishes to show that Christ's touch is more powerful.

17. In the ninth-century *Heliand* Christ is described as a chieftain, and the twelve apostles are his warrior companions. His chief enemy is fate, the crisis occurring when Christ is to meet his own fate at noon on Good Friday. When Peter draws his sword, for example, he is told to put it back into its scabbard, since as Christ tells him, "We cannot by our deeds avert anything." See G. Ronald Murphy, S. J., *The Saxon Savior,* pp. 33–55.

18. *The Heliand, The Saxon Gospel,* pp. 72–73.

multitude of characters in the story, all of whom fall asleep. The enchanted sleep is really more like a communal time of Advent, the time of waiting for the Lord, waiting for the salvation of all the household. When the king's son mounts the stairs to the room where the "old mother," fate, spins, he does not need a key to enter. Nor does fate greet or impede him in any way. It is as though her ability to curse with death, which the twelfth good fairy had ameliorated, has now bowed completely to his coming, just as he then bows to kiss Sleeping Beauty, the good human being. He brings the awakening power of divine love which comes from his Father as well, who, one suspects, knows the little old mother well.

Is all fear of the old mother, the spinner, now gone? Does the story leave her a place at the table of the mystical marriage? She does not vanish as did the equally objectivist father of Cinderella. The story's conclusion gently assures the reader that in the end Chaucer's wise nun was right, *amor vincit omnia*, love conquers all, including death, but nonetheless the wheel still turns. The narrative, I think, advises the readers to rejoice in their hope of rescue by love, by being reborn to eternity through the dove of baptism, but it also suggests that it is appropriate to invite the ancient wise women of the owl and of the raven, and to be appreciative of their feelings and poetry. There is a curious three-word reminder at the story's very end of why one should not fail to have a golden plate of respect ready for "old mother" and her spinning wheel: "And then the marriage of the king's son to Little Thorn Rose was celebrated with great splendor, and they lived in peace and contentment until their end." In Wilhelm Grimm's spirituality of human religious emotions, there is room for reverence for God as our eternal Father in his unity with his Son, the prince, whose loving Spirit saves us from our graves, and also for reverence for our old mother who spins our thread until we fall asleep.

Nine

The identity of the prince within the stories I have often interpreted as a blend of the rescuing hero from three traditions with Christ being the dominant figure. This is true enough, I feel, in the diachronic context of the story and in the style and intent of the narrator. If, however, one looks at the tales in the initially bland and fragmentary form in which many of them first came to the Grimms, and if one considers their remarkable transformation into stories with powers of enchantment, then it is clear that in a creative artistic sense it is Wilhelm Grimm who is the prince. He is the one who kissed these sleeping gems back into life.

As a poet and storyteller he would deny that he was a theologian. Still he has insights that awaken even the theologian. His love of the Two Great Commandments as the key to faith in this life and in an afterlife led him to unusual poetic realizations with the help of the fairy tales. One of these is surely that there is a secret alliance between love and inner beauty on the one hand, and the continuation of life, communion of saints, on the other. Love and life go together and stay together. The God who is love in St. John's Gospel is not stopped by graves.

On the forbidden nature, the evilness, of sin, Wilhelm does not follow the standard synthesis of the Two Great Commandments as is found written in Matthew 25:45: "Whatever you failed to do to these the least of my brethren, you failed to do unto me." Wilhelm's Grimm's basic analogue for the nature of sin comes from the Garden of Eden. Failure to love one's neighbor is a result of being enamored of the serpent's promise, "You will be like God." Thus the failure to love one's own children, his favorite example, is evil not just because it is a violation of nature, nor wrong because the children are family relatives of God, but rather because it is the crude and covert idolatry of self-worship. Self-worship repeats the idolatry of Eden, the desire to be forever the "the fairest in the land," the desire to be "like God." Sin against the least of His brethren is wrong because it violates the First Commandment. God alone is God.

Is the poetry of the Grimms' tales just religious syncretism? The tales are rooted in the diachronic continuity of the act of faith as expressed in the poetic syncretism of myth and story, but not in any syncretistic credal formulation. The concern of Wilhelm is with the amazing continuity over time of the act of belief, hope, and love, the goodness of the human heart and its perversity, expressed in religious poetry. Such religious feelings and poetry are older than any credal formulation, and what Wilhelm makes us realize is that they have been with us for millennia and deserve continuing reverence from Christian believers. There is precedent in the biblical tradition for such reverence in the recognition by Abraham of the priesthood of Melchisedech, in the coming of the alien Magi, and in the Christmas song of the angels addressed to "all men of good will." The attitude of fundamental optimism about life which people of faith, hope, and love have possessed over the centuries has given birth to great stories of the heart, and I do not think one need speak, except perhaps with reverence, of a syncretism of the feelings of the heart.

One of the stories we have not discussed might be given the last word. "The Spirit in the Bottle" ("Der Geist im Glas") may actually give something of a self-portrait of the artist, a symbolic inner autobiography. In it a young man who has gone off to the university to study returns to his hardworking father and helps him in the woods chopping trees. When they take a break, he goes off to look for bird nests in the branches of the trees. He hears a muffled voice calling to him from the roots. There he finds a powerful and dangerous spirit trapped in a bottle whom he lets out, and later, being threatened by the spirit, tricks into returning into the bottle. He then finally decides to take a risk on trusting the spirit's word, and lets him out again. The grateful spirit of the roots gives the young student three wishes and with them he obtains a miraculous bandage with which he becomes the greatest healer in the land.

The story is that of Aladdin, of course, but changed. Aladdin finds his enchanted lamp in a cave, Wilhelm finds his in the roots of an ancient tree. Wilhelm, like the hero, took a chance on leaving his law career and exchanging it for one in which he explored the roots and branches of words, stories, and the languages of birds. In that study in which he "let out" many a pagan genie entrapped for years in oblivion, he succeeded, and it brought him the fulfillment of his wishes for a scholarly family life. In his study of the three birds, the deep and ancient roots of religious consciousness in poetry, he became something his own admired ancestors in the pulpit would have been very proud of, a poet and awakener of the heart.

*The Verses Marked by Wilhelm Grimm in
His Greek New Testament*

The initial and final words of the verses underlined by Wilhelm Grimm in
the Greek of Schott's edition of 1811 are given in each case following the
English translation. This is to clarify the occasional deviation in wording
and in verse numbering from contemporary editions of the Greek New
Testament.

The Spirit of God as the Origin of Life and Awareness

Jn 1:4—"In him was life and the life was the light of men / *en auto zoe en . . . phos ton anthropon."* [from the prologue to St. John's Gospel, also marked with a rectangular paper in the Haldensleben Bible]

Jn 3:6—"That which is born of the flesh is flesh, and that which is born of the spirit is spirit / *to gegennemenon . . . pneuma estin."* [Jesus' conversation with Nicodemus on the need to be born again spiritually]

Jn 4:14—"Whoever drinks of the water that I shall give him will never thirst / *hos d' an pie ek tou hudatos hou ego doso auto ou me dipsesei eis ton aiona."*

Jn 4:24—"God is spirit, and those who worship him must worship in spirit and truth / *pneuma ho theos . . . en pneumati kai aletheia dei proskunein."* [Jesus' response to the Samaritan woman on which temple or mountain is the correct one on which to worship God. Corresponds to Wilhelm's open minded view on Christian churches' and past religions' diverse traditions of religious experience.]

Jn 6:63—"It is the spirit that gives life, the flesh is of no avail / *to pneuma esti to zoopoioun, he sarx ouk ophelei ouden."* [Jesus teaching the disciples, alluding to the creation of Adam by God breathing his breath into clay]

Jn 14:17—"The spirit of truth / *to pneuma tes aletheias"* [Jesus at the Last Supper, promising to send this spirit to his disciples]

Acts 1:5—"John baptized with water, but you shall be baptized with the Holy Spirit / *Ioannes men ebaptisen hudati . . . en pneumati hagio."* [Jesus' promise before the Ascension]

Acts 2:28—"You have made known to me the ways of life / *Egnorisas moi hodous zoes.*" [Peter's Pentecost speech after the coming of the Holy Spirit on the apostles]

Acts 7:[59]60—"Receive my spirit / *dexai to pneuma mou.*" [The last words of Stephen as he was stoned to death]

Acts 10:15—"What God has cleansed, you must not call unclean / *ha ho theos ekathariste, su me koinou.*" [Peter's vision that all animals are good]

Acts 10:36—"He [Christ] is Lord of all / *houtos estin panton kurios.*" [Peter's sermon in the house of Cornelius. Wilhelm might have liked this for its nonsectarian view. In Christ's spiritual kingdom all are equally his subjects]

Acts 11:16—"John baptized with water, but you shall be baptized with Holy Spirit / *Ioannes . . . en pneumati hagio.*" [Peter arguing his view that there is no difference between Jew and Gentile if they are within the Holy Spirit]

Acts 17:28—"In him [God] we live and move and have our being; as even some of your poets have said, 'For we are indeed his offspring' / *en auto gar zomen . . . kai genos esmen.*" [Paul in the Areopagus, preaching to the Athenians. Wilhelm read pantheistic theology with some sympathy, but mainly seems to have had feelings of panentheism: "God in everything." This would make the animism in the fairy tales quite appealing to his religious spirit. "Everything is in God" is the more orthodox formulation found here in Acts.]

Lk 11:13—"If you then who are evil know how to give good gifts to your children, how much more will the heavenly Father give the Holy Spirit to those who ask him! / *ei oun humeis . . . pneuma hagion tois aitousin auton.*" [Jesus' instruction on confident prayer; follows after the teaching of the Our Father. This would make an image of selfish parents such as Hansel and Gretel's truly unnatural and reprehensible.]

Christ and Resurrection

Jn 10:11—"I am the good [lit. 'beautiful'] shepherd / *Ego eimi ho poimen ho kalos.*" [In contrast to a hired man who runs away when the wolf comes, the real shepherd stays to protect the sheep. Perhaps connected to Wilhelm's version of the ending of Red Riding Hood, with the good huntsman's rescue from the wolf]

Jn 10:14—"I am the good shepherd, I know my own and my own know me / *Ego eimi ho poimen ho kalos . . . ginoskousi me ta ema.*" [the context here is on the relationship rather than the wolf above]

Jn 10:38—"that the Father is in me and I am in the Father / *hoti en emoi ho pater, k'go en to patri.*" [Jesus' statement of the mystical relationship between himself and God the Father; parallel to what Wilhelm underlined in *Parzival*]

Jn 11:25—"I am the resurrection and life / *Ego eimi he anastasis kai he zoe.*" [At the raising of Lazarus from the dead, Jesus' identity as bringer of resurrection and life; related, I believe to the resurrection of the heroine by the prince at the end of the Grimms' tales]

Jn 14:27—"Peace I leave with you; my peace I give to you; not as the world gives do I give to you. Do not let your hearts be troubled and do not let them be afraid / *Eirenen aphimini [aphiemi] humin . . . kardia mede deiliato.*" [Jesus, before his death, promises to send the Holy Spirit from heaven to bring his disciples peace. The reference to the untroubled heart may also be a prayer by Wilhelm for his own medical condition with a racing heart and the accompanying panic attacks.]

Lk 10:5—"Peace be to this house / *Eirene to oiko touto.*" [Jesus' instruction on what to say upon entering any house; perhaps Wilhelm's prayer for his own home]

Lk 11:23—"He who is not with me is against me and he who does not gather with me scatters / *Ho me on met' emou kat' emou estin, kai ho me sunagon met' emou skorpizei.*"

Lk 20:36,38—"For they [the deceased] cannot die anymore, because they are equal to angels and are the sons of God being sons of the resurrection. Now he [God] is not the God of the dead, but of the living; for to him all of them are alive / *oude gar apothanein eti dunantai . . . anastaseos huioi ontes. Theos de ouk estin nekron . . . auto zosin.*" [Jesus' strong affirmation of life after death in his debate with the Sadducees. The middle verse, 37, on Moses' address at the burning bush was not underlined.]

Lk 23:42 " 'Remember me when you come into your kingdom' / *Mnestheti mou hotan elthes eis ten basileian sou.*" [the prayer of the good thief on the cross to Jesus, crucified alongside him. Wilhelm seems to have echoed this verse and Jesus' response in his rewriting of the ending of *Snow White* when the prince invites the risen Snow White to come with him to his father's castle.]

Lk 24:36—"Peace be with you / *eirene humin.*" [the appearance of Christ to his disciples after the Resurrection; his first words]

Mk 10:45a—"For the Son of Man came not to be served but to serve / *kai gar ho huios tou anthropou . . . diakonesai.*" [Jesus admonishes James and John, who had been asking for preference.]

[noted on the back flyleaf in Wilhelm's hand in Greek and Latin:] *adelphoi Jesu Christi,* Math xii.46, xii.55, Joh vii.5. [It seems to have made an impression on Wilhelm that there are three references in Scripture to "brothers of Jesus Christ."]

Love One Another

Jn 13:34—"that you should love one another, even as I loved you so you also should love one another / *hina agapate allelous . . . agapate allelous.*" [Jesus before his passion and death]

Jn 15:12—"This is my commandment, that you love one another as I have loved you / *Haute estin he entole he eme, hina agapate allelous kathos egapesa humas.*"

Jn 15:17—"this I command you, to love one another / *tauta entellomai humin . . . allelous.*"

Acts 20:35—"It is more blessed to give than to receive / *makarion estin mallon didonai e lambanein."* [Paul is reminding the Ephesians of one of the sayings of Jesus.]

Lk 6:32a, 33a, 37—"And if you love those who love you, what credit is that to you? And if you do good to those who do good to you, what credit is that to you? And judge not, and you will not be judged / *kai ei agapate . . . charis estin. Kai ean . . . charis estin. Kai me krinete, kai ou me krithete."* [This is within the context of Jesus' teaching that his followers should love their enemies]

Lk 6:45—"The good person out of the treasure of his heart produces good / *ho agathos anthropos . . . to agathon."* [Jesus' extension of his example that a good tree produces good fruit, and a bad tree, bad fruit, and thus it is by their fruits, rather than by their appearances, that you will know what they are. This is ubiquitous in the fairy tales, perhaps most prominently in *Cinderella.*]

Lk 10:27—"You shall love the Lord your God with all your heart, and with all your soul, and with all your mind; and your neighbor as yourself / *Agapeseis kurion ton theon . . . hos seauton."* [The Shema with the neighbor added. Jesus has the Torah scholar recite the great commandments as an introduction to the story, parable, of the Good Samaritan. It is the helpful people, regardless of their appearances, who actually fulfil the commandment to love. Wilhelm may have seen much in the fairy-tale tradition which could readily be harmonized with the Good Samaritan tale, and the Great Commandments, including helpful people and animals assisting the hero/heroine.]

Mk 12:31—"You shall love your neighbor as yourself / *Agapeseis ton plesion sou hos seauton."* [As above, to the question of which commandment is the greatest, Jesus gives this as the second greatest after the command to love God.]

Mt 5:41 [faint]—"And if anyone forces you to go one mile, go with him two miles / *kai hostis se aggareusei milion hen, upage met' autou duo."*

Mt 7:12—"So whatever you wish that people would do to you, do so to them / *Panta oun . . . poieite autois."* [the Golden Rule]

The largest group of scriptural passages has to do with the Spirit of life and the divine milieu of love that bespeaks even the resurrection and eternal life. This is not at all what one would have expected if one solely went by the grim and austere implications of Jacob's phrase that the brothers Grimm were raised "strictly Reformed." The next groups are perhaps less numerically represented, but they are also important for an insight into Wilhelm's spirituality.

Humble Faith

Jn 5:44—"How can you believe, when you accept glory from one another and do not seek the glory that comes from the only God / *Pos dunasthe humeis pisteusai . . . ou zeteite?"* [Jesus is speaking to the Jewish leadership. Wilhelm may have been urging himself to seek a reward only from God for his scholarship to strengthen the realism of his faith. Possibly related to the sin of vanity, a recurrent theme in the fairy tales, "Who's the fairest of them all?"]

Acts 2:21—"And it shall be that whoever calls on the name of the Lord shall be saved / *kai estai pas . . . sothesetai."* [Peter's speech at Pentecost, citing the prophet Joel. Apparently, invoking the common religious phrases of the day, such as "God will help us," was not a cliché to Wilhelm or Jacob but rather a part of their everyday faith in God.]

Acts 5:29b—"We must obey God rather than men / *peitharchein dei theo . . . anthropois."* [Peter's reply to the high priest when ordered not to teach about Jesus or his Resurrection. This may reflect the high moral stance taken by the brothers Grimm at Göttingen against the king's repeal of the constitution, which cost them their jobs and their homeland of Hesse.]

Acts 21:14—"the Lord's will be done / *to thelema tou kuriou genestho."* [Paul insists on going up to Jerusalem despite danger to his life; as above, again Wilhelm did not treat common everyday religious expressions as meaningless.]

Lk 18: 13b—"but he was beating his breast saying, 'God, be merciful to me a sinner' / *all' etupten . . . to hamartalo."* [in Jesus' story of the Pharisee and the publican, the publican's humble prayer. Supports Professor Tatar's theory on the importance of humility for the success or the hero or heroine in the Grimms' tales]

Mk 4:40—"Why are you afraid? Have you no faith? / *Ti deiloi este? Oupo echete pistin?"* [from the scene of the calming of the storm on the Sea of Galilee]

Mt 8:13—"'Be it done for you as you have believed / *Hos episteusas genetheto soi'."* [the curing of the centurion's son, spoken by Jesus to the humble centurion after he said he was not worthy that Jesus come under his roof. Possibly related to the death of Wilhelm's son?]

[The following was found written in Wilhelm's careful hand on the back flyleaf in German and in Greek with his underlining of the phrase *agnoso theo:*] *"Paulus sagt zu den Athenenser, Praxeis xvii.23 Dierchomenos gar kai anatheron ta sebasmata humon, heuron kai bomon, en ho epegegrapto:agnoso theo [sic]."* "Paul says to the Athenians, Acts 17:23, 'For as I passed along and observed the objects of your worship, I found also an altar with the inscription <u>To the Unknown God</u>.'" [Paul associates his God with the one the Greeks and their ancestors had "unknowingly" been worshiping. Obviously very important to Wilhelm from his recopying of the entire passage, this passage of Scripture gives clear justification and Pauline precedent for Wilhelm's great reverence for the pagan faiths of the past, both Greek and Germanic, and for his, and Paul's, association of them with the Christian faith of the present. The owl and the raven, therefore, are related to the dove: All three fly on the air of the same unseeable spirit.]

God's Love and Providence

Acts 7:49—"The heavens are my throne and earth is my footstool / *ho ouranos . . . ton podon mou.*" [Stephen argues before his martyrdom that God does not need a temple since he uses nature as his chair and footstool, citing Isaiah. Wilhelm, and any German Romantic, would be completely at home with this association of God and nature.]

Acts 27:34b—"Not a hair is to perish from the head of any of you / *oudenos humin thrix apo tes kephales apoleitai.*" [Paul to terrified shipmates during a great storm at sea. The remains of a small (red?) flower were found on this page where the above was underlined.]

[faint] Lk 15:10—"There is joy before the angels of God over one sinner who repents / *ginetai chara . . . metanoounti.*" [from the parable of the lost coin]

Lk 21:13—"but not a hair of your head will perish / *kai thrix ek tes kephales humin ou me apoletai.*" [Jesus' warning to his followers that they will be persecuted and put to death, however, not a hair will be lost]

Mt 10:30—"but even the hairs of your head are all numbered / *humin de kai trixes tes kephales pasai erithmemenai eisin.*" [Jesus' reassurance that not even a sparrow falls without the Father knowing of it, but in the case of human beings, every hair is noted. The divine awareness and concern for everything that befalls us must have been a very important point for Wilhelm, thus, again, the prominence of the aware and guiding dove.]

[very faint] Mt 24:2—"the buildings of God / *tas oikodomas tou theou.*" [Jesus predicts the fall of the temple.]

Poverty and Wealth

Lk 12:21—"So is he who lays up treasure for himself, and is not rich toward God / *houtos ho thesaurizon . . . me eis theon pluton.*" [from the parable of the Rich Fool unknowingly making merry on the eve of his death]

Lk 12:25—"Which of you by worrying can add a single cubit to the span of his life? / *tis de ex humin . . . pechun hena?*" [from Jesus's sermon on the lilies of the field: life is more than worrying about clothing and food]

Lk 16:15b—"for, what is prized among human beings is an abomination in the sight of God / *hoti to en anthropois hupselon bdelugma en opion tou theou.*" [Jesus speaking against the Pharisees' love of money; follows the section on "You cannot love both God and Mammon (god of wealth)"]

Mt 6:28—"Consider the lilies of the field, how they grow; they neither toil nor spin / *katamathete ta krina . . . oude nethousin*" [as above. The Grimms almost always had to scrimp to get by. Even in Berlin toward the evening of their lives the two brothers were paid the salary of one professor.]

Mt 6:33—"Seek first the kingdom [of God] and his righteousness, and all these things will be given to you as well / *zeteite de proton ten basileian.*" [Same context as above. One thinks immediately of Wilhelm's handling of wealth in *Hansel and Gretel* and in *Cinderella*.]

Mt 11:8—"Behold, those who wear soft garments are in the houses of kings / *ide hoi ta malaka . . . oikois ton basileon eisin.*" [People went into the desert to see John the Baptist because he was a prophet, not because of the quality of the clothing he was wearing; if you are interested in wealthy clothing, you went to the wrong place.]

[copied in full on the back flyleaf by Wilhelm in his own hand:] Mt 11:8—*ide hoi ta makala phorountes en tois oikois ton basileon eisin.* [transl. as in preceding. Professor Zipes is right that their poverty and unjust treatment was indeed a persistent concern to the brothers. It seems, however, they were also concerned not to put too much store in money or wealth as granting any added importance to one's person. It is possible, judging from the markings in the Haldensleben Bible, that they may also to have feared being led into the sin of envy by being jealous of the wealthy.]

Rejection

Acts 4:11-12—"This is the stone which was rejected by you builders, but which has become the cornerstone. And there is salvation in no one else / *houtos estin ho lithos . . . he soteria.*" [Peter's speech in Jerusalem to the high priest and elders on their rejection of Christ]

[double horizontal line made by Wilhelm next to this verse] Lk 4:24—"I say to you that no prophet is accepted in his own country / *lego humin hoti oudeis prophetes dektos estin en patridi autou.*" [Jesus commenting on his treatment in his hometown. Wilhelm may be thinking of the brothers' rejection in Göttingen and their forced exile from Hesse. As he banished them from their homeland, the king is said to have remarked with little concern: "What did the Grimms ever do for me?"]

Lk 16:8—"because the sons of this world are shrewder in dealing with their own generation than are the sons of light / *hoti hoi huioi tou aionos toutou . . . ten heauten eisin.*" [Jesus explaining the success of the unjust steward in the parable. The misuse of reason in dealing with people is found in the parents' decision in *Hansel and Gretel;* Wilhelm may also have been attracted to the term "sons of light" for those who are not as shrewd.

Mt 5:44—"Love your enemies and pray for those who persecute you / *agapate tous echthrous humon . . . diokonton humas.*" [from the Sermon on the Mount]

Bread

Jn 6:27a—"Do not labor for the food which perishes but rather for the food which endures to eternal life, which the Son of Man will give to you /

ergazesthe me ten brosin . . . humin dosei." [Jesus speaking after the multi-
plication of the loaves and fishes. In *Hansel and Gretel,* the parents choose
the food which perishes over their children's lives, and the strewn breadcrumbs do not show the children the path home, only the dove and the
duck are able to do that.]

Jn 6:50a–51a—"This is the bread which comes down from heaven so that anyone may eat of it and not die. I am the living bread that came down from
heaven / *houtos estin ho artos . . . ek tou ouranou katabas."* [Jesus, alluding
to the manna, identifying himself as the food that prevents death. Echoes
Red Riding Hood's bread and is the opposite of the death-bringing apple of
Snow White's stepmother.]

Acts 2:46b—"They partook of food with happy and sincere hearts / *metelam-
banon trophes en agalliasei kai apheloteti kardias."* [Description of the early
church. Preceding verse: "day by day they were attending temple together
and breaking bread in their homes;" succeeding verse: "praising God and
having favor with all the people." Wilhelm may, perhaps, have been thinking of his own household and the concomitant love of harmony which the
description implies.]

The Word

Lk11:28—"Blessed rather are those who hear the word of God and keep it! /
menoun makarioi oi akouontes ton logon tou theou kai phulassontes!" [There is a
latitude of meaning in phulassontes ("keep") extending from "preserve,
protect" to "observe, obey," which may have appealed to Wilhelm as storyteller, especially since he regarded the fairy tales as small remnants of ancient faith whose words he was trying to preserve and restore as well as to
respect their spiritual content.]

Lk 21:31—"The heavens and the earth will pass away, but my words will not
pass away / *ho ouranos kai he ge . . . ou me pareleusontai."* [Jesus averring
the lasting power of his message. Wilhelm may have seen this remark as a
guarantee for the lasting ability of his religiously rewritten versions of the
tales, insofar as he harmoniously incorporates Christian "words that will
not pass away."]

The Child

Lk 18:16–17—"Let the little children come to me and do not prevent them, for
to such belongs the kingdom of God. Amen I say to you, whoever does not
accept the kingdom of God as a little child will not enter it / *Aphete ta
paidia erchesthai pros me . . . ou me eiselthe eis auten."* [It would be very surprising if this verse had not been noted by Wilhelm Grimm. It was the
credo of Novalis and many contemporary German romantics, and as the

years went on, children became more and more the destined audience for
Wilhelm's rewritten fairy tales. Childlikeness is also a frequent characteristic of the hero/heroine.]

Passages from the Haldensleben German Bible
Probably Marked by a Later Hand

[The marginal lines are in irregular scrawl and in color; Wilhelm used an
extremely fine and straight pen when marking passages.]

Sirach 30:12–14—"Discipline you son while he is still young so that he does not
become stubborn and disobey you. Discipline your child and do not let him
be lazy lest his folly humiliate you. Better to be a poor man but active and
healthy than to be a rich man suffering in a wasted frame."

Sirach 31:2–6—"Concern for one's livelihood banishes slumber; more than a
serious illness it disturbs sleep. That man is rich who labors to accumulate
wealth and then stops and enjoys what is his. That man is poor who toils
for a meager subsistence, and if he ever stops, he finds himself a beggar.
The lover of gold will not be free from sin, and he who pursues wealth will
pass away with it. Many have been brought to misfortune by money, even
though their destruction lay before their eyes.

Sirach 31:12–15—"If you are sitting at a rich man's table do not open your
jaws wide thinking 'what a spread to devour!' but rather remember that a
greedily envious eye is an evil thing. What could be more evil than such
an eye? It weeps whenever it sees anyone else reaching for the food. Do
not reach for everything your eye looks at, and do not grab at everything
it sees in front of it in the serving dish."[1]

Sirach 32:27–32 (31:24–28 in a modern version)—"Everyone in the whole town
grumbles about a stingy skinflint, and they are right to do so. Do not try to
be a hero at wine drinking; wine destroys many people. Immersion in acid
is how steel is proofed; wine proofs the hearts of the irreverent in the same
manner when they are drunk. Wine enlivens human life as long as one
drinks it moderately. What is life if there is no wine? Wine was created in
order to make the hearts of men merry. Wine drunk with restraint brings
joy to body and soul."

---

1. The Meyer translation in this passage is inimitable: "Wenn du bey eines reichen Mannes
Tische sitzest, so sperre deinen Rachen nicht auf, and denke nicht, hier ist viel zu fressen;
sondern gedenke, daß ein neidisches Auge böse ist; denn was ist neidischer, weder ein solches
Auge? und weinet wo es siehet einen zugreifen. Greif nicht zu, wo es hinsiehet; und nimm
nicht, was vor ihm in der Schüssel liegt."

APPENDIX B

Little Red Riding Hood
1st edition, 1812

The following text is from the copy of the first edition of the fairy tales (1812 & 1815) at Yale's Beinecke Library. The two volumes of the first edition contain no frontispiece, and the edition is dedicated: *"An die Frau Elisabeth von Arnim für den kleinen Johannes Freimund."* There is an appendix at the end of each volume giving the source and a few remarks about each tale. The stories are numbered independently in each volume, beginning with number 1 and then to 70 in the second (1815) volume, 1 to 85 in the first (1812). The quotation from Walter Scott (1810) from "The Lady of the Lake" is cited in a short addition to the introduction, p. xxiv, *Zeugnisse für Kindermärchen*, but not the excerpt from the newspaper. This earliest version of "Testimonials for Fairy Tales" has only Strabo, Luther, Johannes Mueller, Sir Walter Scott, and Eloi Johanneau.

The appendix to the first edition contains this brief commentary on *Red Riding Hood*:

> On Red Riding Hood, No. 26: Amazingly, except for our oral saga, we have not come across this story anywhere except in Perrault (chaperon rouge) and in Tieck's reworking of Perrault.
>
> ("Zum Rothkäppchen, No.26: Dieses Märchen haben wir außer unserer mündlichen Sage, was zu wundern ist, nirgends angetroffen, als bei Perrault (chaperon rouge) wonach Tiecks Bearbeitung." p. xxii)

Once upon a time there was a sweet little girl who was liked by everyone who laid eyes on her, but most of all by her grandmother who was always thinking what more she could give to the child. Once she gave her a little cape of red velvet, and since it looked so good on her and she didn't want to wear anything else, people just called her Red Riding Hood; then one time her mother said to her: "Come, Red Riding Hood, here is a piece of cake and a bouteille of wine, take them out to grandmother, she is sick and weak, they will strengthen her; behave yourself properly and say hello to her from me, go straight there and don't run off the path, otherwise you will fall and break the glass and then sick grandmother will have nothing."

Red Riding Hood promised her mother that she would be very obedient. Grandmother lived out in the woods, a half hour from the village. Now as Red Riding Hood came into the woods the wolf met her, but Red Riding Hood did not know what an evil animal it was, and was not afraid of it. "Good day, Red Riding Hood."—"Thank you, wolf."—"Where are you going to so early, Red Riding Hood?"—"To grandmother's."—"What are you carrying under your apron?—"Grandmother is sick and weak, so I am bringing cake and wine. Yesterday we did our baking, and this should strengthen her."—"Red Riding Hood, where does your grandmother live?"—"A good quarter of an hour farther in the woods, under the three oak trees is where her house is, beneath them are the nut hedges. You must certainly know that." The wolf thought to himself, that's a nice fat tidbit for me, how are you going arrange things so that you get it: "Listen Red Riding Hood, he said, haven't you seen the beautiful flowers in the woods, why don't you take a look at what's around you. I think you are not at all listening to how beautifully the little birds are singing, you are walking straight ahead as if you were in the village going to school, and it is so jolly out here in the woods."

Red Riding Hood opened her eyes and saw how the sun had broken through the trees and everything was full of beautiful flowers; then she thought, If I bring grandmother a bouquet she will like it, and it is still early. I will still get there in plenty of time. And [she] jumped into the woods and looked for flowers. And whenever she had picked one, she thought there was another one even prettier over there and she ran over to get it and kept getting farther and farther into the woods. The wolf, however, went straight to grandmother's house and knocked on the door. "Who is out there?"—"Red Riding Hood, I am bringing you cake and wine, open the door."—"Just pull down on the handle," grandmother called out, I am too weak and can't get up." The wolf pulled down on the handle and the door popped open. Then he went in, straight to grandmother's bed, and swallowed her. Then he took her clothes, put them on, put her bonnet on his head, lay down in the bed and closed the bed curtains.

Red Riding Hood had been running around after flowers, and it wasn't until she had so many that she couldn't carry any more that she started on her way to grandmother's. When she got there the door was open, which made her wonder, and as she came into the living room it looked so strange that she thought: Dear God, how frightened I feel today, and usually I enjoy so much being at grandmother's house. Then she went to the bed and pulled the curtains back. Her grandmother was lying there with the bonnet pulled down over her face and she looked so strange. "Grandmother, what big ears you have!"—"So that I can hear you better." "Grandmother what big eyes you have!"—"So that I can see you better." "Grandmother, what big hands you have!"—"So that I can grab you better." "But grandmother, what gigantic jaws you have!"—"So that I can eat you better." With that, the wolf jumped out of the bed, jumped on poor Red Riding Hood, and swallowed her.

When the wolf had finished his fat tidbit, he lay down again in the bed, fell asleep, and started snoring very loudly. The hunter was just passing by and thought how can the old lady be snoring like that, you better take a look. He went in, and when he came to the bed there was the wolf lying there whom he had long been looking for; he certainly must have eaten grandmother, maybe she can still be saved, I won't shoot, thought the hunter. Then he took the scissors and cut open the wolf's belly, and when he had made a couple of cuts he saw the red riding hood beaming and when he cut a little further the girl jumped out and cried: "Oh, was I terrified, it was so dark in the body of the wolf;" and then grandmother also came out alive. But then Red Riding Hood went and got big heavy stones and filled the body of the wolf with them, and when he woke up he wanted to go bounding away but the stones were so heavy for him that he fell down dead.

Then all three were satisfied, the hunter took the wolf's pelt, grandmother ate the cake and drank the wine which Red Riding Hood had brought, and Red Riding Hood thought to herself: for the rest of your life you are never going to go off the path alone and run into the woods when your mother has told you not to.

Es war einmal eine kleine süße Dirn, die hatte jedermann lieb, der sie nur ansah, am allerliebsten aber ihre Großmutter, die wußte gar nicht, was sie alles dem Kind geben sollte. Einmal schenkte sie ihm ein Käppchen von rothem Sammet, und weil ihm das so wohl stand, und es nichts anders mehr tragen wollte, hieß es nur das Rothkäppchen; da sagte einmal seine Mutter zu ihm: "komm, Rothkäppchen, da hast du ein Stück Kuchen und ein Bouteille mit Wein, die bring der Großmutter hinaus, sie ist krank und schwach, da wird sie sich daran laben; sey hübsch artig und grüß sie von mir, geh auch ordentlich und lauf nicht vom Weg ab, sonst fällst du, und zerbrichst das Glas, dann hat die kranke Großmutter nichts."

Rothkäppchen versprach der Mutter recht gehorsam zu sein. Die Großmutter aber wohnte draußen im Wald, eine halbe Stunde vom Dorf. Wie nun Rothkäppchen in den Wald kam, begegnete ihm der Wolf, Rothkäppchen aber wußte nicht, was das für ein böses Thier war, und fürchtete sich nicht vor ihm. "Guten Tag, Rothkäppchen."—"Schön Dank Wolf."—"Wo willst du so früh hinaus, Rothkäppchen,"—"zur Großmutter."—Was trägst du unter der Schürze?—"die Großmutter ist krank und schwach, da bring ich ihr Kuchen und Wein, gestern haben wir gebacken, da soll sie sich stärken."—"Rothkäppchen, wo wohnt deine Großmutter?"—"Noch eine gute Viertelstunde im Wald, unter den drei großen Eichbäumen, da steht ihr Haus, unten sind die Nußhecken das wirst du ja wissen" sagte Rothkäppchen. Der Wolf gedacht bei sich, das ist ein guter fetter Bissen für mich, wie fängst dus an, daß du den kriegst: "hör Rothkäppchen, sagte er, hast du die schönen Blumen nicht gesehen, die im Walde stehen, warum guckst du nicht einmal um dich, ich glaube, du hörst gar nicht darauf, wie die Vöglein lieblich singen, du gehst ja für dich hin als wenn du im Dorf in die Schule gingst, und es ist so lustig haußen in dem Wald."

Rothkäppchen schlug die Augen auf, und sah wie die Sonne durch die Bäume gebrochen war und alles voll schöner Blumen stand; da gedachte es: ei! wenn ich der Großmutter einen Strauß mitbringe, der wird ihr auch lieb seyn, es ist noch früh, ich komm doch zu rechter Zeit an, und sprang in den Wald und suchte Blumen. Und wenn es eine gebrochen hatte, meint es, dort stünd noch eine schönere und lief darnach und immer weiter in den Wald hinein. Der Wolf aber ging geradeswegs nach dem Haus der Großmutter und klopfte an die Thüre. "Wer ist draußen"—"das Rothkäppchen, ich bring dir Kuchen und Wein, mach mir auf."—"Drück nur auf die Klinke, rief die Großmutter, ich bin zu schwach und kann nicht aufstehen." Der Wolf drückte an der Klinke, und die Thüre sprang auf. Da ging er hinein, geradezu an das Bett der Großmutter und verschluckte sie. Dann nahm er ihre Kleider, that sie an, setzte sich ihre Haube auf, legte sich in ihr Bett und zog die Vorhänge vor.

Rothkäppchen aber war herum gelaufen nach Blumen, und erst als es so viel hatte, daß es keine mehr tragen konnte, machte es sich auf den Weg zu der Großmutter. Wie es ankam stand die Thüre auf, darüber verwunderte es sich, und wie es in die Stube kam, sahs so seltsam darin aus, daß es dacht: ei! du mein Gott wie ängstlich wird mirs heut zu Muth, und ich bin sonst so gern bei der Großmutter. Darauf ging es zum Bett und zog die Vorhänge zurück, da lag die Großmutter und hatte die Haube tief ins Gesicht gesetzt und sah so wunderlich aus. "Ei Großmutter, was hast du für große Ohren!"—"daß ich dich besser hören kann."—"Ei Großmutter, was hast du für große Augen!"—"daß ich dich besser sehen kann." "Ei Großmutter was hast du für große Hände!"—"daß ich dich besser packen kann."—"Aber Großmutter, was hast du für ein entsetzlich großes Maul!"—"daß ich dich besser fressen kann." Damit sprang der Wolf aus dem Bett, sprang auf das arme Rottkäppchen, und verschlang es.

Wie der Wolf den fetten Bissen erlangt hatte, legte er sich wieder ins Bett, schlief ein und fing an, überlaut zu schnarchen. Der Jäger ging eben vorbei und gedacht wie kann die alte Frau so schnarchen, du mußt einmal nachsehen. Da trat er hinein und wie er vors Bett kam, da lag der Wolf den er lange gesucht, der hat gewiß die Großmutter gefressen vielleicht ist sie noch zu retten, ich will nicht schießen, dachte der Jäger. Da nahm er die Scheere und schnitt ihm den Bauch auf, und wie er ein paar Schnitte gethan, da sah er das rothe Käppchen leuchten, und wie er noch ein wenig geschnitten, da sprang das Mädchen heraus und rief: "ach wie war ich erschrocken, was wars so dunkel in dem Wolf seinem Leib;" und dann kam die Großmutter auch lebendig heraus. Rothkäppchen aber holte große schwere Steine, damit füllten sie dem Wolf den Leib, und wie er aufwachte, wollte er fortspringen, aber die Steine waren ihm so schwer, daß er sich todt fiel.

Da waren alle drei vergnügt, der Jäger nahm den Pelz vom Wolf, die Großmutter aß den Kuchen und trank den Wein, den Rothkäppchen gebracht hatte, und Rothkäppchen gedacht bei sich: du willst dein Lebtag nicht wieder allein vom Weg ab in den Wald laufen, wenn dirs die Mutter verboten hat.

The alternative ending, with a second occasion and "another wolf" and the warm sausage water, is printed in the first edition and is identical to that in the second edition; the alternative ending in the final edition of the story is very little changed. Perhaps the alternative ending was of less interest to Wilhelm Grimm because there is no death in it to be overcome.

On Charles Perrault's French versions of this and other fairy tales, the Grimms remark in the preface to the 1812 edition:

France certainly still has much more than what was communicated by Charles Perrault, who was the only one who still treated them as children's fairy tales (not his inferior imitators, Madame Aulnoi, Murat); Perrault relates only a few, the ones which are the best known and also among the most beautiful. His contribution is that he added nothing, and except for a few details he left things unchanged as they were. His presentation of the tales deserves praise for being as simple as was possible for him. [This is especially so as the Grimms add, probably based more on their contemporary experience, since French has become so full of refined curlicues (*zusammengekräuselt*) that there is probably nothing harder to do than to tell children's fairy tales in a simple and straight-forward manner in the language.] pp. xvi–xvii

(Frankreich hat gewiss noch jetzt mehr, als was Charles Perrault mittheilte, der allein sie noch als Kindermärchen behandelte (nicht seine schlechteren Nachahmer, die Aulnoi, Murat); er giebt nur einige, freilich die bekanntesten, die auch zu den schönsten gehören. Sein Verdienst besteht darin, daß er nichts hinzugesetzt und die Sachen an sich, Kleinigkeiten abgerechnet, unverändert gelassen; seine Darstellung verdient nur das Lob so einfach zu seyn, als es ihm möglich war.)

APPENDIX C

Yggdrasil, the Cross, and the Christmas Tree

Yggdrasil, "The Universe Tree," "The Tree of Life," is an ancient, mysterious name that has long been forgotten. Or has it?

Several years ago, as I was working to complete a translation of the *Heliand*, a Northern European version of the gospel story dating back to the early ninth century, the middle of the Dark Ages, I was disconcerted by the curious distortions that had entered into the depiction of the Crucifixion. The incident with the lance being thrust into the side of the dead Christ was made into a strangely highlighted action: "One of the enemy came closer, hate in his mind, carrying a well-made spear tightly in his hands. With incredible force he thrust it, cutting a wound in Christ's side with the spearhead, opening up His body." More striking is the description of Christ as dying on the cross by hanging from a rope ("the Protector of the Land died on the rope"). For the hearer or reader of a thousand years ago, the Crucifixion has clearly been made to echo the death of the Germanic god Woden (or Odin) on the Tree of the Universe, Yggdrasil, when he both hanged himself on the tree and stabbed himself to death with his spear. In death he reached down and seized the magic runes. The story is told in the Havamal saga:

> I know that I hung
> on the windswept tree
> for nine whole nights
> pierced by the spear
> and given to Odin
> (myself to myself)
> on that tree
> whose roots
> no one knows.

In both narratives, in the Germanic *Havamal* and in the Christian *Heliand*, the sacrificial death is followed by magic. In the case of Woden, he has seized the mysterious runes (the Germanic alphabet) which magically allow speech to be converted into writing and into potent spells. In the same way, the death of Christ on the cross in the *Heliand* magically enables creatures without language to express themselves in speech:

> As the Protector of the Land died on the rope, amazing signs were worked immediately so that the Ruler's death, His last day, would be recognized by the many speechless beings. Earth trembled, the high mountains shook, hard boulders in the fields cracked apart. The colorful curtain so wonderfully woven which had for many a day been hanging without harm inside the shrine [the Temple] was torn in two down the middle—Jewish people could then see the treasure hoard! . . . What a powerful thing that was, that Christ's death should be felt and acknowledged by so many beings which had never before spoken a word to human beings in this world!

One thinks immediately of the Anglo-Saxon *Dream of the Rood* in which the cross comes to speak of the care with which it tried to bear the burden of Christ crucified upon it.

This ancient tradition of a sacred and universal tree which is invisible but is the very structure, the living energy exchange, of the whole universe, is at the living heart of Germanic mythology. It is upon this evergreen tree "whose nature or species no one knows," that the chief Germanic god comes to realize, through his experience of his mortality, who he is. At its feet is the deepest of all wells, the well of Time, whose bottom no one has fathomed, and around which sit the three blind women, the Norns or Fates, spinning the thread of lives and events, measuring the thread, and then cutting it. The great tree behind them is a dynamic entity, always being consumed by the stags who eat at its leaves [something which reflects observation of the habits of deer in wintertime], and by an enormous evil serpent which continually tries to devour the roots of the tree deep below the surface of the middle world in which human beings live. Yggdrasil survives by continually producing as much as is consumed so that it is never diminished nor increased—an idea not unknown to modern physics. Yggdrasil, the tree of life, really has only two dangerous enemies in the world of Germanic mythology, and these are the primal, non-living forces of cold and heat. To all personal beings, both the Germanic gods and human beings, however, these unthinking, inorganic enemy forces are not merely dangerous but lethal. At Ragnarok, the end of the world, the "Twilight of the Gods," they will put an end to the gods. Human beings will, of course, be even more vulnerable to cosmic cold and heat, unless perhaps. . . . When the end of the world comes, after three terrible unending winters, the great glaciers of the North will begin to move again, irresistibly overwhelming all in their path. The great serpent will attack Thor, the god of personal strength, and will kill him with venomous fangs as, at the same moment, Thor will bury his hammer in the serpent's head, killing the snake. Woden, the god of consciousness and feelings, will be swallowed by the enormous jaws of the wolf Fenrir, whose mouth gapes from one end of space to the other. The whole of the middle world will also be shaken by earthquakes and be enveloped in raging flames that will reach up to the sun and moon. Fireballs will surge from the earth and will fall from the skies as the forces of heat emerge from the South to engage in a terrifying struggle with the massive forces of cold coming down from the North. All the human beings will be destroyed—except for two. Before the final terrifying cataclysm takes place, Yggdrasil will open up its great tree trunk to admit the last boy and girl and will then close around them to protect them and keep them safe throughout the time of the end of the world. When the end is over, the tree will have survived. And as a new sky appears with a new sun and a new moon and stars, and when the meadows first turn green again with new grass, the tree will open up and let the boy and girl go out to start again in the new world. Yggdrasil is, for human beings, the Savior Tree. To parallel Genesis, Yggdrasil is the Germanic name for the "Tree of Life," though definitely not because of edible fruit.

In a mythic world with such a high place for the tree, and in a northern world in which every cold and snowy winter could be seen as a dangerous and prophetic version of the end of the world, it is not surprising that trees which could remain perceptibly alive and green, all through the cold of winter (and survive forest fires, as well), would be seen as visible micro-manifestations of Yggdrasil. They would have been regarded as sacraments, visibly containing the real presence and life force of the unseeable Tree of Life (something which one wishes St. Boniface with his axe might have realized). One tree, down to our own day, has retained in its very name in English the sacramental reverence that the Germanic people of England, Germany and Scandinavia had for it: the holly. "Holly" is, of course, "holy," and thus it was known as the "holy tree," since its holiness enabled it to keep itself alive—green—all through the time of winter cold. All the evergreens in the forest, including the more lowly ivy and laurel, must have been regarded with the same reverence. Christmas carols and Northern custom have long retained a feel for life's green miracle at the winter solstice. "The Holly and the Ivy," "Deck the Halls with Boughs of Holly," in English as well as "O Tannenbaum" in German. Thus it is not surprising to find the most amazing amalgams of Christianity's cross and the tree Yggdrasil in Northern Europe. One that I find most moving is a gravestone from this early period of Christianity found in England. It dates from the tenth century and is found in Yorkshire. At first the gravestone appears to be a normal Celtic-style Latin cross, with the shaft about four or five times as long as the arms. It is immediately clear, however, on even casual observation, that the shaft of the cross does not depict Christ or anything biblical, but rather the body of the man buried beneath the gravestone. It is almost an X-ray of the grave below showing a warrior buried in a wooden box with his spear and shield, his Viking-style helmet and his sax (a single-bladed knife). By depicting the dead warrior on the cross shaft as he lies in the ground below, the observer sees the dead man as a part of the stem of the cross. He is resting, in other words, not really below the cross, rather he is as a Christian within the cross! Only a Northern European familiar with the Yggdrasil story would be at home with the image of seeing himself as protected against the cold cataclysm of death by being safely hidden and defended within the tree of Christ's cross. This beautifully thoughtful grave cross in Yorkshire led me to wonder if perhaps scholars have not been somewhat misled by the touching description in *Beowulf* of a dead chieftain sailing off to his unknown destination in a fiery funeral ship. The common man could not afford such a funeral, but did the myth of Yggdrasil's salvation of mankind from death offer another poetic possibility or model for how to bury the dead? The answer, I think, may lie in the many tree-trunk coffins that have been exhumed in Germany. If a "holy tree" is felled, the stem hollowed out and sawn in such a way as to create a box and a lid, might not being interred in a tree trunk be a sure way to attain survival after death? This burial form seems to be a close poetic and religious imitation of Yggdrasil's saving role. One well-preserved pre-Christian tree casket even has an open-mouthed snake, ready to strike, carefully carved into the lid. The snake has a head carved at both ends and no tail. The snake is most likely an attempt by rather frightening magic to prevent grave robbers from opening the lid, but the fact that the carved snake has "no end," may also be a way through magic to pray or ensure that the interred will one day exit the grave, through the saving power of the tree trunk, to enjoy a new life "without end."

Should one wonder what this might say about the origins of the casket of our current burial practice? It may reveal a good deal. In the Mediterranean world whence Christianity came, burial was often in a tomb, the body washed, anointed, wrapped in a shroud and laid upon a slab to desiccate, as we know from the New Testament. In some places the dried-out bones were eventually placed in a bone house and the tomb reused for more recent deaths, as at St. Catherine's in the Sinai. When a Northern European Christian was buried, the casket of evergreen pine, with a cross carved on the lid, was considered appropriate, and for centuries this has been the common manner of interment (though perhaps mindlessly ridiculed by those who prefer less meaningful metals to "the pine box" of the common person). Although no longer fully understanding why, we somehow continue to follow the poetic ways of Northern ancestors, hoping on the last journey through the coldness perhaps for the protection of Yggdrasil, the Tree of Life, Christ's cross.

The curious concept of salvation by being "within the tree" may also have given birth to the magnificent wooden stave churches of Norway, many of which have lasted even down to our very day. The churches are built with roof upon roof so that they bear some resemblance to a high pagoda. They are most likely descendants of ancient Germanic temples, since the eaves of the upper roofs are still equipped with carved dragon heads to ward off evil spirits from a holy place. The lower roofs are equipped with crosses, no doubt to serve the same function. When Pope Gregory the Great, after much vacillation, arrived at a solution to the problem of whether the new Northern converts would be permitted to worship in their formerly pagan temples, he followed ancient Roman tradition. It would be allowed for the English to continue to worship in the same (pagan) places and temples which they were accustomed to regard as sacred sites, but the altars inside (because of the blood of human sacrifice) would have to be removed and destroyed. From his time forward, this wise solution permitted the continuation of worship inside pagan temples and the construction of churches built in the Northern, pagan style. The stave church, when looked at from the side or from its entrance, is seen clearly to have been built to resemble an enormous pine tree—thus the function of the repeated roofs, growing smaller toward the peak. To walk into such a church-temple is therefore to step "inside the Tree."

When a visitor approaches one of the stave churches he or she will be shocked to see that the sanctuary portal, the doorway, is none other than a representation of Yggdrasil, the Tree of Life. It even has a stag carved into the lower branches, performing his traditional function of devouring the lower branches. Most remarkably, the tree trunk, the central portion of the large carving, opens up, revealing itself to be a door allowing the visitor to enter "the Tree." Inside, the almost excessive hollowed-out woodiness of the interior, as well as (in one case) the face of Woden himself glaring one-eyed from the wooden capital of one of the supports, tells the medieval church-goer in his own mythological tradition that, on entering here, a Christian church, you have found the protection of the real Yggdrasil, Christ's cross, the life tree.

In the High Middle Ages, Northern Europe's "northern barbarians" produced a remarkable new church, the "Gothic" cathedral. "Gothic" was originally a sneer used by admirers of the traditional Romanesque church of Italy and the Mediterranean. To say "Gothic" was a very clear way of saying "Visigoth, Vandal, Germanic, barbarian." It turns out, I believe, that the insult is quite accurate, the architecture is indeed "Germanic." My reason for this is the shape of the new church. Traditional churches in Italy had been variants on the basilica, the Roman long-apse style inherited from Roman civil building, and also, rarely, as in the Pantheon, in a round form, with an occasional short transept. In the East, churches were often shaped in square, octagonal, or Greek-cross (four equal arms) or basilica form, also with an occasional short transept. Curiously enough, the Gothic cathedral, looked down on from above, is always constructed in an unmistakably pronounced cross form, with a very clear and proportional transept, so that the building has the unmistakably distinct footprint on the landscape of a very large cross. Why would the Northern barbarians feel so at home with or in such a shape?

I would venture it was their continued reverence for the cross as the tree (many early medieval manuscripts in England as well as in Germany depict the cross with nubs of sawn-off branches, thereby emphasizing its nature as a tree), as well as for the traditional felt need to "enter into" it, to feel its protection. If this theory is correct, what scene would one expect to see over the main entrance at the foot end of the church? The Nativity? Christ in glory? I would expect that above the main portal there would be, in Christianized version, a depiction of the end of the world, doomsday, from the deadly consequences of which "entering into the tree" provides protection—saving grace. How many cases are there where one looks up before entering a "Gothic" cathedral and sees above the entrance the dead rising from their graves to come before Christ to face The Last Judgment? Thus the Yggdrasil story may be the ancient and silent key to understanding the dynamic and shape of the Northern cathedral.

The evergreen tree has found its most lasting and most emotional place in our culture, without a doubt, in the Christmas tree. Though the custom of having a Christmas tree survived without too much difficulty in Germany, it was given something of a rough time by some Reformers and by Puritans in England and in America (Christmas was forbidden by the good Puritans of the Massachusetts Bay Colony). It was not until the very late 1800s, for example, that the White House felt that it was acceptable to have a Christmas tree, and of course it was unknown in Italy, and in the Mediterranean countries in general, as well as in Mexico and South America. Now that the Christmas tree has spread in our time to many of these more tropical areas, I still get the feeling that the little pine tree is out of place when surrounded by Christmas celebrants in bathing suits and tropical clothing. Snow and coldness are required, methinks, for the evergreen to give its encouraging message that life will be back again. There are very old feelings that encourage "dreaming of a white Christmas."

In December of every year Yggdrasil comes into the house. A tree inside the home after all the centuries that have passed is quite miracle enough. To glorify and celebrate its ancient, compassionate, magic power, it is decorated with lights (with burning candles in Germany!) and with tinsel, to make sure it looks radiantly stolid and happy despite the cold and ice. Then a star is placed at its peak, since Wise Men must surely find their way to this tree. Below the tree, as if he had just emerged from its trunk, the true source of the warmth of the Tree of the Universe and its power to renew life, encouragement, and protection against all the kinds of cold, is lying in a manger: the newborn child.

In the Roman south, it is the unconquered sun, *sol invictus*, that traditionally is the object in nature honored on December 25 as being most like the birth of Christ, since on that day the sun stands still on the horizon and turns around to bring light and heat back north again. In Northern Europe with its cloudy skies and long snowfalls obscuring any view of the sun, it will be the holly tree, the evergreen pine tree, green leaves, and needles faithfully standing their ground, covered with heavy blankets of winter-cold snow, surrounded by the bleak and leafless other trees of the forest, that will speak in their own language, Christmas angels in green, reassuring mankind every winter of the fidelity and invincibility of the loving warmth of the newly born Child of God, the Lord of Life.

> O Tannenbaum, O Tannenbaum,
> Wie treu sind deine Blätter!
> Du grünst nicht nur zur Sommerzeit,
> Nein, auch im Winter, wenn es schneit!
> O Tannenbaum, O Tannenbaum,
> Wie treu sind deine Blätter!

> O pine tree, O pine tree,
> how faithful are your leaves.
> you are ever green, not only during the summer,
> but even during the winter when the snow falls.
> O pine tree, O pine tree,
> how faithful are your leaves.

"Yggdrasil," is an ancient, mysterious name of a faithful tree that has long been forgotten. Or has it?

SELECT BIBLIOGRAPHY

Primary Sources

Kinder- und Hausmärchen, gesammelt durch die Brüder Grimm. Bd.1, 1812; Bd. 2, 1815. Berlin: in der Realschulbuchhandlung [Reimer]. [contains first brief source information and comment given by the brothers; at the Beineke Library, Yale]

Kinder- und Hausmärchen, 2. Auflage, Bd. 1 & 2, 1819; Bd. 3, 1822. Berlin: Reimer. [vol.3 contains expanded annotations and Wilhelm's essay on the nature of fairy tales; at the Firestone Library, Princeton University]

Kleine Ausgabe. Berlin: Reimer, 1825. [contains illustrations by Ludwig Emil Grimm guided by Wilhelm; a later reprint at Firestone Library, Princeton]

Novum Testamentum Graece, ed. Schott. Leipzig: 1811. [at the Humboldt University Library, Berlin]

Die Heilige Schrift in berichtigter Uebersetzung mit kurzen Anmerkungen. Johann Friedrich von Meyer. Frankfurt am Main: Verlag der Hermannschen Buchhandlung, 1819. [at the Grimm Museum in Haldensleben]

Secondary Literature

Appolodorus. *The Library*, trans. Sir James Frazer. Cambridge: Harvard University Press, 1939.

Apuleius. *The Golden Ass*, trans. Jack Lindsay. Bloomington: Indiana University Press, 1962.

Basile, Giambattista. *Lo Cunto de Li Cunti*, a cura di Ezio Raimondi. Milan-Naples: Einaudi, 1960.

Bettelheim, Bruno. *The Uses of Enchantment, The Meaning and Importance of Fairy Tales*. New York: Random House, Vintage Books, 1977.

Bolte, Johannes, and Georg Políkva. *Anmerkungen zu den Kinder- und Hausmärchen der Brüder Grimm*. 5 vols. Leipzig: Dieterich, 1913–32; Hildesheim: Olms, 1963.

Bottigheimer, Ruth B. "From Gold to Guilt: The Forces Which Reshaped Grimms Tales." *The Brothers Grimm and Folktale*, ed. James M. McGlathery.

———. "The Publishing History of Grimms' Tales: Reception at the Cash Register." *The Reception of the Grimms' Fairy Tales*, ed. Donald Haase. Detroit: Wayne State University Press, 1993.

———. *Grimms' Bad Girls and Bold Boys, The Moral and Social Vision of the Tales*. New Haven: Yale University Press, 1987.

Branston, Brian. *The Lost Gods of England*. London: Thames and Hudson, 1984.

Brothers Grimm and Folktale, ed. James M. McGlathery. Chicago: University of Illinois Press, 1991.

Brüder Grimm. Kinder- und Hausmärchen (Jubiläumsausgabe), Ausgabe letzter Hand mit den Original Anmerkungen der Brüder Grimm, I–III, hrsg. Heinz Rölleke. Stuttgart: Reclam, 1993.

Campbell, Joseph. *The Hero with a Thousand Faces*. Bollinger Series 17. New York: Pantheon, 1949.

———. "Folkloristic Commentary." *The Complete Grimms' Fairy Tales*, ed. Padraic Colum. New York: Random House, 1972.

Climo, Shirley. *The Egyptian Cinderella*, illus. Ruth Heller. New York: HarperCollins, 1989. [an appealingly rethought and illustrated version of Strabo's story, with some gifted conjecture, for children]

Colum, Padraic. *Nordic Gods and Heroes*. New York: Dover, 1996.

Complete Fairy Tales of Charles Perrault, trans. Neil Philip and Nicoletta Simborowski. New York: Clarion Books, 1993.

Complete Fairy Tales of the Brothers Grimm, trans. and with an introduction by Jack Zipes. New York: Bantam Books, 1992. [contains brief source notes for each tale]

Complete Grimm's Fairy Tales, trans. Margaret Hunt, revised by James Stern, with an introduction by Padraic Colum, and a folkloristic commentary by Joseph Campbell. New York: Random House, Pantheon Books, 1972.

Davidson, H. R. Ellis. *Gods and Myths of Northern Europe*. New York: Penguin, 1979.

De Vries, Jan. *Altgermanische Religionsgeschichte*. Berlin: Walter de Gruyter, 1957.

Dégh, Linda. "What Did the Grimm Brothers Give to and Take From the Folk?" in *The Brothers Grimm and Folktale*, ed. James M. McGlathery.

Deneke, Ludwig, und Irmgard Teitge. *Die Bibliothek der Brüder Grimm, Annotiertes Verzeichnis des festgestellten Bestandes*, hrsg. Friedhilde Krause. Weimar: Hermann Böhlaus Nachfolger, 1989. [an indispensable aid for locating the scattered books of the Grimms' personal libraries]

Deutsches Wörterbuch, Jacob Grimm und Wilhelm Grimm. Leipzig: Hinzel, 1873.

Die älteste Märchensammlung der Brüder Grimm, Synopse der handschriftlichen Urfassung von 1810 und der Erstdrucke von 1812, herausgegeben und erläutert von Heinz Rölleke. Cologny-Genève: Fondation Martin Bodmer, 1975. [most accessible and useful source for earliest versions]

Dielmann, Karl. *Märchenillustrationen von Ludwig Emil Grimm*. Sonderdruck aus Hanauer geschichtsblätter No. 18. Hanau: 1962. [useful but rare volume of reproductions, can be found at the Grimm archives in Kassel.]

Dundes, Alan. "Interpreting Little Red Riding Hood Psychoanalytically." *The Brothers Grimm and Folktale*, ed. James M. McGlathery.

Ellis, John M. *One Fairy Story Too Many, The Brothers Grimm and Their Tales*. Chicago: The University of Chicago Press, 1985.

Enzyklopädie des Märchens, Handwörterbuch zur historischen und vergleichenden Erzhlforschung, hrsg. Kurt Ranke, Göttingen. Berlin, New York: Walter de Gruyter, 1979.

Flint, Valerie I. J. *The Rise of Magic in Early Medieval Europe*. Princeton: Princeton University Press, 1991. [an excellent interpretation of the early mutual accommodation of European pagan and Christian religious practice and ritual]

Flowers, Stephen E. *Runes and Magic, Magical Formulaic Elements in the Older Runic Tradition*. New York/Berne/Frankfurt: Peter Lang, 1986.

Gerstner, Hermann. *Brüder Grimm mit Selbstzeugnissen und Bilddokumenten*. Reinbeck bei Hamburg: Rohwolt Taschenbuch Verlag, 1973.

Glas, Norbert. *Red Riding Hood*. East Gannicox: Education and Science Publications, 1947.

————. *Once Upon a Fairy Tale: Seven Favorite Folk and Fairy Tales by the Brothers Grimm*, translated and interpreted by the author. Spring Valley, N.Y.: St. George Publications, 1976.

Gott im Märchen, hrsg. Jürgen Janning (im Auftrag der europäischen Märchengesellschaft). Kassel: Erich Röth-Verlag, 1982.

Graves, Robert. *The Greek Myths*, 2 vols. New York: Penguin Books USA Inc., 1990.

Grimm, Jacob. *Selbstbiographie*, hrsg. Ulrich Wyss. München: DTV, 1984.

Grimm, Wilhelm. "Über das Wesen der Märchen." *Jacob und Wilhelm Grimm Werke, Abteilung II, Die Werke Wilhelms*, Bd. 31, hrsg. Otfried Ehrismann. Hildesheim, Zürich, New York: Olms—Weidmann, 1992.

Grimm, Wilhelm. *Selbstbiographie* in Jacob Grimm und Wilhelm Grimm Werke, hrsg. Ludwig Erich Schmitt. Hildesheim, Zürich, New York: Olms—Weidmann, 1992.

Hagen, Rolf. "Perraults Märchen und die Brüder Grimm." *Zeitschrift für deutsche Philologie*, 74 (1955), 4, 392–410.

Herder's Werke, ausgewählte Werke in einem Band. Stuttgart und Tübingen: Cotta, 1844.

Herodotus. *The History*, trans. David Grene. Chicago: University of Chicago Press, 1987.

Hesiod. *Theogony*. Baltimore: Penguin Books, 1973.

Il Pentamerone, trans. Sir Richard Burton. New York: Liveright, 1893 [orig.], 1943.

Jacob and Wilhelm Grimm, Selected Tales, translated with notes by David Luke. New York, Penguin Books USA, Inc., 1982.

Jacob Grimm und Wilhelm Grimm Werke, Forschungsausgabe, hrsg. Ludwig Erich Schmitt. Hildesheim, Zürich, New York: Olms—Weidmann, 1992. [contains the autobiographies and Wilhelm's essay on the nature of fairy tales]

Kamenetsky, Christa. *The Brothers Grimm and their Critics, Folktales and the Quest for Meaning*. Athens, Ohio: Ohio University Press, 1992.

Kemminghausen, Karl Schulte und Ludwig Denecke. *Die Brüder Grimm in Bildern ihrer Zeit*. Kassel: Erich Röth-Verlag, 1963.

Kurfürstin Auguste von Hessen (1780–1841) in ihrer Zeit. Hrsg. Bernhard Lauer. Kassel: Brüder Grimm-Gesellschaft, 1995.

Lange, Günter. "Grimms Märchen aus der Sicht eines Religionspädagogen." *Hanau, 1986–1986, 200 Jahre Brüder Grimm*. Hanau: Stadt Hanau, 1986. [sees the fairy tales' religious use, with some misgivings, as, at best, propaedeutic to faith]

Leges Saxonum et Thuringorum, hrsg. von Claudius Freiherrn von Schwerin. Hannover: Hahnsche Buchhandlung, 1918.

Lüthi, Max. *Once Upon a Time, On the Nature of Fairy Tales*, trans. Lee Chadeayne and Paul Gottwald. New York: Frederick Ungar Publishing Company, 1970.

Michaelis-Jena, Ruth. *The Brothers Grimm*. London: Routledge and Kegan Paul, 1970.

Mieder, Wolfgang. "'Ever Eager to Incorporate Folk Proverbs:' Wilhelm Grimm's Proverbial Additions in the Fairy Tales." *The Brothers Grimm and Folktale*, ed. James M. McGlathery.

Moser, Dietz-Moser. "Christliche Erzählstoffe." *Enzyklopädie des Märchens, Handwörterbuch zur historischen und vergleichenden Erzählforschung*, hrsg. Kurt Ranke. Berlin: Walter de Gruyter, 1979.

Murphy, G. Ronald. "Yggdrasil, the Cross and the Christmas Tree." *America*, Vol. 175, No. 19 (Dec. 14, 1996). New York: America Press, 1996.

————. *The Heliand, The Saxon Gospel*. New York: Oxford University Press, 1992.

————. "From Germanic Warrior to Christian Knight: the Heliand Transformation." *Arthurian Literature and Christianity: Notes from the Twentieth Century*. New York: Garland, 1999.

————. "Magic in the Heliand." *Monatshefte*, 83, No. 4 (1991), 386–97.

————. *The Saxon Savior, The Germanic Transformation of the Gospel in the Ninth-Century Heliand.* New York: Oxford University Press, 1989.

Musäus, Johann Karl August. *Volksmärchen der Deutschen.* Darmstadt: Wissenschaftliche Buchgesellschaft, 1961.

New English Dictionary on Historical Principles, A, ed. James A. H. Murray. Oxford: Clarendon, 1888.

New Greek-English Interlinear New Testament, trans. Robert Brown and Philip Comfort, ed. J. D. Douglas. Wheaton, Ill.: Tyndale House Publishers, Inc., 1993. [uses the Kurt Aland text of the 26th edition, Novum Testamentum Graece, from the Institute for New Testament Textual Research, Münster, Westfalen.

Nibelungenlied, trans. Arthur Thomas Hatto. New York: Penguin Books USA, 1969.

Oberlin, Jeremias Jacob. *Essai sur le patois lorrain des environs du comté du Ban de la Roche, fief d'Alsace.* Strasbourg: Stein, 1775. [Princeton, rare books collection, Firestone Library]

Old Neapolitan Fairy Tales, retold by Rose Mincieli. New York: Knopf, 1963. [too cleaned up to be of much scholarly use, but one of the rare contemporary translations]

Pentamerone of Giambattista Basile, trans. N. M. Penzer. London: John Lane the Bodley Head, 1932.

Peppard, Murray B. *Paths Through the Forest, A Biography of the Brothers Grimm.* New York: Holt, Rinehart, Winston, 1971. [a very good and sensitive biography]

Perrault, Charles. *Contes de ma mère l'Oye, Histoires du temps passé avec des moralités.* Mayenne: Éditions Gallimard, 1977. [illustrated by Gustave Doré]

Reception of the Grimms' Fairy Tales, Responses, Reactions, Revisions, ed. Donald Haase. "Detroit: Wayne State University Press, 1993.

Röhrich, Lutz. "The Quest for Meaning in Folk Narrative Research." *The Brothers Grimm and Folktale,* ed. James M. McGlathery.

Rölleke, Heinz. *Wo das Wünschen noch geholfen hat: Gesammelte Aufsätze zu den Kinder- und Hausmärchen der Brüder Grimm.* Wuppertaler Schriftenreihe Literatur, 23. Bonn: Bouvier, 1985.

————. "Die 'stockhessischen' Märchen der 'alten Marie': das Ende eines Mythos um die frühesten KHM-Aufzeichnungen der Brüder Grimm." *Germanisch-Romanische Monatsschrift,* n.s. 25 (1975), 74–86.

————. "New Research on Grimms' Fairy Tales." *The Brothers Grimm and Folktale,* ed. James M. McGlathery.

Russell, James C. *The Germanization of Early Medieval Christianity, A Sociohistorical Approach to Religious Transformation.* New York: Oxford University Press, 1994.

Ryan, Judith. "Hybrid Forms in German Romanticism." *Prosimetrum, Crosscultural Perspectives on Narrative in Prose and Verse,* ed. Joseph Harris and Karl Reichl. Cambridge: D.S. Brewer, 1997.

Saga of the Volsungs, The Norse Epic of Sigurd the Dragon Slayer, trans. Jesse L. Byock. Berkeley: University of California Press, 1990.

Schoof, Wilhelm. *Zur Entstehungsgeschichte der Grimmschen Märchen: Bearbeitet unter Benutzung des Nachlasses der Brüder Grimm.* Hamburg: Ernst Hauswedell, 1959.

————. "Stilentwicklung der Grimmschen Märchen." *Zeitschrift für deutsche Philologie,* 74 (1955), 4, 424–33.

Seitz, Gabriele. *Die Brüder Grimm, Leben, Werk, Zeit.* Munich: Winkler Verlag, 1984.

Stone, Kay. "Three Transformations of Snow White." *The Brothers Grimm and Folktale,* ed. James M. McGlathery.

Strabo. *The Geography,* trans. literally with notes by H. C. Hamilton and W. Falconer. London: G. Bell and Sons, 1915.

Sturluson, Snorri. *Heimskringla or The Lives of the Norse Kings*, ed. Erling Monsen. New York: Dover, 1990. [contains the story of Snaefrið]

Tatar, Maria M. *The Hard Facts of the Grimms' Fairy Tales*. Princeton: Princeton University Press, 1987.

———. "Beauties vs. Beasts in the Grimms' Nursery and Household Tales." *The Brothers Grimm and Folktale*, ed. James M. McGlathery.

Tieck, Ludwig. *Leben und Tod des kleinen Rotkäppchens. Eine Tragödie*. In Ludwig Tieck's Schriften, 2. Bd. Berlin: Reimer, 1828.

Ward, Donald. "New Misconceptions about Old Folktales: The Brothers Grimm." *The Brothers Grimm and Folktale*, ed. James M. McGlathery.

Warner, Marina. *From the Beast to the Blonde, On Fairy Tales and their Tellers*. New York: Farrar, Straus and Giroux, 1995.

Wolfram von Eschenbach. *Parzival, (Studienausgabe) mittlehochdeutscher Text nach der 6. Ausgabe von Karl Lachmann*. Berlin: Walter de Gruyter, 1998.

Wolfram von Eschenbach. *Parzival*, trans. Helen Mustard and Charles Passage. New York: Vintage Books, 1961.

Zipes, Jack. "Dreams of a Better Bourgeois Life: The Psychosocial Origins of the Grimms' Tales." *The Brothers Grimm and Folktale*, ed. James M. McGlathery.

———. *Fairy Tales and the Art of Subversion: The Classical Genre for Children and the Process of Civilization*. New York: Wildman, 1983.

INDEX

Adam and Eve, 39, 80, 127
adolescent lethargy, 133
aesthetic criteria, 121
Aladdin, 154
Albertus Magnus, 114
alliteration, 122
Anfortas, 9
animism, 39
Apollo, 18
Apostles' Creed, 100–101
apple (as diachronic), 114
Appolodorus, 82
Apuleius, 107
Aquinas, St. Thomas, 6
Ariadne, 53, 149, 151
Artemis, 18
ashes (as diachronic symbol), 109, 111
Auguste, princess of Hesse, 104 n.15

Baptism, 7, 10, 17, 20, 26, 138, 145–146,
    151–152
Basile, Giambattista, 18, 40, 95–100, 105,
    118, 137, 140, 147, 151
bath, the, 144, 145
Beatitude, the second, 103, 105, 130
Bede, 8
Bettelheim, Bruno, 17, 74, 77, 86, 123, 126,
    128, 133
Blanca, 115
Bluebeard, 136

Bottigheimer, Ruth, 23–25, 36
Brabant, 13, 114, 124
Brentano, Clemens, 45
Brynhild (Brunhild), 136, 140, 151

Caedmon, 8
Calvin, John, 7, 38, 62, 101, 149
Carmosina, 97
Catholic Church, 25
Catholics, 31–32
Cendrillon, 93
Cennerentola, 87
Chaperon rouge, 67
Charlemagne, 53
China, 86
Christ, 21, 39, 40–41, 43, 63, 72, 82–83, 101,
    110, 131–132, 146, 149–150, 153
Christmas, 14, 117
Church of St. Catherine (Katharinen-
    kirche), 31–32, 33, 37
Cinderella (Aschenputtel), 34, 40, 85–112
Colum, Padraic, 124
Communion, 7, 31–32, 34, 111, 148
communion of saints, 34, 100, 102–103,
    151
compassion, 28
Condwiramurs, 11, 123
Confirmation, 32, 34
Contes du temps passé. See Perrault
crab, the, 144

Cronos, 82
crown of thorns, 149, 151
Crucifixion, 9

d'Aulnoy, the Countess, 87
diachronic symbolic imagery, 14–15, 29,
    41
    in comment on biblical Joseph, 26
        n.22
    in *Cinderella*, 102–103, 108, 110
    in *Hansel and Gretel*, 59
    in *The Juniper Tree* (Bottigheimer), 25
    in *Little Red Riding Hood*, 75, 79–80,
        83
    in *Sleeping Beauty*, 148–149
    in *Snow White*, 119, 130–131
    in *The Spirit in the Glass*, 154
    in Wilhelm Grimm's life, 34–35, 104
Disney, Walt, 4
Dornröschen, 133–152. *See also Sleeping
    Beauty*
dove(s), the, 11, 18, 39, 58, 62, 83, 86, 89,
    95, 99, 102, 107, 108, 152
duck, the, 19, 63, 145, 147
Dundes, Alan, 27
dwarfs, 127
    in Musäus, 115
    in *Snow White*, 127–130

Egypt, 85
Eliade, Mircea, 26
Ellis, John M., 22–23, 45
English Philological Society, 5
Enlightenment, 47, 115
Erlkönig, 57
Essai sur le patois lorrain, 62 n.15
ethnocentricity, 29
Exodus, 63

Face, The (Lo Caro), 140
fairy godmother, 93–94
faith, 3, 6, 40–43, 62, 83, 127, 149
Fall, the, 60, 76, 80
fatalism, classical, 140

fate(s), the, 8, 98, 100, 133, 146–147, 150,
    152
Feirefiz, 13
Fenrir, 78, 83
Finette Cendron, 87
frog, the, 144–146, 151
Frog Prince, The (Der Froschkönig), 146
    n.14

Gahmuret, 9
galette, 77 n.10
Garden of Eden, 63, 108, 126, 153
Garden of the Hesperides, 108
Genesis, 76, 80–81, 124
Geographikon, 85–86
German Romanticism, 4, 13, 28, 115
Glas, Norbert, 27–28
glass casket, 118, 130
God, 19–20, 32, 40, 62, 79, 110, 127,
    130–131.
    in Rölleke's reading, 19, 24
Goethe, 23, 57
Golden Bird, The (Vom goldenen Vogel),
    26
Good Friday, 11, 149
Gottfried of Ardenne, 115
Göttingen, 33, 42
grail, the, 65
Greek New Testament, 29, 38, 63
Gunderich der Pfaffenfreund, 114

Haldensleben, 14, 41
Hanau, 31, 33, 36, 59
Handwörterbuch des deutschen Märchens,
    24
Hansel and Gretel (Hänsel und Gretel),
    18, 36, 45–65, 145, 147
Harald Fairhair, 116
Haraldsaga, 116
Harris, Joseph, 28 n.34
Hassenpflug, Jeanette, 68
Hassenpflug, Marie, 119, 121, 124, 135, 137,
    140, 142
hazel, the, 86

Heimskringla, 116
Heliand, 7–8, 24, 40
Herder, 28
Herodotus, 85 n.1
Hesiod, 82
Hesse, 36, 50-51, 86, 113
Hildebrandslied, 5
Hjalmgunnar, 141
holy coat of Trier, 104 n.16
Holy Spirit, 8, 10, 39, 59, 62, 65, 101, 107,
    110
Hop O' My Thumb (Petit Poucet), 47
Hugin and Munin, 18
Huguenots, 22, 67
Humboldt University Library, 14, 36

Indo European roots, 14
Institutes of the Christian Faith, 7
Irish and Slavic tales, 29

Jacob Grimm, *Autobiography*, 31, 119
Jesus. *See* Christ
Juniper Tree (Der Machandelboom), 25

Kamenetsky, Christa, 28–29
Karoline, princess of Hesse, 104
Kitchen Maid, The (The Young Slave), 118
Kunstmärchen, 22

La Belle au bois dormant (Sleeping
    Beauty), 133–152
labyrinth, the, 148–149
Lessing, 115
Leto, 118
L'Histoire de Fleur d'épine, 135
Library, The (see Appolodorus)
*Life and Death of Little Red Riding Hood,
    A Tragedy*, 71ff.
Lilla, 118
Little Red Riding Hood (Rotkäppchen), 27,
    67–84
Little Thorn Rose (Dornröschen), 133–152
Lord's Supper. *See* Communion
Lucifer, 126–128

Luther, Martin, 6–7
Lutherans, 31, 62
Lüthi, Max, 26

magic, 21, 93, 141
Marburg, 10
Mass, 114
menstruation, 134
Meyer, Johann Friedrich von, 43
Middle Ages, 5
Minotaur, 148–149
mortality, 18 n.4, 135, 148
mortal sin, 57
Moser, Dietz-Rüdiger, 25
Munsalvaesche, 11
Murray, James A.H., 5 n.4
Musäus, 114, 119, 124

New Testament. *See* Greek New
    Testament
norns, 133, 135. *See also* fate

Oberlin, Jeremias Jacob, 62 n.15
objectivity, 109, 111
Odin. *See* Woden
Oedipus the King, 53, 111, 124, 147
ogre, 49
ogress, 137
Ölenberg, 45, 51
original sin, 60, 76
owl, the, 83, 152
Oxford English Dictionary, 5

Parcae, 13, 100, 133, 135. *See also* fate
Parzival, 9, 24, 65, 123
passage of time, 133–134, 149
Paths Through the Forest. *See* Peppard
pelagianism, 62
Pentamerone, 118
Pentecost, 71
Peppard, Murray B., 32
Perrault, Charles, 22, 40, 47–48, 50,
    67–70, 77, 80, 86–87, 92, 105, 119,
    136–138, 144, 151

Petit Poucet. See Hop 'o My Thumb
phoenix, the, 25–26, 26 n.22
poverty, 41
predestination, 149. *See also* fate
Protestant dialect, 32
Protestant work ethic, 27
Providence, 130
Psamathe, 82 n.13
Psyche and Cupid, 106, 111
Psychopannychia, 101 n.13
pulpit, 37, 154

Ragnarök, 58, 78, 148
rape, 151
raven, the, 83, 152
Reformed Church, 7, 31–33, 38, 62
Regin, 124
rejection, 41
Resurrection, 25, 40, 83, 103–104, 117, 131, 150
Rhea, 82
Rhodopis, 85–86
Richilde, 114
Röhrich, Lutz, 22 n.14
Rölleke, Heinz, 19, 21, 24, 25, 39, 45, 68, 115, 117
Romanticism. *See* German Romanticism
Ryan, Judith, 28

salvation, 74, 149, 152
Sardinia, 102
Saturn, 9
Savigny, Karl von, 5, 119
Schmeller, J.A., 8
Scott, Walter, 85 n.2
Seven Ravens, The (Die sieben Raben), 17
sexual maturity, 74, 77, 134
shepherd, 40
Sigurd (Siegfried), 136, 140–141, 146, 149, 151
Sleeping Beauty, 118, 133–152. *See also* Dornröschen
sleep motif, 131 n.15, 133, 144, 147–150
Snaefrid, 116

Snorri Sturluson, 116
Snow White (Sneewittchen), 113–132
origin of name, 114 n.2, 116, n.6
Song of Roland (Ruolandsliet), 104
Sophocles, 53
soul, 101, 146
Sparrow and His Children, The (Der Sperling und seine vier Kinder), 24
Spirit in the Bottle, The (Der Geist im Glas), 154
Steinau, 7, 13, 31, 33, 35
Stories of Mother Goose, 47
Strabo, 85–86
Summa Theologica, 100–101
Sun, Moon and Talia, 140

tachycardia, 35, 40, 147
Talia, 18, 137
Tatar, Maria, 28
Theseus, 146
Thor, 78
Three Languages, The (Die drei Sprachen), 18
Three Sisters, The (Die drei Spinnerinnen), 132 n.1
Tieck, Ludwig, 67, 71, 81
tree, the (as diachronic symbol), 34, 36 58–59, 79, 102–103, 141
Trinitarian Christianity, 39, 43, 79, 100, 132

Valkyrie, 141–142
Venus, 106
Viehmann, Dorothea, 22, 86
Virgin Mary, 18
Volksmärchen der Deutschen, 114
Volsung saga, 141

Ward, Donald, 21–22
Warner, Marina, 29
Wiener Oswald, 60 n.14
Wild, Henriette Dorothee (Dortchen), 36, 45

Wilhelm Grimm, *Autobiography*, 33–36

Woden, 8, 78–79, 141

wolf, 28, 68

Wolfram von Eschenbach, 9, 65, 123

Word, 41, 42

Yggdrasil, 25, 58, 148–149

Yule, 116–117

Zaubermärchen, 4

Zeus, 18, 82

Zezolla, 97–99, 103

Zipes, Jack, 27